Study Guide for the Telecourse

Faces Of Culture

Study Guide for the Telecourse

Faces Of Culture

by
Richard T. Searles

with special essays by
Mari Womack

for
The Coast Community Colleges
Costa Mesa, California

Holt, Rinehart and Winston
New York Chicago San Francisco Philadelphia Montreal Toronto
London Sydney Tokyo Mexico City Rio de Janeiro Madrid

The Coast Community Colleges

Norman E. Watson, Chancellor
The Coast Community Colleges

Leslie N. Purdy, Senior Instructional Designer
Office of College Development

Louise Matthews Hewitt, Telecourse Editor

Judith D. Lindow, Assistant Telecourse Editor

Ira R. Abrams, Series Producer

Arthur Barron, Creative Consultant

Study guide consultant Frances F. Berdan, Professor and Chair, Department of Anthropology, California State College, San Bernardino

Map illustrations by Lou Bruno

Cover photo: Napoleon A. Chagnon

"Faces of Culture," a telecourse, is produced by The Coast Community Colleges and KOCE-TV, Channel 50, in cooperation with Holt, Rinehart and Winston, in association with City Colleges of Chicago, Dallas County Community College District, Miami-Dade Community College, Southern California Consortium for Community College Television, and State of Florida Department of Education.

ISBN 0-03-069543-0

CBS COLLEGE PUBLISHING
Holt, Rinehart and Winston
The Dryden Press
Saunders College Publishing

Preface

To the Student

Welcome to the telecourse "Faces of Culture," a course introducing the principles and information of cultural anthropology. Whether you are planning a career in anthropology or taking the course to gain insights into your own and other cultures, we believe that you will find it interesting, entertaining, and enriching.

"Faces of Culture" is designed according to the philosophy that culture as the expression of human values, behavior, and social organization exists in unique and varied forms throughout the world, in past and present times. The course attempts to document that diversity and demonstrate the inherent logic of each culture in light of the problems people need to solve and environments to which they must adapt. While the behavior and customs you will see may, at times, strike you as odd, or even unpleasant, we urge you to try not to make value judgments, but rather to look for the purpose and function of the action within the context of that culture and its values. Other times in this course, you will see human behavior which expresses universal needs and feelings, albeit expressed through diverse cultural customs and practices. Thus, as you progress through this course, your own feelings will probably range from a sense of awe at the differences between people to a sense of respect for, and oneness with, people around the world. We hope that you will be touched by, as well as learn from, the people you will see and read about in this course.

As with most classroom courses, "Faces of Culture" has a textbook, a study guide, tests, and assignments. The text is *Cultural Anthropology* by William A. Haviland (New York: Holt, Rinehart and Winston, 1983). This book, *Study Guide for the Telecourse Faces of Culture*, will guide your study through the course, providing reading and viewing assignments, study activities, and practice test questions. You may also be required to purchase and read additional books for this course—case studies which describe particular cultures in depth. In addition, "Faces of Culture" has a special learning element that most classrooms do not have: a companion half-hour television program for each of the twenty-six lessons in the course.

The Course Goals

The designer, academic advisors, and producer of this television course have specified nine major goals for students taking "Faces of Culture." By the end of the course, students should be able to:

- Understand and appreciate the concept of culture from the perspective of anthropologists as the adaptive mechanism which provides for survival of the human species.

- Recognize underlying similarities as well as the wide range and variability of human cultures.

- Recognize and appreciate that there are a number of valid "cultural solutions" to living on the earth.

- Appreciate the duration of total human history and prehistory.

- Understand the relationship between culture and the individual.

- Understand the factors involved in culture change.

- Gain a broad cross-cultural background against which to view their own culture as well as contemporary social problems.

- Know the meanings of the basic concepts and terms used by cultural anthropologists.

- Understand some of the procedures used by anthropologists in studying cultures.

How to Take This Television Course

If you are new to college courses in general, and television courses in particular, you can perhaps profit from a few suggestions offered by students who have successfully completed other television courses.

Television courses are designed for busy people—people with full-time jobs or family obligations—who want to take a course at home, fitting the study into their own personal schedules. To do this, you will need to plan in advance how to schedule your viewing, reading, and study. Buy the books before the course begins and look them over; familiarize yourself with any materials supplied by your college and estimate how much time it will take you to complete special tests and assignments for each lesson. Write the dates of midterms, finals, review sessions, and special projects in your calendar so that you can plan to have extra time to prepare for them. Discuss with your family and friends your needs for study and television viewing time. While you may find it enjoyable and instructive to watch the programs with other people, save the talking and discussion until *after* the program so that you won't miss important information. You may find it helpful to take five minutes at the end of the program to write a brief summary of what you have seen, the meaning of key concepts and terms, and the names of the cultural groups presented.

This study guide will be especially helpful to you as you progress through the course. Begin your study of each lesson by reading the lesson Overview, the Learning Objectives, and the Assignments for the lesson. Follow the

Preface

To the Student

Welcome to "Faces of Culture," a telecourse which introduces the principles and information of cultural anthropology. Whether you are planning a career in anthropology or taking it to gain insights into your own and other cultures, we believe that you will find the course interesting, entertaining, and enriching.

"Faces of Culture" is designed according to the philosophy that culture as the expression of human values, behavior, and social organization exists in unique and varied forms throughout the world, in past and present times. The course attempts to document that diversity and demonstrate the inherent logic of each culture in light of the problems people need to solve and environments to which they must adapt. While the behavior and customs you will see may, at times, strike you as odd or unpleasant, we urge you to try not to make value judgments about the cultures under study, but look instead for purpose and function of the action within the context of those cultures and their values. Other times in this course, you will see human behavior which expresses universal needs and feelings, albeit expressed through diverse cultural customs and practices. Thus, as you progress through this course, your own feelings will probably range from a sense of awe at the differences between people to a sense of respect for, and oneness with, people around the world. We hope that you will be touched by, as well as learn from, the people you will see and read about in this course.

As with most classroom courses, "Faces of Culture" has a textbook, a study guide, assignments, and tests. The text is *Cultural Anthropology* by William A. Haviland (New York: Holt, Rinehart and Winston, 1983). This book, *Study Guide for the Telecourse Faces of Culture*, will guide your study through the course, providing reading and viewing assignments, study activities, and practice test questions. You may also be required to purchase and read additional books for this course—case studies which describe particular cultures in depth. In addition, "Faces of Culture" has a special learning element that most classrooms do not have: a companion half-hour television program for each of the twenty-six lessons in the course.

The Course Goals

The designer, academic advisors, and producer of this television course have specified nine major goals for students taking "Faces of Culture." By the end of the course, you should be able to:

- Understand and appreciate the concept of culture from the perspective of anthropologists as the adaptive mechanism which provides for survival of the human species.

- Recognize underlying similarities as well as the wide range and variability of human cultures.

- Recognize and appreciate that there are a number of valid "cultural solutions" to living on the earth.

- Understand the relationship between culture and the individual.

- Understand the factors involved in culture change.

- Gain a broad cross-cultural background against which to view your own culture as well as contemporary social problems.

- Know the meanings of the basic concepts and terms used by cultural anthropologists.

- Understand some of the procedures used by anthropologists in studying cultures.

How to Take This Television Course

If you are new to college courses in general, and television courses in particular, you can perhaps profit from a few suggestions offered by students who have successfully completed other television courses.

Television courses are designed for busy people—people with full-time jobs or family obligations—who want to take a course at home, fitting the study into their own personal schedules. To do this, you will need to plan in advance how to schedule your viewing, reading, and study. Buy the books before the course begins and look them over; familiarize yourself with any materials supplied by your college and estimate how much time it will take you to complete special tests and assignments for each lesson. Write the dates of midterms, finals, review sessions, and special projects in your calendar so that you can plan to have extra time to prepare for them. Discuss with your family and friends your needs for study and television viewing time. While you may find it enjoyable and instructive to watch the programs with other people, save the talking and discussion until *after* the program so that you won't miss important information. You may find it helpful to take five minutes at the end of the program to write a brief summary of what you have seen, the meaning of key concepts and terms, and the names of the cultural groups presented.

This study guide will be especially helpful to you as you progress through the course. Begin your study of each lesson by reading the lesson Overview, the Learning Objectives, and the Assignments for the lesson. Follow the sequence of reading and viewing recommended there and then use the Study Activities section as a way to review and study the information in the lesson. As a final step, take the Self-Test and check your answers with the answer key at the end of the lesson.

To further ensure that you will complete "Faces of Culture" to your satisfaction, you should heed these additional suggestions:

- Buy your own copies of the text and study guide for this course. You will not be able to pass the course without following the assigned exercises in these books.

- Watch all of the television programs. You will need to study both the books and television programs to complete the tests and assignments.

- Keep up with your work *every week*. Set aside time for reading, viewing, and study, then stick to your schedule.

- Contact the instructor at your college or university if you have questions, need advice or help, or wish to review television programs or watch ones you've missed. More than likely, broadcasts will be repeated at least once by your local station, and videocassette copies of programs are generally available through your college media center or library.

About the Television Programs

The twenty-six television programs in this course are made up of films or portions of films showing many different societies and cultures. Many of the films have been photographed by or under the supervision of anthropologists, and some show people who have been rarely filmed. Some films come from Japanese and French anthropologists and film makers and have been rarely, if ever, seen in this country. Thus, in this course, you have an opportunity to see authentic film of a wide variety of cultures and people from around the world. Because of this, you will be able to experience these cultures in a more thorough and in-depth way than you could by just reading or hearing about them.

In the field of anthropology, a special kind of research has developed around the use of ethnographic filming—the recording on film of the life-styles of people in one culture. Photographs and filming allow anthropologists to document cultural practices, capturing all aspects of human behavior visually including language, gestures, clothing, social interactions, rituals, and ceremonies, in a more complete way than a written record can do. This has allowed study of many cultures by many anthropologists and also permits recording some practices and customs which, for one reason or another, are becoming rare, perhaps never to be repeated again. Much of the film you will see is ethnographic film, taken for the express purpose of being an accurate and authentic record of the people and practices of other cultures.

As part of the effort to be accurate and let the people of the culture speak for themselves, many of the programs will contain simultaneous English translations in the form of subtitles or narration. Because the subtitles carry important information, be sure your television set has a clear focus so that you can read them.

One of the characteristics of culture is that it integrates all aspects of the society. However, you will be studying various aspects of culture, such as political organization, religion and magic, family patterns, and the economy, as distinct and separate entities. Even though the television programs will focus on these distinct topics, never forget that all parts of culture work together. For example, when you watch the programs on political systems, you will also be seeing practices that relate to a culture's patterns of marriage and family and kinship. So look beyond the specific focus of a program and be alert to the *total* pattern of a culture.

We hope you will enjoy this course and will come to a new and deeper understanding of the variety and richness of human cultures.

Office of College Development
Coastline Community College

Acknowledgments

Producing the "Faces of Culture" television course has been a complex team effort by many people with many skills over a period of many months. Several of those persons responsible for this course are listed on the copyright page of this book.

In addition to those people, appreciation is expressed for the contributions of a number of academic advisors to the course. First, William A. Haviland, Ph.D., professor of anthropology at the University of Vermont, and author of the text, served as a technical advisor to the series and helped in numerous ways throughout course production.

Production of the course was made possible with grants from several educational institutions. Each of them, in turn, provided a faculty advisor who helped to formulate the overall course outline and reviewed print and video materials as produced. These reviewers and the institutions they represent are:

- *Parker Nunley, Ph.D.* Dallas County Community College District

- *Elvio Angeloni, M.A.* Southern California Consortium for Community College Television

- *Dennis Shaw, D.A.* Miami-Dade Community College

- *Howard White, Ph.D.* Chicago City Colleges

- *Marjorie Nam, M.A.* Tallahassee Community College

- *Richard Behnke, Ph.D.* Pensacola Junior College

- *Joseph Sasser, M.A.* Florida Junior College, Jacksonville

Advisors White, Nam, and Sasser all represented the Florida State Department of Education.

Others also provided academic assistance for the course. Joe Filson, M.A., instructor at Golden West College, helped to formulate the course goals and instructional objectives. Frances Berdan, Ph.D., professor of anthropology at California State College, San Bernardino, reviewed the study guide. Consultants provided specialized information used in several programs. Their names are included in the program credits.

In addition, appreciation is expressed to Richard T. Searles, M.A., free-lance writer and classroom teacher, who wrote this study guide as well as other guides for several Coast telecourses, and to Mari Womack, Ph.D. (anthropology), free-lance writer and editor of educational materials, who contributed background notes to this guide.

Administrative assistance was provided by J. Warren Binns, Jr., Florida State Department of Education; Sally Beaty, Southern California Consortium for Community College Television; Rodger Pool, Dallas County Community College District; J. Terence Kelly, Miami-Dade Community College; and John H. Thissen, City Colleges of Chicago.

Appreciation is also expressed to Holt, Rinehart and Winston for their support of the telecourse production. David Boynton, formerly their anthropology editor, provided a great deal of important advice and assistance during the planning stages of the telecourse.

The twenty-six programs of "Faces of Culture" were produced by KOCE-TV, Channel 50, in its studios located on the Golden West College campus in Huntington Beach, California. An affiliate of the Public Broadcasting Service (PBS), Channel 50 is owned and operated by the Coast Community College District, Costa Mesa, California. This study guide, test materials, and instructor's materials for this course were developed for publication by the Office of College Development, Coastline Community College, Fountain Valley, California, a member of the three Coast Community Colleges.

Contents

The Nature Of Anthropology

Overview

This first lesson in "Faces of Culture" introduces you to the discipline of anthropology, or "the study of humankind," as anthropologists define it. The subject matter of anthropology is, in a sense, shared with psychology and sociology, but anthropology differs from these social sciences in at least two significant ways. The first of these differences might be called the "focus of interest" of anthropology. Anthropologists take special interest in the wide diversity of human groups, including those groups which are distant both in space and time. The second way in which anthropology differs from other social sciences is in its methods of research, or methodology. Investigators in this field seek knowledge of human activity from both the present and the past, using specially developed techniques. These techniques include the sifting of massive amounts of minute data in search of patterns, conducting field research, and making comparative cross-cultural studies of specific aspects of culture. In an effort to discover new general principles that explain human behavior, anthropologists also compare the results of their research with the findings of scientists from other disciplines.

In this lesson, you are asked to approach this important question: In what ways is anthropology a science? To answer this, you will have to consider both the nature of science and the nature of anthropology. You may find it helpful to watch for evidence that anthropologists, like other scientists, constantly collect new information, and, in the process, revise and even discard explanations that no longer apply to anthropological fields.

In the lessons that follow, you will learn something about the many discoveries anthropologists have made in their studies of humans in a variety of times and places. After *your* studies, you will undoubtedly have a deeper appreciation for the creativity and adaptability that humankind exhibits everywhere, greater admiration for the drama of human life, and a clearer understanding of your own society and your place within it.

Learning Objectives

When you have completed all assignments in this lesson, you should be able to:

1. Describe ways in which anthropology attempts to be a scientific study of humankind. (Text pages 7, 8, 12-14, 20-23; television program.)

2. Identify ways in which anthropology is distinct from other disciplines that study human beings. (Text pages 10-16, 18-10, 22-23.)

3. Describe the focus of the field of physical anthropology. (Text pages 11-12.)

4. Define cultural anthropology and the subfields of archaeology, ethnology, and linguistics. (Text pages 12-15; television program.)

5. Explain the difference between ethnology, ethnography, and ethnohistory. (Text pages 15-16, 23.)

6. Define the terms "hypothesis" and "theory." (Text pages 7, 20-23.)

7. Identify some of the ways the study of anthropology is relevant to today's world. (Text page 24.)

Assignments For This Lesson

Before Viewing the Program

Read the overview and the learning objectives for this lesson. Use the learning objectives to guide your reading, viewing, and thinking.

Read the preview to Chapter 1 in the text, and look over the topic headings in the chapter.

Read Chapter 1, "The Nature of Anthropology."

View Program 1, "The Nature of Anthropology."

As you view the program, look for:

the story of what happened to the Tasmanian Aborigines as a result of British colonialization.

the classic film taken of the war rituals of the Kwakiutl Indians of the Pacific Northwest of Canada.

the reasons—told in the words of a Turkana leader named Lorang—why the Turkana men customarily have several wives.

After Viewing the Program

As a follow-up to the television program, you may wish to read brief descriptions of some of the anthropologists discussed in the program. Check the index of your text for information about Franz Boaz and Margaret Mead.

Review the terms used in this lesson. Check your understanding of all unfamiliar terms appearing in the learning objectives and the glossary notes in the text.

Review the reading assignments for this lesson. A thorough second reading is suggested. Include the chapter summary in your review.

Complete each of the study activities and the self-test in this study guide; then check your answers with the answer key at the end of this lesson.

According to your instructor's assignment or your own interests, complete one or more of the suggested activities. You may also be interested in some of the readings suggested at the end of Chapter 1 in your text.

Study Activities

Vocabulary Check

Check on your understanding of terms by matching those on the left with the definitions on the right. Check your choices with the answer key at the end of the lesson.

1. __C__ physical anthropology
2. __a__ cultural anthropology
3. __b__ archaeology

a. the study of cultures from a comparative or historical point of view

4. __A__ ethnology
5. __D__ ethnography
6. __H__ hypothesis
7. __E__ theory

b. the study of material objects, from the past or present, to describe and explain human behavior
c. systematic study of humans as biological organisms
d. systematic description of a culture based on firsthand observation
e. an explanation incorporating validated hypotheses that provide a systematic explanation of phenomena
f. scientific study of all aspects of language
g. focuses on the patterns of life in a society
h. a tentative explanation of the relationship between phenomena

Completion

Choose the best word or phrase from the lists provided to fill the blanks in the paragraphs below.

1. One example of the use of the scientific approach in anthropology is the work of the ethnographer, who gathers extensive ____data____ about a culture before attempting to describe cultural patterns.

data
cross
cross-cultural
linguistics
archaeology
description
ethnology

2. Ethnological theories in anthropology usually are the result of careful ____CROSS____-cultural comparisons.

3. Anthropologists, in contrast with psychologists or sociologists, seek understanding of the ____CROSS-CULTURAL____ basis of human behavior.

4. The field of anthropology is divided into two major parts: physical and cultural anthropology. The subdivisions of cultural anthropology are ____Ethnology____, ____ARCHAEOLOGY____, and ____linguistics____.

5. Ethnography is the _descriptions,_
   of a culture that is used by ethnologists in making generalizations.

Short-Answer Questions

1. How does anthropology differ from other social sciences in its approach to studying people?

2. List and briefly describe the three specializations within the field of cultural anthropology.

3. Give at least one reason why anthropological research is important in today's world.

Self-Test

(Select the one best answer.)

Objective 1
1. One of the major problems facing an anthropologist doing research is
   a. identifying a culture which is different from his own.
   b. forming an objective and culture-free hypothesis about phenomena in another culture.
   c. formulating a theory before beginning to study a culture.
   d. constructing a satisfactory questionnaire before interviewing members of a society.

Objective 2
2. Anthropology generally differs from sociology and psychology because sociology and psychology do not
   a. make generalizations about groups of people.
   b. study human beings.
   c. compare behaviors occurring in different cultures.
   d. develop hypotheses and theories.

Objective 3
3. Which of the following is a major concern of physical anthropology?
   a. natural environments
   b. evolution
   c. present-day cultures
   d. nutrition

Objective 4
4. Which of the following best describes the focus of interest of cultural anthropology?
   a. humans as biological organisms
   b. human activity as revealed by material remains
   c. the scientific study of language
   d. patterns of life in societies

Objective 5
5. A field particularly concerned with studies of cultures of the recent past is
   a. ethnology.
   b. physical anthropology.
   c. ethnohistory.
   d. linguistics.

Objectives 1, 5, and 6
6. In ethnographic studies, the anthropologist usually forms a hypothesis
   a. before beginning the study.
   b. as soon as he has comparative data from two or more cultures.
   c. after close contact and gathering data in the field.
   d. after compiling information from a questionnaire.

Objective 6
7. When constructing a *theory*, the theory should be supported by
   a. a system of validated hypotheses.
   b. data from other theories.
   c. material objects.
   d. a tentative conclusion.

Objective 7
8. The "garbage survey" of the University of Arizona suggests that
   a. techniques of anthropology are best employed in studying isolated societies.
   b. techniques of archaeology can be employed in studying present-day America.
   c. the questionnaire is always a valid research tool.
   d. ethnographic studies are best accomplished in a present-day industrial environment.

Suggested Activities

1. Do library research on the Tasmanians, the destruction of their people and culture, and the opinion of English-speaking scientists of the Tasmanians in the nineteenth century.

2. Read the review article concerning Derek Freeman and his book, *Margaret Mead and Samoa*, which appeared in *Time*, February 14, 1983 (Volume 121; page 68). As you read this article, consider whether the information given there suggests that Freeman's data was collected from a different data base and with a different point of view from that of Mead.

3. Set up a "garbage study" in your own household to test ideas about your life-style and values. Design your study, deciding what you will look for and what your findings might indicate. Write a report describing your findings and conclusions.

Answer Key

Vocabulary Check

1. c
2. g
3. b
4. a
5. d
6. h
7. e

Completion

1. data
2. cross
3. cross-cultural
4. linguistics, archaeology, ethnology
5. description

Short-Answer Questions

1. How does anthropology differ from other social sciences in its approach to studying people? Your answer should include:

   Anthropologists are generalists who look at the broad bases of human behavior rather than any one aspect.

   Anthropology is unique among the social sciences because it is based on the study of human behavior and biology in all known societies rather than in European and North American societies alone.

2. List and briefly describe the three specializations within the field of cultural anthropology. Your answer should include:

Archaeology, which usually focuses on ancient cultures, material objects which help to identify and describe life-styles and cultural patterns.

Ethnology is based on historical and contemporary studies of specific cultures; it makes comparisons between cultures to arrive at more general principles about human behavior and culture.

Linguistics, the scientific study of all aspects of language.

3. Give at least one reason why anthropological research is important in today's world. Your answer should include:

The potential for widespread communication and travel in the world today make it especially important to achieve better understanding between societies.

Rapid changes occurring in our own and other societies require better understanding of the principles underlying the behavior of people in their cultures and societies.

Changes occurring in relatively isolated traditional societies may cause many such societies to disappear as they adopt Western life-styles. If they disappear, another example of the range of human culture and adaptation is lost from our study and observation.

Self-Test

1. b	5. b	9. a
2. a	6. d	10. b
3. d	7. c	
4. c	8. c	

The Nature Of Culture 2

Overview

Every field of knowledge possesses certain key concepts or
understandings that are crucial to its full appreciation. For example,
the concept of *numbers* is essential to understanding mathematics,
element to chemistry, and *force* to physics. Anthropology is no
exception. As a branch of the social sciences which attempts to
understand and explain human behavior, anthropology, too, has
basic ideas which are crucial to any study of the discipline.

There are two especially important concepts you should
understand from the beginning of your study of anthropology. The
first is *culture*, the second is *society*. Although those terms are
already familiar to you, you probably don't use them in the same
senses that they are used by anthropologists.

Before you begin your study of this lesson, you might find it
helpful to think about the popular meanings of culture and society
and be aware that, for you, these two words will take on more
complex dimensions throughout the rest of this course. Culture
means much more than manners and the arts; society involves more
than a select and highly publicized status group. And, you should
note one other precaution: Culture and society have separate
meanings. The two words are not, strictly speaking, interchangeable.
However, they *are* firmly related, because culture cannot exist
without society, and all human societies have a culture.

In this lesson, you will be introduced to anthropological definitions of culture and society and to some of the many varieties of cultures in existence around the world. You'll also learn what anthropologists observe to be some universal characteristics of cultures and how culture is involved in every significant part of the lives of members of any society. By the end of this lesson, you probably will realize that you truly are a "person of culture," if not in the popular sense, at least in the anthropologist's view. But then, so is every other human on planet Earth today.

Learning Objectives

When you have completed all assignments in this lesson, you should be able to:

1. Identify E.B. Tylor's classic definition of culture. (Text page 30; Background Notes.)

2. Explain what anthropologists mean when they say that culture is "shared." (Text pages 31-32; Background Notes.)

3. Define "society" and explain its relationship to culture. (Text pages 31-34; Background Notes.)

4. Define and give an example of "subcultural variation." (Text pages 32-34; Background Notes.)

5. Explain what anthropologists mean when they say culture is "learned." (Text pages 34-35; television program; Background Notes.)

6. Explain how culture is based on symbols. (Text pages 35-36; television program.)

7. Define integration as a characteristic of culture, and recognize that cultures can tolerate some internal inconsistencies. (Text pages 36-38; television program; Background Notes.)

8. Explain how adaptation is an important aspect of human culture. (Text pages 44-46; television program; Background Notes.)

9. Recognize that all cultures change over time. (Text pages 46-48; television program.)

10. Explain how culture must balance the needs of both individuals and groups in order for the society to survive. (Text pages 48-49.)

11. Contrast "cultural relativism" and "ethnocentrism." (Text pages 49-50; television program.)

12. Discuss the reasons why cultural relativism is emphasized by anthropologists, and describe Haviland's view of a "scientific" criterion for evaluating culture. (Text page 50; television program.)

Assignments For This Lesson

Before Viewing the Program

Read the overview and the learning objectives for this lesson. Use the learning objectives to guide your reading, viewing, and thinking.

Read the preview to Chapter 2 in the text, and look over the topic headings in the chapter.

Read text Chapter 2, "The Nature of Culture."

View Program 2, "The Nature of Culture."

As you view the program, look for:

the varied influences of different cultures upon their respective societies.

an example of ethnocentrism from one of the first European contacts with the New World.

the culture of the Indian tribes of the Xingu River region of Brazil, how their cultures have enabled these societies to survive in a challenging environment, and the crisis facing these Indians today (summarized near the end of the program.)

the Boran society and some aspects of its culture.

scenes showing the great variety of human cultures, as revealed in clothing, ceremonies and rituals, ways of finding and eating food, and ways of organizing members of societies into families and work groups.

After Viewing the Program

Read the background notes for this lesson.

Review the terms used in this lesson. In particular, check your understanding of these:

culture   symbol
society   integration
social structure   adaptation
subcultural variation   ethnocentrism
enculturation   cultural relativism

Review the reading assignments for this lesson. A thorough second reading of the text chapter and the background notes is suggested. Include the chapter summary in your study.

Complete each of the study activities and the self-test in this study guide, then check your answers with the answer key at the end of this lesson.

According to your instructor's assignment or your own interests, complete one or more of the suggested activities. You may also be interested in some of the readings suggested at the end of Chapter 2 in your text.

Background Notes

Aspects of Culture and Society

We are all bearers of culture. We carry around with us an intricate set of rules for appropriate behavior, as well as instructions on how to survive in our social and physical environment. We can use and manufacture tools. We also have coherent and unified explanations for how the world came to be the way it is. We can communicate our understanding of the world with others like us. These are all aspects of culture. Anthropologists sometimes speak of culture as "patterns" for behavior, meaning that a culture consists of all one needs to know to behave as a member of a particular society is expected to behave.

We acquire this knowledge as members of society. We are *enculturated* as members of social groups. Culture is not invented anew by each new baby that is born. It is accumulated and transmitted to each new member of the group. This process is not always a conscious one, and sometimes the individual is not aware of the extent to which culture influences his or her behavior.

A society is a group of people sharing a common culture and locality. Every society has institutions for enculturating its members. Individuals first learn about their cultural traditions as members of a family. Later, they may learn by observing people outside the family or through especially established institutions, such as apprenticeships or schools.

Anthropologists sometimes also use the term "culture" to refer to a specific cultural system, as when William A. Haviland, the author of your text, refers to Kapauku culture (pages 36-38). However, it is sometimes difficult to understand the difference between society and culture when culture is used to describe specific societies. It is simplest to think of culture as the total pattern of human behavior, and society as a group of people who behave according to a set of cultural assumptions. One anthropologist has suggested that culture is like a musical composition and society is like the orchestra which performs it.

It's not quite that simple, of course, since not all social groups are societies. Students in a classroom are a social group behaving according to a set of cultural assumptions. They are members of a society, but they do not constitute a society, according to most anthropological definitions. A society is generally defined as a group that has all of the institutions necessary to sustain itself through time. This includes ways of obtaining food, protecting its members from environmental extremes and hostile outsiders, of reproducing itself, and of passing on cultural traditions to new members.

Cultural knowledge underlies all areas of our lives, from getting and preparing food to gaining favor with influential elders in the community. It guides our behavior in economic, political, and other spheres. Within a given cultural tradition, different aspects are likely to form a coherent system. That is, they are *integrated*. In our society, for example, the predominance of nuclear families may be related to geographical and social mobility, which in turn may be related to industrialization.

In this course, there will be many other examples of integration among different institutions within a society or cultural system. However, there is *variability* within any culture, more than many early anthropologists expected or believed. Intracultural variability is especially marked in complex societies, such as our own. For example, not everyone in our society lives the same way. The life of an inner-city family will not be the same as that of a farm family and neither will duplicate the experience of a wealthy jet-setter. Religious institutions in the United States range from the unstructured practices of the Quakers (Friends), who have no formal creed or other ecclesiastical forms, to the Roman Catholic Church, with its hierarchical character and long tradition of emphasis upon ritual and symbol. Yet, geography, economic status, and religion notwithstanding, we all share common cultural assumptions. We agree that mashed potatoes should be eaten with a fork instead of our hands. We drive our cars on the right-hand side of the road and recognize that a red light means "stop," while a green light means "go." We can even generalize this very useful cultural information by understanding that when someone speaks of giving us the "green light," we can go ahead with some project or action we've been considering.

When there is much diversity, as in our own society, it is appropriate to speak of *subcultural variation*. This means that some groups share an identity that distinguishes them from others in the society, but they still partake of the common cultural heritage and participate in some of the society's overarching institutions. For example, Vietnamese who have immigrated to the United States may retain their way of preparing food, maintaining a household, and observing religious beliefs, but they are subject to the same federal, state, and local laws and systems of taxation as everyone else in the United States.

Even in small-scale societies, which anthropologists once thought of as uniform, there is a degree of variation. Young people do not have access to the esoteric knowledge of elders, and men and women may have different roles and associated cultural knowledge. Also, any cultural system contains and can tolerate inherent inconsistencies and conflicts. Folk wisdom in our society advises us both that "a penny saved is a penny earned" and "you can't take it with you." These inconsistencies usually do not cause great difficulty for us as members of society, since we can apply whichever rule is compatible with our goals. We learn how and when to apply the rules at the same time we learn the rules.

Most anthropologists consider the environment to be an important influence on culture and a factor in culture change and adaptation. When anthropologists go into the field, they note the physical environment, as well as the customs and social institutions of the people they are studying. However, the physical environment is not the only influence on the development of specific cultures. This is demonstrated by the fact that different groups have different solutions for problems posed by one particular environment.

The television program describes in some detail the cultural practices of two groups, the Txukarrame of Brazil, and other similar Indian groups in the same region, and the Boran of Ethiopia and Kenya. Note the role of the environment in these cultures in the following descriptions. The Txukarrame and the Boran cultures represent different adaptations to two vastly different types of environment.

The Txukarrame of Brazil

There are several closely related Indian groups that live near the Xingu River of Brazil, a river that runs into the Amazon. One group, the Txukarrame, typify the cultural practices of these Indians. They use slash-and-burn techniques for growing food. First, they cut down trees in the jungle to form a garden plot, then plant it with manioc, a bitter tuber that provides nutritious starch. They plant season after season, until the land begins to lose its fertility. Then they clear a new plot of land, allowing the jungle to reclaim the older one. This is a form of agriculture well suited to the jungle environment, because it does not deplete the soil and jungle resources as much as more intensive forms of agriculture. Large-scale agriculture using commercial fertilizer and heavy equipment destroys delicate jungle soils. Slash-and-burn agriculture allows the Txukarrame to live close to the jungle, where they can hunt for monkeys and other small animals and gather honey from wild bees. The Txukarrame also fish with bows and arrows from dugout canoes.

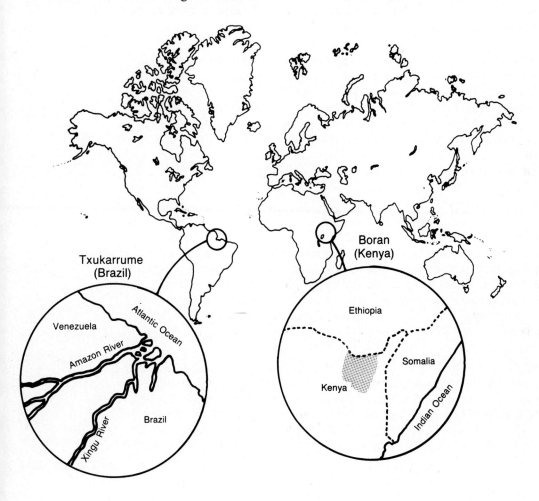

Figure 2.1 The Txukarrame of Brazil's Amazon River basin and the Boran, nomads of Kenya, are two societies whose cultures reflect different environmental conditions.

This seems a simple life, but carving a living out of the jungle requires many skills and a large stock of cultural knowledge. Young males must learn to hunt and fish. Girls must learn to prepare manioc, which is poisonous if not prepared properly.

Young boys and girls of the Txukarrame society learn the cultural knowledge they must have by watching their parents and other adults, but their training becomes more formal at adolescence. At this time they go into a period of seclusion which marks their passage from childhood to adulthood. They must also learn their place in society. The *kuarupe* ceremony symbolizes the permanence of Txukarrame society and the link of present-day members with their ancestors. Young women coming out of seclusion during the kuarupe ceremony symbolically take the place of members of the village who have died. This ceremony perpetuates cultural knowledge by providing a context for teaching all that people must know and do as members of Txukarrame society.

The Boran

The Boran live in southern Ethiopia and northern Kenya, an entirely different environment from the jungles of Brazil. They are pastoral nomads, meaning that they are herders who move from place to place. The Boran live in a sparse environment, to which they have adapted culturally. Anthropologist Asmarom Legesse writes, "Their entire sociopolitical system is so flexible that it allows them to circumvent all but the most extreme droughts and to rehabilitate their communities and herds after every disaster."

The Boran herd cattle and their principal source of food is cow's milk. They use their few sheep and goats primarily for meat and sometimes buy grains from neighboring agricultural communities. But they value their cattle more than any other livestock. As noted in the television program, the Boran believe that humans and their cattle were created at the same time, whereas other animals were created later. They can trace the pedigrees of their cattle, and no important ceremony can be conducted without cattle sacrifice.

Sharing and openness are pervasive aspects of Boran society. Their dwellings have no doors, food is readily shared, and they readily answer questions, even when asked by strangers. The social organization is very flexible. Local communities consist of a few families that come together for a single season. Each camp has a leader whose primary responsibility is to call together meetings of elders, whose advice governs the leader's ability to keep order in the camp. The camp leader is chosen on the basis of seniority, but seniority is determined by lineage or kinship, not by age.

The Boran live in huts that are easily carried from place to place, since they are built of branches covered with skins. The entire possessions of a household can be loaded onto a single camel.

Every year, Boran herdsmen return to their ancestral wells, when temporary watering places dry up. These wells, not their huts, are considered home. Wells are owned by lineages and controlled by the senior male member of the lineage. Wells are a kind of gathering place where kinsmen can exchange information. The wells are important sources of water in an area that is plagued by recurring drought, but they are also centers of social activity.

There is division of labor by sex among the Boran. Women construct houses, process dairy products, and manufacture leather goods, whereas woodcarving, care of cattle, performance of ritual, and political and military activities are carried out by males. Training of boys and girls is informal and emphasizes practical aspects of Boran life. Girls learn how to thatch a roof and milk cows, tend a hearth, and care for children. All children must learn how to manage cattle, how to find water, and how to live through a drought. Additionally, boys are taught tribal lore and religious beliefs, as well as an understanding of relationships with neighboring tribes.

The television program shows how Boran beliefs about cattle and herding practices are integrated with other social institutions and how all members work to help the group survive in a hostile environment. However, the Boran way of life is threatened by modernization: pressures to settle in one place; give up traditional ways of training and send their children to schools; and pay taxes and fit into either Kenya or Ethiopian systems of government.

The way in which the Boran adapt to these pressures will be, in part, determined by their cultural assumptions. A change in one part of a cultural system has implications for the rest. Whether the Boran can retain a cultural identity and viability as a society in the face of changes being introduced remains to be seen.

Study Activities

Vocabulary Check

Check on your understanding of terms by matching those on the left with the definitions on the right. Check your choices with the answer key at the end of the lesson.

1. ___D___ Edward Burnett Tylor
2. ___G___ society
3. ___H___ social structure
4. ___B___ culture

a. social movements designed to reform the society

b. set of rules or standards that, when acted upon, produce behaviors that

5. __M__ subcultural variation
6. __K__ enculturation
7. __C__ language
8. __L__ integration of culture
9. __F__ adaptation
10. __E__ ethnocentrism
11. __J__ cultural relativism

          fall within the range the members of the group consider proper and acceptable

c. the most important symbolic aspect

d. wrote the first comprehensive definition of "culture"

e. belief that one's own culture is superior to all others

f. a term used both for the process, and the results of a process, by which organisms (or cultures) achieve a beneficial adjustment to their environment

g. a group occupying a specific locality and possessing the common cultural institutions necessary to sustain itself through time

h. the relationships of people and groups within a society that hold it together

i. a basis for scientific evaluation of a culture

j. concept that a culture can be evaluated only according to its own standards

k. process by which culture is transmitted from one generation to the next

l. tendency for all aspects of a culture to function as an interrelated whole

m. a distinctive set of values and standards by which a group operates within a larger society

Completion

Choose the best word or phrase from the lists provided to fill the blanks in the paragraphs below.

1. When members of a society share a common __culture__, they can usually __predict__ the actions of others in a particular set of circumstances. Although a society may have a

uniform
predict
culture
cultural

common _cultural_ tradition, not all members have _uniform_ roles.

2. Culture is accumulated and _transmitted_ to each new generation. The chief means by which culture is thus shared is _language_. Although all aspects of the culture are interrelated, their "harmony" need not be perfect. There is usually room for individual _differences_ in a culture; thus, there is always potential for _change_.

differences
change
language
transmitted

3. Animals which have survived environmental changes over many generations have done so by developing _physical_ characteristics that result in a _beneficial_ adjustment. Humans, however, depend primarily on cultural _adaption_ for survival.

adaption
physical
beneficial

4. As anthropologists discovered that people called "primitive" and "savage" were fully human in their own right, they reacted to the ethnocentrism of earlier "civilized" observers by declaring that each culture should be evaluated only in terms of its own _standards_ and _values_. Haviland states that this view, called cultural _relativism_, is also an extreme position and suggests instead a scientific criterion for judging the worth of a culture: the ability of the society to _survive_ through the means given it by the culture.

values
relativism
standards
survive

Short-Answer Questions

1. Briefly contrast Sir Edward Burnett Tylor's definition of culture with that suggested by Haviland in your text. What is the most significant difference between the two definitions?

2. Summarize the characteristics of culture which have been observed by anthropologists to be common to all cultures.

3. According to your text author, William A. Haviland, what are the dangers of an excessive tendency to meet only the needs of the society or only the needs of the individual?

4. Contrast the type of environments to which the Txukarrame and Boran societies have adapted, indicating how they have adapted, and briefly summarize the cultural threat that each society faces today.

Self-Test

(Select the one best answer.)

Objective 1
1. Which one of the following is a key phrase from Edward Burnett Tylor's classic definition of culture?
   a. a group of people who occupy a specific locality and depend upon each other for survival
   b. set of rules or standards which, acted upon by members, produce behavior considered proper and acceptable
   c. complex whole which includes knowledge, belief, art, law, morals, custom, and any other capabilities and habits
   d. the observable behaviors that reveal the relationships between various groups within the larger society

Objective 1
2. Which of the following contains key phrases from William Haviland's definition of culture?
   a. a group of people who occupy a specific locality and depend upon each other for survival
   b. set of rules or standards which, acted upon by members, produce behavior considered proper and acceptable
   c. complex whole which includes knowledge, belief, art, law, morals, custom, and any other capabilities and habits
   d. the observable behaviors that reveal the relationships between various groups within the larger society

Objective 2
3. Cultures are "shared" in the sense that
   a. elements of culture are frequently passed on to societies in other areas.

20

b. people in the same locality learn to work together.
c. some members of the group will try to teach their beliefs to others.
d. members of the group generally hold the same ideals, values, and standards.

Objective 3
4. "A group of people occupying a specific locality and sharing the same traditions" is Haviland's definition of a
   a. society.
   b. subcultural variation.
   c. culture.
   d. social structure.

Objective 4
5. The Old Order Amish in the United States are an example of a
   a. pluralistic society.
   b. variable society.
   c. world culture.
   d. subcultural variation.

Objective 5
6. What happens in the process called enculturation?
   a. The individual flees from the influence of culture.
   b. One learns the culturally appropriate ways of satisfying one's needs.
   c. One can select any of the available subcultural variations.
   d. The major traits of the culture are inherited biologically.

Objective 6
7. Why is language important in the transmission of culture?
   a. Language is the only means for transmission of culture.
   b. Language is the only nonsymbolic means of communication.
   c. Language is helpful in explaining the symbols of a culture.
   d. Language provides the foundation upon which human culture is built.

Objective 7
8. Anthropologists have found that the parts of a culture tend to function as an interrelated whole. This phenomenon is called
   a. enculturation.
   b. harmony.
   c. integration.
   d. pluralism.

Objective 8
9. Identify the phrase which is *not* an aspect of cultural adaptation, as defined in the text.
   a. process by which organisms make a beneficial adjustment to the environment

b. results achieved through changes in biological or physical structure over many generations

c. possession of characteristics that enable organisms to overcome hazards and secure needed resources

d. results of the process by which the adjustment was made

Objective 8

10. Why is the human race unique among animals in its adaptations?
    a. Humans have not needed to adapt to varying environments.
    b. Humans have usually made cultural adaptations.
    c. Humans depend primarily on biological adaptation.
    d. Humans make adaptive adjustments only to changes in the natural environment.

Objective 9

11. Which one of the following is a factor which is forcing cultural changes in the Boran society?
    a. introduction of metal tools
    b. physical changes in the environment
    c. new patterns of education for youth
    d. a breakup of kinship and lineage patterns

Objective 9

12. What cultural change caused disastrous cultural upset among the Yir Yoront?
    a. educational policies from another culture
    b. introduction of a metal axe head
    c. removal of the people from their land
    d. modification of pig-raising customs

Objective 10

13. If the culture emphasizes the needs of the society at the expense of individual needs and interests, the danger
    a. is comparatively little, because survival of the society is assured.
    b. of social upset is great, because a culture is usually unable to affect the values and standards of large numbers of people.
    c. is slight, because people within a society do not recognize that their own activities are restricted.
    d. from excessive stress and alienation experienced by many individuals is great.

Objective 10

14. What is generally the most important incentive for members of the society who adhere to its cultural standards?
    a. economic advantage
    b. greater freedom of action
    c. social approval and acceptance
    d. leadership positions

Objective 11

15. The belief that one's own culture is superior to any other in all ways is called
    a. ethnocentrism.
    b. cultural relativism.
    c. cultural materialism.
    d. maladaptation.

Objective 12

16. The view that individual cultures should be evaluated only according to their own standards is
    a. generally not held today, although nineteenth century observers favored it.
    b. unrealistic, because it is impossible to learn what these "standards" are.
    c. generally favored by anthropologists today.
    d. impossible in light of subcultural variation.

Objective 12

17. Identify the aspect listed which is most closely related to a "scientific criterion" for evaluating culture.
    a. technology
    b. survival
    c. environmental resources
    d. individual needs

Suggested Activities

1. Write an essay contrasting the popular use of the terms "society" and "culture" with their meanings in anthropology.

2. What harmful effects might result from a purely ethnocentric bias when one culture comes in contact with another? What harm might result from the other extreme, cultural relativism, when two cultures first contact each other? Answer each of these questions in a single paragraph, then examine each answer for evidences of values and standards ("rules") that you have learned from your own culture. Finally, comment on whether or not you can anticipate any difficulties in being truly objective in learning about cultures other than your own, evaluating them only by William Haviland's "scientific" criterion.

3. In addition to Tylor's and Haviland's definitions of culture, anthropologists have suggested many other definitions. Using library resources, find at least five other definitions of culture and write a brief paper comparing the definitions. Comment on why you feel it has been difficult to develop one definition that is generally accepted.

Answer Key

Vocabulary Check

1. d	5. m	9. f
2. g	6. k	10. e
3. h	7. c	11. j
4. b	8. l	

Completion

1. culture, predict, cultural, uniform

2. transmitted, language, differences, change

3. physical, beneficial, adaptation

4. values, standards, relativism, survival

Short-Answer Questions

1. Briefly contrast Sir Edward Burnett Tylor's definition of *culture* with that suggested by Haviland in your text. What is the most significant difference between the two definitions? Your answer should include:

   Tylor's definition: "that complex whole which includes knowledge, belief, art, law, morals, custom and any other capabilities and habits acquired by man as a member of society."

   Haviland's definition: "a set of rules or standards that, when acted upon by the members of a society, produce behavior that falls within a range of variance the members consider proper and acceptable."

   Tylor's definition is much more general than Haviland's. In particular, Haviland's definition reflects the emphasis upon values and beliefs, rather than on observable behavior, as the essential aspect of culture.

2. Summarize the characteristics of culture which have been observed by anthropologists to be common to all cultures. Your answer should include:

   Culture is shared by all the members of the society.

   Culture is learned as a person grows up in the culture.

   Culture is based on symbols and transmitted from one generation to the next, primarily through symbols; language is the most important form of symbolism.

Culture is integrated. Although some degree of individual differences is permitted, all parts of the culture must be more or less harmonious with each other.

Cultures change over time.

3. According to your text author, William A. Haviland, what are the dangers of an excessive tendency to meet only the needs of the society or only the needs of the individual? Your answer should include:

If society's needs are met at too great expense of individual needs, the individual is placed under excessive stress, which may lead to antisocial behavior and eventually a loss of social cohesion.

If individual needs are met at too great expense of society's needs, the result can be social breakdown and violent change.

4. Contrast the type of environments to which the Txukarrame and Boran societies have adapted, indicating how they have adapted, and briefly summarize the cultural threat that each society faces today. Your answer should include: .

The Txukarrame have adapted to the forest lands of Brazil, becoming agriculturalists, but they also hunt and fish.

The Boran live in a sparse environment in Kenya and Ethiopia that periodically suffers drought. They are nomadic, primarily herding cattle, although they also raise a few sheep and goats.

The Txukarrame and the other Indian cultures of the region are being pushed away from their forest lands and even hunted and killed by people seeking to claim the land for other purposes.

The Boran are being pressured to settle in one place, as well as live according to the requirements of the "modern" governments of Ethiopia and Kenya. Boran children are being introduced to more formal schooling, which ignores and replaces the learning of their own cultural traditions.

Self-Test

1. c	7. d	13. d
2. b	8. c	14. c
3. d	9. b	15. a
4. a	10. b	16. c
5. d	11. c	17. b
6. b	12. b	

How Cultures Are Studied

3

Overview

Do you remember Yahohoiwa, the violent Yanomamo tribesman who assaulted an anthropologist with both his fists and a bow and arrow? You met Yahohoiwa in the "original study" for text Chapter Two, your reading assignment for Lesson Two. Anthropologist Napoleon Chagnon's vivid description of his confrontation with Yahohoiwa, who was the younger brother of the village headman, undoubtedly made you aware that, during the course of their research and fieldwork, anthropologists may face some challenges which we don't usually think of as being associated with the "scholarly" life.

In this lesson, you will learn more about Yahohoiwa's people, the combative Yanomamo, who dwell in a jungle environment on the common border between Venezuela and Brazil. You will also come to know more about Chagnon and his experiences as both *observer* and *participant* in the Yanomamo society for nearly two years. How Chagnon earned the trust of the Yanomamo and achieved a new understanding of their culture is a story that is both instructive and entertaining. As a result of Chagnon's work, we, in turn, have been able to learn and understand much more about the Yanomamo than would be possible had we been restricted to looking at their society only from the "outside."

But the scientist is not the only one who faces unusual challenges, learns, and is changed by such contacts. An anthropologist can introduce changes into a society that will disrupt cultural patterns, making it difficult or impossible for the society to remain the same. As a scientist, the anthropologist may want to observe a society which is untouched by outside ideas and practices, but in order to *understand* the culture, it is necessary that the anthropologist *participate* in it. Participation requires "give and take" and presents thorny ethical problems for the anthropologist. This lesson looks at some of the scientific, ethical, philosophical, and personal questions raised while "studying" cultures firsthand.

Learning Objectives

When you have completed all assignments in this lesson, you should be able to:

1. Contrast ethnology and archaeology. (Text pages 13-16, 18-20.)

2. Identify the difference between ethnology and ethnography. (Text pages 15-16.)

3. Describe the anthropologist's commitment to a scientific approach to studying culture. (Text pages 20-23.)

4. Describe the purposes of participant observation (ethnographic fieldwork). (Text pages 15-19; television program.)

5. Put in the correct order and define: theory, hypothesis, hypothesis testing. (Text pages 20-21.)

6. Describe ways fieldworkers attempt to deal with the problems of culture-bias and subjectivity. (Text pages 20-23, 49-50; television program; Background Notes.)

7. Identify three aspects of the Yanomamo culture studied by Napoleon Chagnon. (Text pages 41-44; television program; Background Notes.)

8. Discuss the ethical questions raised by studying an isolated group, such as the Yanomamo, where the fieldworker becomes a source of change and modernization. (Text page 48; television program; Background Notes.)

Assignments For This Lesson

Before Viewing the Program

Read the overview and learning objectives for this lesson. Use the learning objectives to guide your reading, viewing, and thinking.

Review Chapters 1 and 2 in the text, particularly pages 13-23, 41-44, and 48-50. (The pages listed for each of the learning objectives will help to guide your review.) Include the chapter summaries in your study.

View Program 3, "How Cultures are Studied."

As you view the program, look for:

these unfamiliar names: Mishimishimabowei-Teri (the village); Nanokawa, Dedeheiwa, Rerebawa, Moawa (villagers), hekura (spirits).

cultural practices which Napoleon Chagnon adopted in order to make the villagers accept and trust him.

the techniques used to develop records of families and villages.

examples of the fierce and combative behavior of the Yanomamo.

Chagnon's statements about participant observation and cultural relativism.

After Viewing the Program

Read the background notes, which follow the assignments in this study guide lesson.

Review the meaning of these terms:

ethnology	cross-cultural comparison
ethnography	village fissioning
holistic perspective	participant observation
theory	cultural relativism
hypothesis	ethnographic present

Review the reading assignments for this lesson.

Complete each of the study activities and the self-test; then check your answers with the answer key at the end of this lesson.

According to your instructor's assignment or your own interests, try to complete one or more of the suggested activities. You may also be interested in the readings suggested at the end of Chapters 1 and 2 in your text.

Background Notes

Studying the Yanomamo

Part of anthropology's appeal for fledgling anthropologists and the public alike is reports of fieldwork among "primitive" people in exotic lands. But the reality of doing fieldwork is often more harsh than glamorous. In his book, *Yanomamo: The Fierce People* (New York: Holt, Rinehart and Winston, 1977), Napoleon Chagnon describes his first meeting with the Yanomamo, the people he was to live among and study:

> I looked up and gasped when I saw a dozen burly, naked, filthy, hideous men staring at us down the shafts of their drawn arrows! Immense wads of green tobacco were stuck between their lower teeth and lips, making them look even more hideous, and strands of dark-green slime dripped or hung from their noses....My next discovery was that there were a dozen or so vicious, underfed dogs snapping at my legs, circling me as if I were going to be their next meal. I just stood there, holding my notebook, helpless and pathetic. Then the stench of the decaying vegetation and filth struck me and I almost got sick. I was horrified. What sort of welcome was this for the person who came here to live with you and learn your way of life, to become friends with you? (p. 5)

Chagnon stayed among the Yanomamo for nineteen months, learning to understand their way of life and eventually to view some of them as friends. He also returned to the field many times to conduct detailed studies. As a result of his research, Chagnon came to view the Yanomamo way of life as being a coherent, internally consistent way of coping with the Yanomamo's jungle environment and their experience of the world.

The Yanomamo live in a jungle area of southern Venezuela and adjacent portions of northern Brazil in about 125 widely scattered villages. There are usually from seventy-five to eighty people living in each village, some of whom have never had contact with an outside culture. The Yanomamo tribe is one of the largest in North and South America that retains its traditional way of life.

One reason the Yanomamo have not had extensive contact with outsiders is that they occupy a region that has been largely inaccessible. They live in hilly terrain that is difficult to cross on foot. During the wet season, in summer, many trails between villages are covered with water, and rivers in the area become impassable torrents. Even in the dry season, the dense jungle forms a canopy that keeps the sun from reaching the ground. Thorns, snakes, and small biting insects also make travel through the region uncomfortable or hazardous.

Figure 3.1 Anthropologist Napoleon Chagnon studied the Yanomamo, isolated tribal peoples living in the jungle headwaters of the Orinoco River.

Yanomamo tools are simple. They hunt with bows and arrows tipped with *curare*, a poison obtained from a jungle vine. They make fire with wood drills and fashion knives from the incisor teeth of a large rodent, the *agouti*. They also make crude, poorly fired clay pots, which break very easily. Women, who are considered to be very clumsy, are rarely allowed to handle them. Consequently, men do the cooking that requires use of the clay pots.

The Yanomamo live in circular houses constructed from poles, vines, and leaves. They make crude, temporary canoes from the bark of a tree.

The jungle furnishes many varieties of plants and animals which the Yanomamo use for food. They hunt monkeys, wild turkey and pigs, armadillos, anteaters, tapir, deer, a small species of alligator, small rodents, and several species of small birds. They also gather palm fruits, Brazil nuts, and edible roots. In addition, they eat wild honey and several species of grubs, which are the fat, white larvae of certain kinds of insects.

Additional food comes from simple farming. The Yanomamo clear a section of jungle, plant a garden, then continue to plant crops there until the soil begins to lose its fertility. When this happens, a new garden spot is cleared. In these gardens, the Yanomamo plant bananas and plantain, a starchy fruit which is similar to the banana. Important root crops are manioc, taro, and sweet potatoes, which are boiled or roasted over coals. They also cultivate corn, tobacco, and cotton, from which they make yarn fibers for hammocks.

Chagnon calls the Yanomamo the "fierce people," adding, "The thing that impressed me the most was the importance of aggression in their culture" (p. 2). Incidents of aggression described by Chagnon include wife beating, chest-pounding duels (in which two men hit each other in the chest with their fists), and fights with clubs and axes. In an axe fight, the men usually hit each other with the flat side of an axe, but this often causes serious injury. Warfare takes the form of raids, in which the object is to enter an enemy village, kill one or more of the men living there, and flee without being discovered. If members of the raided village do not retaliate in kind, they are considered cowardly. Chagnon reports that one village in the area he studied was raided twenty-five times in the nineteen months he spent doing his fieldwork.

The Yanomamo believe it is in the "nature of man" to fight, because men were born "in the blood of the Moon." According to Yanomamo myth, Moon used to steal remains of the dead, so the original Yanomamo tribesmen shot him with arrows. When Moon's blood flowed over the earth, it became men who were warlike and fierce.

The Yanomamo spirit world is also potentially hostile, and Yanomamo shamans, who are healers and workers of magic, spend much of their time trying to bring these spirits under control. The men blow up their noses a hallucinogenic drug in the form of a dark green powder. Much of it, mixed with mucous, runs back out again. This was the green slime which so startled Chagnon when he saw it hanging from the men's noses on his first visit to the Yanomamo. The drug is produced from the bark of a particular tree, the *ebene* and, according to the Yanomamo, the drug produces colored visions and allows the user to get in touch with his *hekura*. Hekura are miniature demons that live on rocks and mountains. As the drug begins to take effect, the men begin to chant to the hekura, inviting them to come and live in their chests. When a man can control a number of hekura, by luring them into his chest, he can become a shaman and heal the sick or work magic against the enemies of his people. Shamans send their hekura to capture the souls of enemy children and use magic to ward off the hekura of their enemies. When a Yanomamo child becomes ill, the illness is often thought to be caused by soul loss, brought about by hekura sent by an enemy.

Chagnon argues that these beliefs are consistent with the Yanomamo view of people as being fierce, living in a world dominated by warfare. He writes, "The...relationship between man and spirit is largely one of hostility" (p. 52). He notes that this permits the Yanomamo to deal with their jungle environment and their experience of the world as a potentially hostile place, and he adds "...each individual Yanomamo enters the world with the physical, social, and ideological traditions at his disposal that will permit him to confront and adjust to the jungle, his neighbors, and the demons that cause sickness" (p. 53).

Coping With Ethical Problems

Chagnon was able to overcome his initial repugnance for the Yanomamo and conduct extensive fieldwork among them. But the problems in doing fieldwork do not end there. An anthropologist studying a group of people who are little known to outsiders collects information which may be harmful to the people under study if it is not treated carefully. Therefore, the anthropologist must abide by a professional standard of ethics designed to minimize potentially harmful effects of fieldwork.

In the television program, Chagnon says that he exchanges machetes and other goods for information, but adds that he has concern about the impact of these exchanges on the Yanomamo culture. Each new implement introduced into a culture like that of the Yanomamo can have a major impact on the environment and disrupt traditional social relationships. For this reason, Chagnon tried to limit the amount and kinds of goods he offered the Yanomamo for exchange.

In his book, *The Fierce People*, Chagnon explains that tribesmen who live close to missions try to borrow shotguns from the missionaries, claiming to need them for hunting game. But the shotguns are often used in fights, giving one group an advantage over the other and escalating the violence.

Even if the shotguns were used only for hunting, they might upset the Yanomamo's adaptation to their environment. The Yanomamo are limited in the amount of game they can take by their reliance on the bow and arrow. Even though they are skilled hunters, they kill only enough game to meet their needs. With shotguns, they would be more efficient killers and, perhaps, deplete the jungle of its game resources. If the Yanomamo overtaxed the jungle's capacity to support life, they might be faced with starvation or the need for drastic change in their way of life. In the anthropological literature, there are many examples of people who have upset their delicate balance with the natural environment and subsequently faced population crises or famine.

Another ethical dilemma arises from the fact that the anthropologist may have information, medicines, and other artifacts which could improve the health of the people being observed. Yet the anthropologist is not trained to diagnose illness or administer drugs and does not have the financial resources to solve major health problems of those under study.

Introducing new technology can also upset established social ties and alliances. If a missionary or anthropologist gives an axe or steel knife to a young boy or outsider who, unknown to the anthropologist, is in the group only temporarily, he gives that person the means and prestige to challenge traditional authority. At the same time, customs for keeping the peace and ensuring the security of the group will be overthrown and hostilities may be escalated. Thus, a "generous" gesture can cause unintended harm.

Sometimes the mere presence of the anthropologist can exert a disruptive influence upon the group. Chagnon mentions in the television program that each group wanted him to remain with them because they desired a monopoly on his trade goods. Having an anthropologist in the village can also bring prestige to its inhabitants, giving them power over their neighbors.

The anthropologist must always be aware of his potential for changing the group he is studying and make every attempt to minimize harmful effects of his fieldwork. At the same time, he must avoid taking a proprietary attitude toward "his" people, resisting all change in an attempt to preserve his "laboratory."

All people change, of course. Change is a natural process that occurs within all human groups. Even people who seem to us to be "primitive" have undergone a long evolutionary history. Groups split apart and join with others. Climatic variations introduce new types of plants and animals into their environment and eliminate others, requiring new types of adaptations. The anthropologist cannot put a glass jar over a people to keep them "unchanged."

The term "ethnographic present" is used to convey the idea that an ethnography is a slice of history, a description of a particular group at a particular time. The group may change considerably as they are contacted by others after the anthropologist leaves them. But ethnographic books and films are written in the present tense because they represent the "present" at the time the anthropologist conducted the study. Thus, cultures can be compared across barriers of time and space, and ethnographies can form the basis for ethnology. Their usefulness for cross-cultural comparison is limited only by the accuracy and thoroughness of the ethnographer.

Ethnographic fieldwork techniques can also be used for studying complex societies. Anthropologist William Pilcher made a widely acclaimed study of Portland longshoremen. James Spradley studied urban transients, and

Hortense Powdermaker studied the Hollywood film industry in the 1940s. Today, studies are being conducted among such diverse populations as ethnic minorities, urban policemen, and professional athletes.

Anthropological fieldwork is an intensive research strategy which produces information that would be missed by the sole use of questionnaires and other survey methods. For all of its hazards, frustrations, and discomforts, ethnographic fieldwork is considered the best way to find out how people really live.

Overcoming Limits and Responding to Change

Although anthropologists try to be as free of cultural bias as possible, they are still products of their own culture. Anthropology as a discipline is a product of the Western tradition of scientific inquiry and, therefore, reflects our cultural assumption that research into human social interaction is both important and necessary.

As the field develops, theoretical assumptions underlying anthropological fieldwork change. Early in this century, anthropologists were very concerned with the question of defining "race," eventually defining the term as a cultural concept, rather than a biological one. More recently, they have become interested in the relationship of economics to other social institutions, and the degree of variability within cultures.

Anthropology also changes in response to changes within our society. Traditionally, when an anthropologist studied a society, he or she talked primarily to men, so that fully one-half of the population was not represented in a "holistic" study of a culture. Since the 1960s, the importance of women's contribution to society is being recognized, so that studies are more balanced. Even the sex or temperament of the anthropologist can affect access to data. Men wouldn't be allowed to witness childbirth practices or women's rituals in many or most societies, and women would probably be barred from men's secret rituals. However, an anthropologist must recognize that some limitations on the ability to collect data are beyond his or her control. All scientific research is limited in opportunities to observe naturally occurring phenomena. However, the anthropologist tries to overcome limitations by being as systematic and thorough as possible in collecting data.

Study Activities

Vocabulary Check

Check on your understanding of terms by matching those on the left with the definitions on the right. Check your choices with the answer key at the end of the lesson.

1. __G__ ethnology
2. __a__ archaeology
3. __D__ ethnography
4. __J__ hypothesis
5. __B__ theory
6. __F__ holistic perspective
7. __E__ cultural relativism
8. __K__ hekura
9. __I__ shotguns

a. study of material objects, both from the past and present, to describe and explain human behavior and culture
b. a belief which may generally be accepted as true but is not beyond challenge
c. a series of tests or trials designed to prove or disprove a supposition
d. systematic description of a culture based on extensive firsthand observation
e. a view that states that a culture can be judged only according to its own standards and values
f. learning how all the institutions within a culture fit together meaningfully
g. observation of human behavior for the study of culture from a comparative point of view
h. one of the ancient myths of the Yanomamo which explains the origins of man
i. example of a borrowed technology that upset a cultural balance in Yanomamo society
j. an interpretation made by a scientist about the relationship between two or more phenomena
k. in Yanomamo mythology, little spirits which are supposed to live in rocks and mountains

Completion

Choose the best word or phrase from the lists provided to fill the blanks in the paragraphs below.

1. Although it is true that scientists begin a study by forming a __hypothesis__, the ethnographer usually immerses himself totally in his study until previously unseen __patterns__ become clear to him. Such an approach requires closest observation of the tiniest details, and

bias
hypothesis
patterns

is time consuming; however, this approach best assures an objective approach and protects against culture ___*bias*___.

2. Anthropologists attempt to be as objective as possible in their studies of other cultures. They try to avoid judging other cultures on the basis of their own cultural standards. In its extreme form, judgment of other social groups by one's own cultural standards is known as *ethnocentrism*. However, gaining an objective view is not easy; it requires that one study another culture while *participating* in it. For example, Napoleon Chagnon learned the language and customs of the Yanomamo in order to study settlement patterns. Only after gathering extensive data did he develop a hypothesis regarding village growth and break-up, which he called village *fissioning*.

ethnocentrism
fissioning
participating

3. Chagnon obtained much of his information from *informants*, like Dedeheiwa, who related information about the society and its culture. In addition to learning customs and traditions, Chagnon developed records of ___*kinship*___ ties and created maps showing village *gardens* cultivated by the Yanomamo for food crops.

kinship
gardens (or garden plots)
informants

Short-Answer Questions

1. Briefly describe the general procedure followed by scientists as they attempt to understand and explain natural phenomena.

2. Explain how ethnographers attempt to avoid preconceptions which might bias their studies.

3. What were some of the aspects of the life of the Yanomamo people that Napoleon Chagnon studied extensively?

4. What are some adverse effects that an ethnographer or others who come in contact with an isolated society may unwittingly have on a society?

Self-Test

(Select the one best answer.)

Objective 1
1. Archaeology is defined as the study of
   a. material objects.
   b. ancient ruins.
   c. food production techniques.
   d. behavior by firsthand observation.

Objective 2
2. Which of the following is most likely to make cross-cultural comparisons?
   a. evolutionist
   b. ethnologist
   c. ethnographer
   d. sociologist

Objective 2
3. Napoleon Chagnon was engaged in what kind of study during his stay with the Yanomamo?
   a. archaeology
   b. ethnology
   c. ethnography
   d. none of the above

Objective 3
4. Ethnocentrism is best defined as
   a. belief that one's own culture is superior to others.
   b. the study of individuals in isolated societies.
   c. belief that each society must be judged according to its own values.
   d. the study of material objects left by humans.

Objective 3
5. Which of the following best describes the scientific approach?
   a. rejection of theories on the basis of logic
   b. development of imaginative explanations for observed phenomena

c. development of testable explanations for observed phenomena
d. development of sufficient proof of an explanation to ensure that it cannot be challenged

Objective 4

6. The most important reason for ethnographic fieldwork is that it
   a. provides an opportunity for making a photographic record of a society.
   b. eliminates the need for a more rigid scientific approach.
   c. is a means of becoming familiar with the traits of primitive cultures.
   d. provides an opportunity to discover previously unknown patterns in culture.

Objective 4

7. The *most* desired result of participant observation by the ethnographer is
   a. a wide variety of factual data from which others can make generalizations.
   b. a recorded history based on the traditions of the people studied.
   c. sufficient facts to judge whether or not the society studied is superior to others.
   d. an explanation of how the society's practices and traditions fit into a meaningful whole.

Objective 5

8. Which of the following is *not* true of hypothesis testing?
   a. Alternate hypotheses should be disproven.
   b. The hypothesis begins as a tentative explanation.
   c. One item of supporting data will verify a hypothesis.
   d. A hypothesis must be testable.

Objective 5

9. How does science define the term "theory"?
   a. a set of validated hypotheses that systematically explain phenomena
   b. a tentative supposition about how certain phenomena are related
   c. a proven explanation of phenomena that should remain accepted despite any further discoveries
   d. an explanation generally accepted as true, although it cannot be verified

Objective 6

10. Napoleon Chagnon states that anthropology must teach "cultural relativism" because he believes
    a. that the Yanomamo are in danger of losing their culture in the near future.
    b. that modern technology and practices must be taught to primitive cultures quickly.

c. that many cultures have developed unique, consistent, and valuable ways of solving problems of living.

d. the customs and traditions of many primitive peoples are superior to Western culture.

Objective 7

11. Which of these aspects of human relationship was studied in considerable detail by Chagnon, according to the television program for Lesson Three?

a. courtship customs

b. communication between villages

c. marriage ceremonies

d. combativeness

Objective 7

12. Chagnon took extensive photographs of individuals during his fieldwork with the Yanomamo in order to

a. learn kinship ties.

b. determine total population.

c. help remember names.

d. record effects of aging.

Objective 8

13. Why was Chagnon especially careful about the kinds of things he traded with Yanomamo villagers?

a. The items traded could become too expensive during extended field study.

b. Many normal trade items are taboo to Yanomamo.

c. New technology can cause unexpected harm to a traditional culture.

d. Government regulation prohibits the trade of many items.

Objective 8

14. Which of these statements comes *closest* to an ethical standard for ethnologists who are in contact with an isolated society?

a. Ethnologists should make every effort to prevent any change in societies being studied.

b. Ethnologists should be aware of the harmful effects on the societies they study that could result from their contact.

c. Ethnologists should avoid any participation in societies under study.

d. Ethnologists should introduce improved technology as rapidly as possible, except for weapons.

Suggested Activities

1. Imagine that you will construct a time capsule to let a future generation know what American culture was like during the last years of the

twentieth century. You have only a limited space in a protected vault. What material items could you select (excluding books and photographs) that would best reflect the *non-material* parts of your culture that seem most important to you? Write a brief essay justifying your selection of artifacts for such a time capsule.

2. The term "culture shock" is frequently used to describe the reactions of persons (especially those who are not prepared) who suddenly find themselves in a society markedly different from their own. You might wish to consult Philip Bock's book *Culture Shock* (New York: Borzoi Books, 1970). You might also locate one or more periodical articles on this subject and read guide books published by the government or private sources to aid servicemen, Peace Corps volunteers, employees, and other persons preparing for duty involving contact with cultures other than their own. Try to make a list of the situations and behaviors which might cause culture shock.

3. Develop a suggested "code of ethics" to apply to ethnographers and others who come into contact with previously isolated societies such as the Yanomamo. You should recognize a reality of today's world: Modern means of travel and communication make it inevitable that all humans will be affected by technological advancement. For example, the frontiers of Venezuela and Brazil will be pushed back, just as the American frontier receded in the nineteenth century, and the jungle-dwelling Yanomamo will have more and more contact with other cultures.

4. Because this lesson introduces you to Napoleon Chagnon, as well as to participant observation as the chief methodology of the ethnographer, you may be interested in reading and writing a report on Chagnon's vivid and comprehensive book, *Yanomamo: The Fierce People* (New York: Holt, Rinehart and Winston, 3rd edition, 1983). Read reviews of this book. Discuss areas of research which Chagnon did not explore when he first visited the Yanomamo but which might be considered important by anthropologists today.

Answer Key

Vocabulary Check

1. g
2. a
3. d
4. j
5. b
6. f
7. e
8. k
9. i

Completion

1. hypothesis, patterns, bias

2. ethnocentrism, participating, fissioning

3. informants, kinship, gardens (or garden plots)

Short-Answer Questions

1. Briefly describe the general procedure followed by scientists as they attempt to understand and explain natural phenomena. Your answer should include:

   Scientific approaches require both imagination and skepticism.

   A scientist first forms a hypothesis, or a tentative explanation, about the relationship between certain phenomena.

   A hypothesis is tested by gathering data which support it and which disprove alternate hypotheses.

   A system of proven hypotheses may constitute a theory, or a "most probable truth." However, theories are subject to later challenge and revision.

2. Explain how ethnographers attempt to avoid preconceptions which might bias their studies. Your answer should include:

   Anthropologists attempt to be as objective as possible by gathering and studying data extensively, using the participant-observer method as their major data-collecting technique.

   Anthropologists try to find patterns that were not previously known before starting to frame hypotheses.

   Anthropologists try to avoid ethnocentrism, that is, they do not judge the culture studied by the standards of their own culture.

3. What were some of the aspects of the life of the Yanomamo people that Napoleon Chagnon studied extensively? Your answer should include at least three or four of the following:

   Social organization of the Yanomamo—including kinship ties, genealogy, dwelling patterns, movement from village to village.

Village patterns—organization and layout of villages, location of present and former villages, village fissioning.

The Yanomamo language.

Myths, traditions, beliefs, and practices concerning magic and spirits.

The fierce combative behaviors of the Yanomamo.

4. What are some adverse effects that an ethnographer or others who come in contact with an isolated society may unwittingly have on a society? Your answer should include:

Fieldworkers and others in contact with a relatively isolated society may introduce new technologies which may alter cultural practices.

For example, the Yir-Yiront of Australia, when introduced to the metal axe, stopped using stone axes, which had served important symbolic functions related to masculinity, authority, and tribal traditions.

Both new tools and the very presence of a fieldworker may upset established social relationships and alliances. For example, shotguns among the Yanomamo have given some villages great advantage over others in their battles. It is also possible that such weapons could lead to depletion of game in the forests.

Anthropologists should be aware of the ethical considerations inherent in participant observation and follow various standards to minimize problems of impact, while realizing that it is impossible to prevent a culture from changing.

Self-Test

1. a	6. d	11. d
2. b	7. d	12. a
3. c	8. c	13. c
4. a	9. a	14. b
5. c	10. c	

Patterns Of Subsistence:

Hunter-Gatherers and Pastoralists

4

Overview

In the United States today most of us do not have to worry about
producing or gathering the basic necessities of life, which means
enough food and water just to stay alive and shelter adequate for
protection against the outside environment. These means of
subsistence are easily purchased in the marketplace or provided for
in our communities. Instead, our concerns are usually about *income*,
the money which we must use to buy these necessities (and the
luxuries of life, as well). You will learn in this lesson, however, that
some of the basic fabric of our modern social relationships may
come directly from ancient ages when food was never purchased,
but was taken directly from the environment. You will also find,
perhaps to your surprise, that some societies subsist this way today,
still following the ancient patterns of the hunter-gatherers and their
successors, the pastoralists. This lesson introduces you to a few
remaining examples of these vigorous and long-lasting lifestyles.

The hunting-gathering way of life, the oldest and most basic
adaptation of the human species to the environment, has been the lot
of more than 90 percent of all humans who ever lived. Hunting and
gathering demanded much of a people, while, at the same time, it
solved specific problems of existence for members of the society. For
example, suppose the game which provides the society with meat
moves to new grounds. What does the society do? How can the
resources be distributed through the group so that the group
remains large enough and strong enough to care for itself? How do

the people of the culture organize to guarantee a steady and adequate food supply? What do you think that a group which depends on hunting and gathering for its livelihood might do to ensure the protection and survival of its young?

About ten thousand years ago, major changes in the hunting and gathering subsistence pattern began to appear. In some parts of the world, humans began to *produce* food instead of hunting or gathering it randomly from the environment. In pastoralist cultures people began to domesticate animals, collecting cattle, sheep, goats, donkeys, pigs, and camels in herds to provide food and other needs. When you see some examples of these cultural groups on your television screen and read about them in your text materials, you may experience another surprise: The people of these societies sometimes enjoy a leisurely, abundant existence, and their daily lives are neither drab nor lacking in courage and spirit.

Two other patterns of subsistence will be described in the next lesson.

Learning Objectives

When you have completed all assignments in this lesson, you should be able to:

1. Understand that culture is the mechanism by which humans meet their basic survival needs. (Text pages 163-164, 174-175; Background Notes.)

2. Define adaptation. (Text pages 164-168.)

3. Describe the concept of culture area. (Text pages 168-174.)

4. Compare the European settlers' use of the Great Plains culture area with that of the native American Indians. (Text pages 168-175.)

5. Describe the importance of the hunting-gathering subsistence pattern. (Text pages 175-186; television program.)

6. Describe the characteristics of a hunting-gathering way of life, and cite examples of this kind of society. (Text pages 180-186; television program; Background Notes.)

7. Identify several elements of human social organization that developed as a result of the hunting-gathering way of life. (Text pages 183-186; television program.)

8. Explain why the hunting-gathering way of life promotes "egalitarianism" among its members. (Text pages 185-186; television program; Background Notes.)

9. Describe the characteristics of the pastoral way of life and cite examples of pastoral cultures. (Text pages 189-191; television program; Background Notes.)

Assignments For This Lesson

Before Viewing the Program

Read the overview and the learning objectives for this lesson. Use the learning objectives to guide your reading, viewing, and thinking.

Read the preview to Chapter 6 in the text and look over the topic headings in the chapter.

Read Chapter 6, "Patterns of Subsistence," in the text, pages 162-186, and 189-191. The remaining pages in this chapter will be studied in connection with the next lesson.

View Program 4, "Patterns of Subsistence: Hunter-Gatherers and Pastoralists."

As you view the program, look for:

the importance of the woman's role in hunting-gathering cultures.

the technology and skill used in hunting by the Netsilik.

examples of social patterns of the hunter-gatherers.

two examples of pastoral peoples, the Nuer and the Basseri. These scenes emphasize the striking differences between the environments for each and some of the challenges that each tribe must meet in order to survive.

After Viewing the Program

Read the background notes for this lesson.

Check your understanding of these terms:

horticulture   ethnoscientists
ecosystem   hunter-gatherers
parallel evolution   density of social relations
culture type

Review the reading assignments for this lesson. A thorough second reading of the text chapter and Background Notes is suggested. Include the chapter summary in your study.

Complete each of the study activities and the self-test in this study guide; then check your answers with the answer key at the end of this lesson.

According to your instructor's assignment or your own interests, complete one or more of the suggested activities. You may also be interested in some of the readings suggested at the end of Chapter 6 in your text.

Background Notes

The Egalitarian Society

There probably never has been an egalitarian society in the sense that all *individuals* have equal access to resources and prestige and perform identical tasks. Age and sex are universal bases for social distinction. A newborn baby does not have the same rights and responsibilities as a venerable elder and, in all societies, women don't do the same work as men or have the same social position.

Although these differences are rooted in biology—a baby cannot do the work of an adult man or woman and the childbearing role of women is protected in all societies—the precise nature of the differences is culturally determined. Babies are treated differently from culture to culture and the work of women may vary from raising pigs or growing yams in New Guinea to gathering Mongongo nuts among the !Kung Bushmen of the African Kalahari Desert.

Among the Tsembaga of New Guinea, women raise the pigs and men cook them. In the United States, men usually care for livestock and women do the cooking. But one pattern does seem to hold true cross-culturally: Men operate in the public realm and women's work is defined as domestic.

It sometimes confuses students that anthropologists speak of *egalitarianism* when all societies make status distinctions on the basis of age and sex. In fact, *individuals* rarely have equal access to resources, nor do they make equal contributions to subsistence. But individuals are part of a social group, the family. In an egalitarian society, families are equal in status. No family unit is singled out for preferential access to resources and prestige, nor is it released from an obligation to provide labor for subsistence activities. Thus, in an egalitarian society, individuals have rights and obligations conferred on them by virtue of membership in a kin group, and all kin groups have equal access to resources.

Anthropologists distinguish *egalitarian* societies from *stratified* societies, which are characterized by specialization of labor and unequal access to resources. Status differences occur when individuals or families accumulate wealth or privilege through their own efforts or through inheritance. In an egalitarian society, no individual or family group may rise above others by inheritance, accumulation of wealth, or specialized knowledge. (The characteristics of stratification will be described in more detail in Lessons 13 and 14.)

Subsistence Patterns

Producing food and allocating resources such as water or hunting rights are *subsistence* activities. All groups everywhere must have ways of caring for the survival needs of their members. People must feed themselves and shelter themselves from extremes of cold and heat, but the means for doing this vary from group to group, depending on environment and custom.

Obviously, resources available in the environment limit the types of foods people eat and the materials available to construct shelter and clothing. But resources are defined by the people who use them, and not all people exploit their environment in the same way. Some things defined as food by one group of people may be considered repulsive by others. For example, some South American Indians eat grubs, which are fat worms. Guinea pigs are raised for food in Peru. But neither would be considered food for humans in modern North American society.

When anthropologists analyze subsistence patterns, they must consider three variables: biological needs for food and shelter, environmental resources, and social adaptations for converting environmental resources into forms that can be used by people to meet their survival needs. These three variables are the basis for an anthropological definition of subsistence: A cultural means for making environmental resources available for human consumption.

The three peoples viewed in some depth in the television program—the Netsilik, the Nuer, and the Basseri—live in widely varying environments. They represent two subsistence modes, hunting-gathering and pastoralism. Hunter-gatherers typically range over a territory, hunting animal life and gathering plants and other materials. They do not cultivate crops or domesticate animals. Pastoralists, on the other hand, live by herding. They may also move from place to place, but their migrations are determined by grazing lands and other resources needed by their animals.

The Netsilik

The Netsilik live along the Arctic coast northwest of the Hudson Bay. There are no trees, and plant life consists primarily of lichen, mosses, and various grass-like plants. The Netsilik are almost exclusively hunters, since there is little to gather in this inhospitable environment.

Yet the Netsilik must use the limited resources available to them to feed, house, and clothe themselves. Asen Balikci, an anthropologist who has studied them extensively, wrote, "The Netsilik, living in one of the harshest areas of the inhabited North, were able to survive in this cold desert environment because of their efficient and remarkably adapted technology." (*Netsilik Eskimo.* New York: Natural History Press, 1971, p. 3.) They build houses out of snow and ice and make children's toys of ice. Caribou and sealskins are used for making clothes (including waterproof boots), sleeping bags, and kayaks. Because wood is scarce, most tools are made of bone. Lamps and pots are made of soapstone.

Like many other hunter-gatherers, the Netsilik migrate seasonally. Their lives are organized around two seasons, which present radically different environments and different resources to be exploited and give rise to different social interactions. Winter, the long season, lasts from late September to July. During this time, the sea is covered with ice and temperatures may drop as low as 20 to 40 degrees below zero fahrenheit. July and August make up summer, the short season.

In summer, temperatures average about 50 degrees fahrenheit in the daytime, the sea ice melts, and the Netsilik migrate inland to fish and hunt caribou. Food is relatively plentiful in the summer. There is greater variety and it is easier to obtain than in the winter. The Netsilik construct sealskin tents on the marshy tundra near fishing places, where they have built permanent stone weirs, or dams. They trap and spear salmon trout in the weirs and harpoon trout in the lakes.

In late summer, the Netsilik hunt caribou with bows and arrows, but they are not very good archers. They are more effective in hunting from their kayaks, which are outfitted with two long spears. Men in kayaks spear the caribou at lake crossings.

When food is plentiful in summer, each man hunts and fishes for himself and his extended family. But by January the Netsilik gather in large winter camps of fifty to a hundred people for seal hunting. Seal hunting is the primary subsistence activity for the Netsilik from January until the end of May. Seals are air-breathing animals, so they must have breathing holes in the ice. The hunter waits at a breathing hole and harpoons the seal as he comes to the surface to breathe. Seals roam over a wide area, so they must use a number of breathing holes. A single Netsilik, hunting for his own family, could not hope to keep guard at all the holes or predict which hole the seal will use. It would be difficult for a single hunter to catch a seal, since he could not possibly watch all the breathing holes. Cooperation among a group of hunters increases the probability that one, or several, will get a seal.

Cooperation in the large winter hunting camps is encouraged by "sharing partnerships." In addition to providing seal meat for members of their extended families, Netsilik men give meat to their partners according to a rigid set of rules. Ideally, a man should have twelve partners, each of which is entitled to receive a specific part of the seal. If a man is absent from the camp and cannot take part in division of the seal, one of his relatives takes his place. These sharing partnerships form a permanent set of alliances that extend loyalties beyond the hunter's family and give the sealing camp social cohesion.

Summer camps are smaller and are held together by kinship ties, but winter camps draw together hunters who are not bound together by kinship. The sharing partnerships extend the "kinship" tie and stabilize social networks in the winter camps.

In the sharing of resources, the lack of systems of social stratification and specialization of roles, the Netsilik exemplify the egalitarian qualities of all hunting and gathering cultures.

The Nuer

In French detective lore, the good inspector says *"cherchez la femme"* if you want to solve the crime. Anthropologist E. E. Evans-Pritchard says *cherchez la vache* (look for the cow) if you want to understand the Nuer (*The Nuer: A Description of the Modes of Livelihood and Political Institutions of a Nilotic People.* London: Oxford University Press, 1968.). The Nuer are pastoralists who live in the Sudan, near the headwaters of the Nile. They raise cattle for milk and other subsistence needs, figure their wealth in cattle, and use them as links in social relationships. Evans-Pritchard writes, "Cattle are their dearest possession and they gladly risk their lives to defend their herds or pillage those of their neighbors."

The area in which the Nuer live is extremely flat and covered with tall grasses. During the rainy season, which reaches its peak in July and August, the area is flooded by the many rivers which cross the region, and the Nuer move their cattle to villages on sandy ridges. When the rains stop in December and January, water supplies near the villages are soon exhausted and the Nuer begin to move near lakes, marshes, and rivers. In late November or early December, the young people take the cattle to camps near watering places, leaving the older people to harvest grain and repair huts and cattle shelters. As water gets scarcer, the young people are joined at their camps by married people and the camps grow to contain as many as several hundred people.

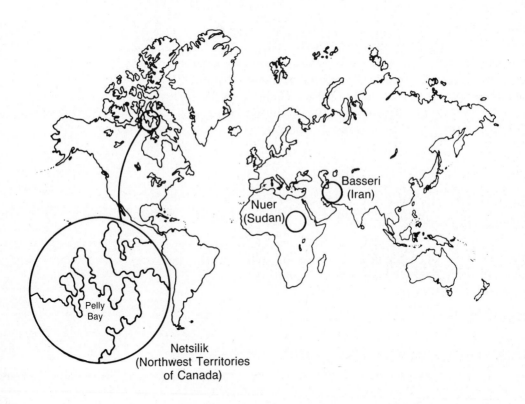

Figure 4.1 The Netsilik, native people of northern Canada, are a hunting-gathering culture; the Nuer of the Sudan and the Basseri of Iran follow a pastoral way of life.

When the rains begin in May, the older people return to the village to prepare the ground for planting millet and corn. The young people bring the cattle back to the village by June. After about ten years, a village site is farmed out or grazed out and the Nuer move on to a new location.

The cattle are chiefly used for milk, and milking is done by women and children. The Nuer drink fresh milk, eat it soured, and make cheese of it. They do not slaughter their cattle for food, but they eat cows that die of natural causes. They also sacrifice cattle during ritual observances and eat their meat.

The area does not have either iron or stone, two materials traditionally used in tool making. Wood is also scarce, but their cattle provide many subsistence needs for the Nuer other than food. Bedding, thongs, and various utensils are made from the skin, bones, and horns. The Nuer use dung to plaster walls and floors and burn it for fuel. In an area where there is little wood, dung is a useful fuel for cooking. The ashes of burnt dung are used for dyeing and straightening hair, tooth powder, and mouthwash. Cow's urine is used in making cheese, tanning leather, and for bathing one's face and hands. The Nuer bleed their cows frequently, boiling the blood for drinking or allowing it to coagulate and then cooking it.

Generally, the Nuer consume fish during the dry season and grain and meat during the wet season. Milk is a staple year round. The Nuer are never able to achieve a food surplus and famine is always a threat. In the Nuer pastoral culture, each household owns its own food and provides independently for the needs of its members, but much food sharing takes place formally and informally at the village level. When cattle are sacrificed, the food is widely distributed, and members of the group are expected to share when food is scarce. Food sharing and the cattle economy allows the Nuer to survive in an area with little plant resources and where there are seasonal fluctuations in availability of water.

The Basseri

Like the Nuer, the Basseri of Southern Iran and the Bakhtiari of Western Iran (described in the text, pages 189-191) are pastoralists. But the Iranian environment presents an entirely different set of challenges from that of the Nuer. The Basseri are tent-dwellers, who migrate seasonally through a mountainous area.

In winter, when the mountains are covered with snow, the Basseri pasture their large herds of sheep and goats on the plains and foothills. During the spring, the herds graze on a well-watered plateau near the center of the territory. By summer, most of the lower-lying pastures have dried up and the Basseri move their herds to the mountains, nearly 6,000 feet above sea level.

The Basseri get milk, meat, wool, and hides from their herds, but their primary foods are sour milk and cheese. During summer, when pastures are rich, they can settle temporarily and build up food surpluses to help them through the leaner winter months. The Basseri also eat agricultural products, most of which are obtained by trade, but they also grow some wheat at their summer camps. They do little hunting or gathering.

The Basseri trade wool and hides and they are skilled weavers. The women weave saddle bags, carpets, and sleeping rugs from homespun wool and hair. Goat hair is woven to make tents. Woven goat hair is especially useful for the Basseri, since it retains heat and repels water in winter, and, in summer, it insulates against heat and permits free circulation of air.

Donkeys and camels are used for pulling or carrying loads and some of the more wealthy men have horses for riding.

Basseri social life and traditions are organized around migration. They do not own land, and individuals do not own property. But family groups, known as "tents," hold full rights over such possessions as bedding, cooking equipment, a herd of sheep and goats (usually numbering about a hundred), and from six to twelve donkeys. In winter, the Basseri live in groups of from two to five tents, but they gather in larger camps of from ten to forty tents the rest of the year.

The tribe has rights over migration routes, which are recognized by local populations and authorities. Thus, though the Basseri do not own the land, they have access to it on a seasonal basis. The "tribal road," or *il-rah*, is regarded as the property of the tribe.

Like the Nuer, the Basseri live by their herds and use their products for shelter as well as for food. Both groups have sexual division of labor, but *women and children* do the cattle herding among the Nuer and Basseri *men* herd the sheep and goats. The Nuer occupy a relatively flat area, threatened only by mosquitos and other pests, but the Basseri must drive their herds along steep mountain trails. Women's work usually does not involve great danger, because their reproductive role is too important to the survival of the group and must be safeguarded. However, their work is no less important. Among such groups as the Nuer and the Basseri, all able-bodied individuals must make a major contribution to subsistence, but the nature of that contribution is determined by survival needs of the community.

Study Activities

Vocabulary Check

Check on your understanding of terms by matching those on the left with the definitions on the right. Check your choices with the answer key at the end of the lesson.

1. _I_ adaptation
2. _C_ preadaptation
3. _D_ convergent evolution
4. _J_ culture area
5. _G_ culture core
6. _A_ cultural ecology
7. _E_ carrying capacity
8. _F_ egalitarian
9. _B_ pastoralist
10. _H_ subsistence

a. the study of the interaction of specific human cultures with their environment

b. a subsistence pattern in which food production is based largely upon the maintenance of animal herds

c. in the study of culture, existing customs with the potential for a new cultural adaptation

d. in the study of culture, the development of similar adaptations to similar environmental conditions by peoples of quite different cultural backgrounds

e. the number of people who can be supported by the available resources at a given level of technology

f. societies in which family groups are equal in status and have equal access to resources

g. the features that play a part in the society's way of making a living

h. the culture's means for making environmental resources available for human consumption

i. the possession of characteristics that foster the survival of organisms in the special environmental conditions in which they are usually found

j. a geographic region in which a number of different societies follow a similar pattern of life

True-False Questions

Circle the correct letter.

1. T (F) Heredity accounts more for adaptation than does learned skills or shared customs.

2. (T) F By taking advantage of their earlier small-game hunting patterns, Comanche tribe members illustrate the value of preadaptation in their adjustment to the Great Plains.

3. (T) F The adaptation pattern of hunting and gathering primarily involves changes in the society's skills and tools, rather than changes in the environment.

4. T (F) The many tribes inhabiting the Great Plains before the coming of the Europeans made up a culture core.

5. (T) F Generally, there is as great a diversity among societies within a culture area as there is among those living in different culture areas.

6. (T) F The European settlers in the Great Plains were of a different culture type than the Indians in that region.

7. (T) F The experience of European settlers in the Great Plains is evidence that a culture area requires similar adaptation by all dwellers.

8. (T) F Food sharing on a regular basis has generally been related to hunting cultures.

9. T (F) The egalitarian societies studied in this lesson generally make no distinctions based on rank, age, or sex.

10. (T) F In hunting-gathering cultures, all men in a group generally performed the same tasks and mastered the same skills.

11. (T) F The hunting-gathering cultures generally developed a stratified social system.

12. (T) F Unlike hunter-gatherers, the pastoralist cultures tend to remain in a single location throughout the year.

54

Completion

Choose the best word or phrase from the lists provided to fill the blanks in the paragraphs below.

1. The ways in which a society utilizes the resources to meet basic human needs are studied as _patterns of sub_ by anthropologists. The specific ways employed by a society are determined by those shared skills and standards called its _culture_. Humans, more fortunate than the lower animals, can _adapt_ to the environment, both by making changes in the environment and by modifying their own _customs_. For example, the Comanche and the Cheyenne, who came from different backgrounds to the Great Plains, made similar _adaptations_ to the area, a phenomenon called _convergent_ evolution.

   culture
   adapt
   convergent
   adaptations
   patterns of subsistence
   customs (or technologies)

2. It is likely that the majority of hunting and gathering societies lived in environments that provided relatively plentiful amounts of food. One anthropologist calls hunter-gatherers the "original _affluent_ society." Because they do not raise crops or animals, it is necessary for such societies to _move_ from place to place in search of food resources. A typical group of hunter-gatherers probably has no more than _25-50_ members. Membership in the group does not remain static, however. There are moves from one group to another by

   gatherers
   affluent
   25-50
   move
   marriage
   hunters
   food sharing

individuals or families for the purpose of visiting, _MARRIAGE_, or seeking a more congenial setting. In all groups, men have been the _hunters_, while women generally were the _gatherers_. Although the hunting may or may not be co-operative, _food sharing_ is customary within the group.

3. Pastoral cultures derive their name from the practice of raising _domesticated_ animals. These are _nomadic_ peoples, moving in response to the seasons. The Nuer move to _villages on_ in the summers to avoid lowland floods, while the Bakhtiari and Basseri move to _mountains_ during the summer months. The lands in which the pastoralist societies dwell contrast strongly with those of hunter-gatherers, who are found today only in inaccessible forests and the most marginal areas, such as _arctic tundra_ and _deserts_. Pastoralists are found in areas that do not lend themselves to agriculture, such as _grasslands_, _mountains_, and deserts.

villages on sandy ridges
deserts
domesticated
nomadic
mountains
arctic tundra
mountains
grasslands

Short-Answer Questions

1. Suggest several reasons which make study of the hunting-gathering cultures important to understanding both early human beings and modern industrial societies.

2. Briefly describe the concept of an _egalitarian_ society from an anthropological perspective, and identify the characteristics of hunting-gathering cultures that illustrate egalitarianism.

Self-Test

(Select the one best answer.)

Objective 1
1. It is a society's ___*cul+uRE*___ that determines the way in which it will meet its need for subsistence.
   a. heredity
   b. environment
   c. culture
   d. intelligence

Objective 1
2. The attitudes, beliefs, labor patterns, and other factors that help determine how a society will subsist are called its
   a. cultural ecology.
   b. culture area.
   c. convergent evolution.
   d. culture core.
   e. ethnology.

Objective 2
3. Which of the following is *not* central to the concept of *adaptation?* Adaptation is
   a. both a process and the results of the process.
   b. characteristic of organisms that aid in adjusting.
   c. an aid in the development of skills for hunting and gathering.
   d. a beneficial adjustment to the present environment.

Objective 2
4. An example of maladaptation is provided by the
   a. presence of sickle-cell anemia in nonmalaria regions.
   b. pastoralism of the Basseri.
   c. Nuer in the Sudan environment.
   d. drinking of blood by the Nuer.

Objective 3
5. A culture area can best be described as a
   a. set of similar cultural adaptations by widely separated societies.
   b. geographic region in which several cultures follow a similar life pattern.
   c. limited geographic region in which various societies have widely varying cultures.
   d. specific trait or behavior that is found in many different cultures.

6. The Indians in the Great Plains region adapted to their environment in a
   _____ pattern, while Europeans in that region adapted in a
   _____ pattern.
   a. hunting and gathering; horticulture
   b. horticulture; hunting
   c. farming; industrial
   d. hunting and fishing; farming

7. Why did the Indians and the later settlers in the Great Plains adopt
   different subsistence patterns?
   a. Myths and taboos among the Indian tribes prevented any change in
      the culture core.
   b. The Indian culture lacked technology for a different adaptation, but
      the Indians were able to make a good living from their own subsistence
      pattern.
   c. The later settlers adopted from the Indians most of the techniques for
      exploiting the environment, but added their own technology.
   d. Some important features of the environment changed and the
      Indians' subsistence pattern would no longer provide a living for a large
      group.

8. The concept of "home" or "community" probably originated from the
   a. early preindustrial city.
   b. family unit within the larger group.
   c. campsite of ancient hunters and gatherers.
   d. seasonal dwelling sites of the pastoralists.

9. Which of these statements best describes the role of women in the
   hunting and gathering society?
   a. Women generally provide the larger share of the diet from their
      gathering activities.
   b. Women generally undergo greater risk in obtaining food than men.
   c. Women generally travel great distances to obtain food supplies.
   d. Women usually held the accumulated wealth of a family.

10. For what period of time were all peoples involved in the hunting and
    gathering pattern?
    a. The hunting-gathering pattern persisted for approximately 10,000
       years.
    b. This pattern involved all peoples from the beginnings of man to about
       10,000 years ago.
    c. The pattern lasted from about 10,000 years ago to recent times.
    d. Hunting and gathering was never a universal subsistence pattern.

Objective 6

11. What was the pattern of food sharing as practiced by hunting and gathering societies?
    a. Food-sharing practices of humans were similar to those of other primates.
    b. Food sharing was practiced only when game and wild vegetation was plentiful.
    c. Food sharing was done rarely and only as part of religious ceremonies.
    d. Food sharing was generally practiced in hunting and gathering societies.

Objective 6

12. The _Netsilk_ are an example of a hunting and gathering society still in existence.
    a. Basseri
    b. Netsilik
    c. Bakhtiari
    d. Nuer

Objective 7

13. Which of these descriptions correctly lists factors of social organization that can be traced to the hunting and gathering cultures?
    a. sexual division of labor, accumulation of wealth, and concept of a home or community area
    b. regular sharing of food, inherited social status, concept of home or community area
    c. sexual division of labor, stratified social organization, regular sharing of food
    d. sexual division of labor, regular sharing of food, and concept of home or community area

Objective 7

14. The division of labor in hunting and gathering cultures probably grew out of
    a. the relatively greater strength of men, since they generally worked harder and longer.
    b. the necessity for women to remain close to their young.
    c. the need to have a camp or food preparation site under guard at all times.
    d. all of the above factors.

Objective 8

15. The term "egalitarian" implies
    a. equality.
    b. primitive.
    c. wealthy.
    d. civilized.

Objective 8

16. Which of the following is *not* an egalitarian aspect of hunting-gathering cultures?
    a. Families share food.
    b. Group membership is changed easily.
    c. A pattern of giving rather than receiving is practiced.
    d. Women share equal tasks and responsibilities with men.

Objective 9

17. Which of the following pairs best describes pastoralist cultures?
    a. nomadic, herders
    b. gatherers, urban dwellers
    c. farmers, nomadic
    d. animal herders, urban

Objective 9

18. Pastoralists move from one location to another to
    a. obtain fertile land for growing crops.
    b. find ample wild game for the tribe.
    c. provide adequate water and grazing lands.
    d. avoid conflict with other families in the tribe.

Objective 9

19. What was one reason given for the Nuer initiation ceremony shown in the television program?
    a. Undergoing the initiation demonstrates calmness and consideration of others.
    b. Undergoing the initiation demonstrates traits worthy of a warrior.
    c. Undergoing the initiation demonstrates abilities as a leader.
    d. Undergoing the initiation demonstrates willingness to share with others.

Suggested Activities

1. Before the coming of Europeans, your area was probably inhabited by one or more Indian tribes. Seek information at your local library about the lifestyle and customs of one of these tribes as they existed before European influence arrived. Which subsistence pattern did this tribe seem to follow? Write a brief report or summary of the information you find. In particular, try to include in your report any seasonal migratory patterns, information on the exact division of labor, and information on the kinds of social status or stratification that existed within the tribe.

2. Write a short paper on how your life would change if you had to live without such basic items of technology as television, telephones, refrigerators, hot and cold running water, and automobiles.

3. Cultural adaptation has enabled humans to survive and expand in a variety of environments. As an exercise in helping understand how you have adapted to your sociopolitical environment either at home, at college, at work, or in some other environment, keep a detailed one-week log of your travel in and out of your community and the ways in which you deal with the contingencies of daily life.

Answer Key

Vocabulary Check

1. i	5. g	8. f
2. c	6. a	9. b
3. d	7. e	10. h
4. j		

True-False Questions

1. F	5. F	9. F
2. T	6. T	10. T
3. T	7. F	11. F
4. T	8. T	12. F

Completion

1. patterns of subsistence, culture, adapt, customs (or technologies), adaptation, convergent

2. affluent, move, 25-50, marriage, hunters, gatherers, food sharing

3. domesticated, nomadic, villages on sandy ridges, mountains, arctic tundra, deserts, grasslands, mountains

Short-Answer Questions

1. Suggest several reasons which make study of the hunting-gathering cultures important to understanding both early human beings and modern industrial societies. Your answer should include:

   Although only a small fraction of earth's population today belong to hunting and gathering cultures, over 90 percent of all humans who ever lived were hunters and gatherers.

   Hunting and gathering is the oldest of the adaptations man has made to his environment.

Many of the ways that individuals, communities, and nations relate to each other today had their beginnings in the patterns of hunting and gathering cultures.

Some of the basic concepts and practices which can be traced to hunting and gathering cultures are sexual division of labor, the identification of "community" or "home," a profound respect for nature, sharing (especially of food) within the community, and egalitarianism.

2. Briefly describe the concept of an *egalitarian* society from an anthropological perspective, and identify the characteristics of hunting-gathering cultures that illustrate egalitarianism. Your answer should include:

Egalitarianism implies the ideal of equality of all people. In an egalitarian society, all members would ideally have equal access to resources and prestige, and all would have equal abilities to perform the work to be done.

In practice, the egalitarianism of hunter-gatherer peoples extends to families and to hunters. Status distinctions based on age and sex are universal.

Hunters and their families share equally with other family groups in their larger group. Each hunter shares equal responsibility for obtaining game.

Hunter-gatherers do not accumulate property or other forms of wealth. Thus, distinctions based on wealth do not occur in such societies.

Group composition changes frequently in hunting-gathering cultures, because of needs for insuring reproduction, marriage, avoiding conflict, or adapting to changing seasons.

Self-Test

1. c	8. c	14. b
2. d	9. a	15. a
3. c	10. b	16. d
4. a	11. d	17. a
5. b	12. b	18. c
6. d	13. d	19. b
7. b		

Patterns Of Subsistence:
The Food Producers

5

Overview

It is obvious, from the preceding lesson, that cultures neither change at the same rate nor necessarily in the same directions. Did it occur to you during Lesson Four that a logical progression would be from hunting-gathering to pastoral, then to agricultural subsistence patterns? In fact, changes in these patterns have *not* necessarily occurred in such order. As you know, hunting-gathering and pastoral societies still exist, retaining the practices of their ancestors with little change. In this lesson, which investigates two food production subsistence patterns (horticulture and intensive agriculture), you will again meet examples of cultures which use the same technology and skills as their forefathers.

Some societies have changed, of course, from food gathering to food producing, but it is not at all certain what caused such a development. Perhaps a settled agrarian life appears more attractive to you than migratory food hunting, but there is evidence that such a change may not have been very attractive to those who made it.

Still another important change in subsistence patterns is the change from relatively simple agricultural practices, or horticulture, to intensive farming of the land. Again, the evidence does not show conclusively what caused the change. Intensive agriculture, however, did set the stage for yet other developments, including the accumulation of substantial surpluses, the development of cities, and the emergence of more complex political and social patterns designed to meet new social problems.

A full appreciation of these two subsistence patterns requires more than merely understanding the social changes that resulted from them. The text and television materials attempt to portray for you examples of horticultural and agricultural life, in the context of both daily work and seasonal cycle. Taking time to learn some details of rice farming or the growing of a "prestige garden" seems particularly important to a study of anthropology, especially if you come from an urban industrial environment.

Appreciation also involves the many institutions and social practices, still a part of our culture today, that arose together with (and often because of) advances in agricultural methods. The village and the city are only two of many important cultural patterns that developed as human beings adapted to the new ways of food production.

Learning Objectives

When you have completed all assignments in this lesson, you should be able to:

1. Describe the significance of the transition from hunting-gathering to a food-producing way of life, and identify when this transition first occurred. (Text page 186; television program; Background Notes.)

2. Describe the characteristics of the horticultural pattern of subsistence and cite examples of horticultural societies. (Text pages 164-166, 186-189; television program; Background Notes.)

3. Describe the natural environments in which food-producing ways of life are found. (Text page 188; television program; Background Notes.)

4. Describe intensive agriculture and its relationship to the rise of cities. (Text pages 191-192; television program; Background Notes.)

5. Briefly describe the characteristics of preindustrial urban life. (Text pages 191-195; television program; Background Notes.)

Assignments For This Lesson

Before Viewing the Program

Read the overview and the learning objectives for this lesson. Use the learning objectives to guide your reading, viewing, and thinking.

Review the preview to Chapter 6 in the text.

Review pages 164-166, and read pages 186-195 in the text (omitting the section "Pastoralism").

View Program 5, "Patterns of Subsistence: The Food Producers."

As you view the program, look for:

the practice of slash-and-burn horticulture among the Maya of the Yucatan in Mexico.

an extremely dangerous fertility ritual among the "land divers" of Melanesia, a horticultural society.

intensive agriculture, seen in Taiwan, Afghanistan, and Western industrial societies. In these scenes, note the description of social conditions and social problems growing out of advancements in agriculture.

the crucial relationship of modern civilization to advances in agricultural techniques.

After Viewing the Program

Read the background notes for this lesson.

Review the terms used in the lesson. In addition to terms used in the learning objectives, you should be familiar with these:

seasonal uplands   craft specialization
tropical wetlands   slash-and-burn horticulture

Review the reading assignments for this lesson. A thorough second reading of the text chapter and the background notes is suggested. Include the chapter summary in your study.

Complete each of the study activities and the self-test in this study guide; then check your answers with the answer key at the end of this lesson.

According to your instructor's assignment or your own interests, complete one or more of the suggested activities. You may also be interested in some of the readings suggested at the end of Chapter 6 in your text.

Background Notes

The Change from Hunting-Gathering to Food Production

Popular writers sometimes make it sound as if the transition from hunting and gathering to food producing occurred overnight as a result of invention. They imply that people learned for the first time that planting a seed will allow it to grow into a plant or learned how to domesticate a wild animal. This is misleading because it implies that the development of agriculture is based entirely on acquisition of knowledge and that food production is always "better" than hunting and gathering.

Hunter-gatherers possess quite a sophisticated body of knowledge about the plants and animals in the territories they occupy. Their survival depends on being able to identify edible plants, know the seasonal developmental cycles of plants, and distinguish them from poisonous varieties which may appear very similar. Hunter-gatherers acquire sophisticated information about biological processes by butchering the animals they kill for food. Their cultural heritage includes all the information members of a hunting-gathering society need to know to survive in their environment.

An individual reared in a modern city would be faced with a bewildering array of survival choices if set down in the middle of an African savannah or in a tropical rain forest. Even a farmer would starve before his knowledge of agriculture could bear fruit. The change from hunting and gathering to food production represents an acquisition of new kinds of knowledge, but a loss of some other kinds of subsistence skills.

Another misconception about subsistence patterns is that a switch to agriculture frees people from working long hours and ensures a secure food supply. However, ethnographic studies have shown that hunter-gatherers spend fewer hours in subsistence activities than do agriculturalists. The modern factory worker works longer hours than either hunter-gatherers or small-scale agriculturalists. Also, people relying on domesticated plants and animals are more susceptible to weather variations and disease than hunter-gatherers, who can readily move to another area if the game yield in one part of their territory is insufficient.

Clearly, agriculture is not necessarily a "better" way of life for all people. However, the ability to produce and store food has profound implications for social organization.

The change from hunting and gathering to agriculture implies a shift from migration to a more sedentary way of life. People who grow food tend to stay in one place instead of traveling from place to place in search of food. This allows a greater accumulation of material goods. People can live in more or less permanent dwellings, which means they can devote more time and energy to the construction of their buildings. They can accumulate more and heavier household goods. Pottery is an inconvenience to a hunter-gatherer, who is better served by containers made of lightweight materials, such as animal skins.

Hunter-gatherers have no need to "own" their territories. However, a horticulturalist, who invests time and resources in planting seeds, must be assured access to the plants when they mature. With the accumulation of material goods and need for year-round access to a particular plot of land, property rights and inheritance become more important.

Large-scale agricultural projects, such as irrigation systems, require coordination of labor. Conversely, innovations in agriculture may allow production of a surplus. Grain crops, such as rye, corn, and wheat, can be stored. Producing a storable food surplus can free some members of a society from subsistence activities. At the same time, storing food resources requires management and allocation.

Freeing individuals in a society from direct involvement in subsistence activities allows development of skilled artisans, specialists, and managers, with the authority to control labor and settle disputes involving property. The authority to command the labor of others makes it possible to construct monumental architecture and develop urban centers. Specialization of labor and development of an authority structure is the basis for different classes and different access to resources. Thus, the development of a complex, stratified society is directly dependent on the ability to produce large food surpluses, which in turn is dependent on intensive agriculture.

Thus, anthropologists maintain that social organization is directly tied to subsistence. (Anthropologists usually distinguish between horticulturalists, or people who grow only enough for subsistence needs, and intensive agriculturalists.) Small-scale horticulturalists do not, as a rule, develop large cities and highly stratified social systems, as is possible with an intensive agriculture pattern.

The following examples illustrate the relationship between agriculture and political systems.

Afghanistan Wheat Farming

The people of Aq Kupruk, a settlement in Afghanistan near the border of the Soviet Union, have farmed wheat since prehistoric times. Seventy percent of the adult males own land and the rest work as tenant farmers. In April, wheat is planted in the high fields near the town. The fields are plowed with a pair of oxen and a wooden-frame plow with an iron plowshare or point. At harvest time, usually in July, the men move to temporary quarters near the fields. If there aren't enough adults to do the harvesting, hired laborers are brought in.

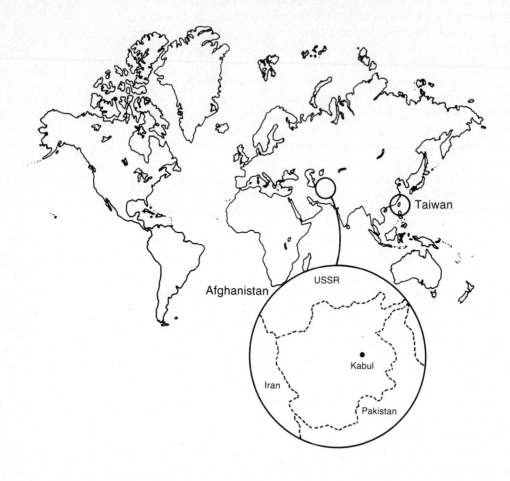

Figure 5.1 The characteristics of an intensive agriculture subsistence pattern are exhibited by wheat farmers in Afghanistan and wet rice farmers in Taiwan.

The wheat is cut with small, curved hand sickles, which are much more efficient for use on the hillsides than large scythes. Teams of oxen are walked over the wheat to separate the grain from the chaff; then the farmers toss the wheat into the air with pitchforks to let the wind blow the lighter chaff away from the heavier grain. Finally, the wheat is taken to the mills to be ground into flour.

The village mills are powered by water from a canal, which also irrigates produce gardens in the village. Every summer, the canal must be dredged and the mill rebuilt. Everyone who uses the mill or who benefits from the irrigation is expected to help. Most of the irrigated gardens are planted in corn, turnips, carrots, millet (a cereal grass), lentils, chick peas, onions, potatoes, cucumbers, tomatoes, eggplant, sesame, linseed, spinach, coriander, cumin seed, and squash. Melons are grown on a small scale and many fruit and nut trees are also grown. Some cotton is grown, but it is almost exclusively for personal use. Sheep and goats are also herded. The people also fish and hunt birds, such as pigeons, doves, and partridges.

Traditionally, sons inherit full shares of land from the father, while daughters receive half-shares, which become part of their dowries. To prevent dividing the land into smaller shares, one son may inherit all the land, with cash shares going to the other children.

The village of Aq Kupruk is the political and economic center of the farming area around it. Its market bazaar is an especially important part of the local economy. Two linguistic groups, Tajiki and Uzbaki, make up the town. The Tajik outnumber the Uzbak by about two to one and the most affluent residents of Aq Kupruk are a subgroup of Tajik.

No formalized association exists among the shop owners of the bazaar, but a chief of merchants is informally chosen among the resident shop owners. The chief serves as a mediator between the bazaar merchants and the district governor. Tradesmen and shop owners sell rugs, household goods, and items from Kabul, the capital of Afghanistan. Farmers bring produce to sell in the open market. Most transactions are on a cash-and-carry basis. However, some shop owners lend money at high interest rates. In some cases, the money is not meant to be repaid. However, the borrower is expected to support the lender in factional disputes.

Taiwan Rice Farming

Among Taiwanese rice farmers, agriculture provides the basis for a strong, centralized, bureaucratic government.

Most of Taiwan's sixteen million people are Chinese. Approximately 38 percent are descendants of immigrants who came to the island from the southeastern provinces of China prior to 1900. The remaining 15 percent are primarily mainland Chinese who immigrated in the late 1940s in the political upheaval on mainland China following World War II. When Chiang Kai-shek's Nationalist Chinese government was defeated by the Chinese Communists, he fled to the island along with about a million of his followers. The Nationalist Chinese leader planned to use the island as a base to regain the mainland. Aided by the United States, the Nationalist government began to develop the agricultural and industrial resources of the island.

Rice is the primary crop in Taiwan. When the Japanese governed the island, from 1895 until the end of World War II, they wanted Taiwan to serve as a rice-producing area, so they built a number of large-scale irrigation systems to encourage wet rice production.

Growing rice is demanding work. In Taiwan, spring rice is planted early, vegetables are grown in the summer, and a second rice crop is planted early in the fall. The first job before planting is to clear the straw from the earlier rice harvest. Straw may be hauled off to use as cattle forage or burned to add fertility to the soil.

Rice fields are flooded a week before plowing to soften the soil. Plowing is done with a water buffalo or, more recently, with a power tiller. After the field has been thoroughly plowed, the soil is broken up further with a harrow, a pronged framework that is dragged over the ground. Then the soil is treated with chemical fertilizer that is sometimes augmented with manure or other natural fertilizers. Chemical fertilizer represents the rice grower's greatest single expense.

At least two weeks before the start of plowing, rice seeds will have been planted in a specially prepared seedbed. Transplanting the rice seedlings into the plowed field requires a great deal of labor. First, the rice seedlings are cut from the seedbed, then carried in baskets on bamboo poles to the fields, where they are planted 10 to 12 inches apart in the flooded fields.

After planting, the field is flooded with at least four inches of water. While the plants are growing, the fields must be weeded three times, as well as sprayed with carefully selected insecticides and fungicides. Rice plants are prey to a number of insects and diseases, so selecting the right spray requires expertise.

Rice is harvested by using a sickle. After the fields have been drained and dried for several weeks, portable threshers are brought to a convenient location. These are powered by foot pedal or a small gasoline engine and have wire teeth that separate the grain from the stalk. Then the heavy sacks of rice are carried to the nearest road, where they are loaded on a farm wagon and hauled to the farmhouses.

Rice from the fields is dried on cement courtyards. It must be repeatedly turned to ensure even drying and, if a rain shower threatens, the rice must be piled and covered. This is usually the job of the farm wife.

Rice farming requires intensive labor and sophisticated knowledge in order to choose the best varieties to plant during spring and fall, the ones that resist disease and yet provide the greatest yields, and to select the proper fertilizers and chemicals. Nearly all Taiwanese rice farmers belong to farmers' associations which provide experts on the latest techniques in rice farming. Farmers can also borrow money from the associations to buy farming equipment and machinery. Since 1950, agricultural experiment stations have been established in Taiwan. These are often funded by the Chinese and American Joint Commission on Rural Reconstruction.

Clearly, the Taiwan rice farming complex is not a locally based, locally controlled system like that of the Afghanistan wheat farmer. The Taiwan system has traditionally been based on a large governmental bureaucracy and local sociocultural institutions. Before the Nationalist Chinese took over, most of the population consisted of peasants who cultivated the land as small landowners or tenants and laborers who had no rights to land. Most of the land and nearly all of the power was held by a small group of highly educated government officials and influential people, often referred to as gentry. The government handled problems by dealing with the resident gentry rather than with the peasants.

Through a series of laws, the Nationalist government reduced tenant rents to 37.5 percent of the annual main crop and protected the tenant against arbitrary eviction. Then the government took part of the landlords' land away and sold it to former tenants on an installment arrangement, spreading payments over ten years. The landlords were paid in land bonds, redeemable in two semiannual installments, and by stock shares in the paper, mining, and cement industries.

The object of redistribution was to increase rice production. However, the Nationalist government also expanded the irrigation network. Increased rice production was necessary to feed Taiwan's expanding population. But the government also wanted to produce a surplus to export to foreign markets for cash to finance its multilevel bureaucracy and military establishment. Also, cash from agriculture was used to finance a move toward industrialization.

The Taiwan and Afghanistan examples represent two different approaches to intensive agricultural systems. However, these do not begin to exhaust the number of potential approaches which are possible.

Study Activities

Vocabulary Check

Check on your understanding of terms by matching those on the left with the definitions on the right. Check your choices with the answer key at the end of the lesson.

1. _D_ horticulture
2. _I_ intensive agriculture
3. _F_ New World seasonal uplands
4. _C_ New World tropical wetlands
5. _H_ preindustrial cities
6. _E_ craft specializations
7. _G_ slash-and-burn farming
8. _A_ landownership

a. first became necessary in horticultural communities
b. produced such crops as rice and yams
c. produced such crops as manioc
d. subsistence food production using simple hand tools
e. became possible in preindustrial cities

f. produced such crops as maize, beans, and squash
g. a form of horticulture
h. urban settlements made possible from intensive agricultural subsistence
i. employ irrigation and technology to produce a surplus

Completion

Choose the best word or phrase from the lists provided to fill the blanks in the paragraphs below.

1. Evidence suggests that the first changes from hunter-gatherer to food producer may have occurred as long ago as _ELEVEN_ thousand years. It is possible that many societies made this change out of necessity, such as a shortage of game and plants for food. The change was dramatic in its consequences, involving the development of new _SKILLS_ and the loss of old ones. It was pointed out that a contemporary farmer probably could not survive if he were placed in a wilderness area and had to hunt for food. For example, he would lack such basic knowledge as which wild plants were _edible_.

- edible
- eleven
- skills

2. Farming, however simple, made it possible for groups to develop _PERMANENT_ settlements to replace the camps of nomadic peoples. Material goods could be accumulated to a greater extent when people stayed in one area. Heavy utensils and tools became practical. At some point, some individuals began _specializing_ in the new crafts, eating food produced by others, thus beginning a new division of labor.

permanent
specializing

3. Horticulture is a distinctive type of farming marked by the use of ___*hand*___ tools on comparatively small plots of land. Individual plots of land, or gardens, are frequently centered around a ___*village*___. Even though complex social systems are usually not developed by horticulturalists, some kind of arrangement of ___*landownership*___ is necessary.

village
landownership
hand

4. In an intensive agricultural society, there may also be a division of labor. The Aq Kupruk, however, are chiefly farmers, although there are some ___*tradesman*___ and shop owners; they maintain an existence comparatively isolated from urban centers. The Aq Kuprak are ___*intensive*___ agriculturalists, rather than horticulturists, because they use more advanced technology, such as animal-drawn plows and ___*irrigation*___, in addition to hand tools.

irrigation
tradesmen
intensive

5. Horticultural farming has been introduced both in dry ___*upland*___ regions and in ___*tropical*___ wetlands. In the Old World, the crops planted in the dry regions included wheat and ___*barley*___, while in the wet regions ___*rice*___ and tubers are cultivated. In the New World, different plants have been cultivated: maize, beans, squash, and ___*potatoes*___ in the dry regions and manioc in the wet areas. Thus, distinct crop complexes have developed with these and other plants.

tropical
rice
upland
barley
potatoes

6. Preindustrial urban areas are associated with many changes in the social order. Specialization of crafts, social _CLASSES_ based on occupation or family, and specialized _political_ institutions develop to meet new needs. In the Aztec city of Tenochtitlan, the production of food surpluses made increasing population size and density possible. Many were employed in nonagricultural pursuits: craftsmen, warriors, merchants, _priests_, and nobles. In Taiwan, great effort has been expended to produce agricultural surpluses to support international trade and _industrialization_.

industrialization
priests
political
classes

Short-Answer Questions

1. Explain why kinship units probably became important as people began farming in groups.

2. Why did preindustrial cities develop in conjunction with intensive agriculture, rather than horticulture or pastoralism?

Self-Test

(Select the one best answer.)

Objective 1
1. Which of these was the most significant result of the change from hunting and gathering to food production?
   a. Humans could spend less time and effort to obtain food.
   b. Kinship ties were weakened, allowing greater individuality.
   c. The nature of human society itself began to undergo significant change.
   d. Food shortages became more severe.

Objective 1
2. It is believed that the transition from hunting and gathering to food production began
   a. six to eight thousand years ago.

74

b. nine to eleven thousand years ago.
c. twelve to fifteen thousand years ago.
d. sixteen to twenty thousand years ago.

Objective 2
3. Which of the following is *not* usually considered a part of the horticultural pattern?
   a. little or no surplus food production
   b. use of hand tools
   c. individual garden plots
   d. irrigation from canals

Objective 2
4. The "prestige garden" kept by Gururumba families is maintained principally for
   a. a decorative "front yard" for the family dwelling.
   b. a supply of good quality vegetables to give as gifts.
   c. growing ornamental plants and flowers used at festivals.
   d. growing a surplus which can be sold for profit at the end of the season.

Objective 3
5. Maize, beans, squash, and potatoes are typically grown in the
   a. New World dry uplands.
   b. New World tropical wetlands.
   c. Old World dry uplands.
   d. Old World tropical wetlands.

Objective 4
6. Which of the following is typical of intensive agricultural farming, but not of horticulture?
   a. new strains of food plants
   b. use of hand tools for cultivation
   c. use of fertilizers
   d. ownership of land by individual or kin group

Objective 4
7. The development through intensive agriculture that made possible the rise of preindustrial cities was
   a. new strains of food plants.
   b. kinship group organization.
   c. complex political structures.
   d. surplus food production.

Objective 5
8. A stratified society, in which people were ranked according to their work or their family, first appeared in

a. hunting-gathering societies.
b. horticultural societies.
ⓒ preindustrial urban societies.
d. pastoral societies.

Objective 5
9. Which of these best describes the governmental structure of the Aztec city of Tenochtitlán?
ⓐ a huge bureaucracy managing social order, taxation, and storehouses
b. an informal government of the leading farmers of the community
c. a king and a few advisors who settled disputes between landowners
d. a council of elders based on kinship groups

Objective 5
10. The immediate purpose of the Nationalist Chinese redistribution of land to peasants in Taiwan was to
a. decrease the rigid stratification of the society into social classes.
b. increase the variety of crops grown.
ⓒ increase rice production.
d. return to traditional farming methods.

Suggested Activities

1. Use the *Statistical Abstract of the United States* (which you can find in your local library) and other references to learn what proportion of United States population is directly engaged in agriculture at the present time, fifty years ago, and one hundred years ago. What developments in agricultural techniques have changed this proportion?

2. For an in-depth picture of the culture, organization, and urban life of the Aztecs, read *The Aztecs of Central Mexico: An Imperial Society*, by Frances F. Berdan (Holt, Rinehart and Winston, 1982).

3. Read Gideon Sjoberg's *The Preindustrial City: Past and Present* (Free Press, 1965), then compare the preindustrial "agricultural revolution" with industrial city patterns.

Answer Key

Vocabulary Check

1. d	5. h
2. i	6. e
3. f	7. g
4. c	8. a

Completion

1. eleven, skills, edible

2. permanent, specializing

3. hand, village, landownership

4. tradesmen, intensive, irrigation

5. upland, tropical, barley, rice, potatoes

6. classes, political, priests, industrialization

Short-Answer Questions

1. Explain why kinship units probably became important as groups began farming. Your answer should include:

   Ownership of land became important when people began to invest their time and efforts in planting and harvesting. The horticulturalist or agriculturalist needed to know that the land and the crop would be "his" at harvest time.

   The growth of settlements meant that more and more people were sharing the same resources, such as land and water.

   Strong kinship groups probably served as the organizing units to determine ownership of parcels of land; the same organizations probably helped settle the question of obtaining adequate work parties for gardens or farms. Kinship organizations also provided a structure for sharing crops and inheritance of property.

2. Why did preindustrial cities develop in conjunction with intensive agriculture, rather than horticulture or even pastoralism? Your answer should include:

   Population growth is one key factor in the rise of cities. Such growth is related to improved agricultural techniques and higher crop yields, but the cause-and-effect relationship is not certain.

   Production of substantial food surpluses makes it possible to free some people from food-producing activities. Thus, individuals can specialize in arts and crafts, or become politicians, priests, or warriors on a full-time basis. The surpluses also require a system of distributing the food and other products, usually a marketplace for the exchange of goods. The market becomes the focal point of the region and the basis of a village or a city. Some people accumulate greater wealth and prestige and become leaders with authority to command the labor of others.

Development of formal political organizations, new inventions, and wider trade created opportunities for construction and other large-scale projects. A modern example of the impact of strong political organization is the island of Taiwan, which has directed large agricultural efforts to make industrialization possible.

In contrast, hunting-gathering and pastoral societies required population mobility. The lack of food surpluses made it impossible for large communities of people to develop and survive.

Self-Test

1. c	5. a	8. c
2. b	6. c	9. a
3. d	7. d	10. c
4. b		

Language And Communication 6

Overview

Talk is so much a part of our daily lives, language is so complex and so universal that it is difficult indeed to conceive of a world without communication. But pretend for awhile that you belong to a society in which there is no verbal or written language. How will you communicate with others in your world? Presumably, you would have some capacity to remember and this could at least create some sort of images in your mind; but, if you can't describe them, and if no one understands their meaning even if you could describe them, your mental "pictures" would be meaningless. To communicate, you would have to make do with body gestures and whatever sounds you are able to make, such as laughing, crying, grunting. Screaming, perhaps?

Some anthropologists think that the make-believe state in which you've placed yourself briefly here is probably just about where our early human ancestors were when the need to communicate stimulated the development of language. It is probable that spoken language evolved from body gestures, particularly of the face and mouth, and a few basic sounds. Evolution of body parts, such as the vocal cords, must also have contributed to the emergence of speech.

From these beginnings, humans today speak between 3,000 and 5,000 different languages and have developed many more in the course of human history. All of these languages are based on only about 50 sounds, which all human beings are capable of making. Even the simplest of these languages is remarkably complex and sophisticated—so much that the scientific study of language is a well-established discipline of its own, with numerous subdisciplines, and is called *linguistics*.

Why should scientists—or you, for that matter—study language? First of all, language is the central means by which every society expresses its cultural values and ideas. Second, all human culture depends upon our capacity to learn and to share our information, beliefs, and experience with the generations that succeed us; unless we can communicate what we learn, human culture would not be preserved beyond our own generation. Culture is based on symbols, and symbols are sounds or gestures to which we've assigned common meanings which are agreed upon by the group as a whole. Symbols make it possible to communicate, and language, which is the verbal and written expression of symbols, is the *primary* tool of human communication. Thus, language is indispensable to human culture.

In this lesson, you will probably wonder, along with the anthropologists, just how such a sophisticated and complex phenomenon as language actually did begin. Did a warning cry eventually become a word? Did imitations of natural sounds eventually become names? Or did a threatening gesture eventually become a warning through association with a particular sound? Even though there are no conclusive answers, you'll study some interesting possibilities. You'll also explore some of the ways humans communicate without words and some interesting experiments in teaching sign language to other primates.

Learning Objectives

When you have completed all assignments in this lesson, you should be able to:

1. Explain the difference between "symbols" and "signals." (Text pages 100-101.)

2. Discuss how human language is symbolic, has meaning, and follows a set of rules. (Text pages 100-101; television program.)

3. Discuss the implications of teaching symbolic communications to chimpanzees and gorillas. (Text pages 64-66, 100, and 125-129; television program.)

4. Explain how language is an aspect of any human culture. (Text page 100; television program.)

5. Define linguistics. (Text page 101; television program.)

6. Distinguish between descriptive and historical linguistics. (Text pages 104, 108-112.)

7. Define the following terms found in the field of descriptive linguistics: phonetics, phonology, phoneme, morphology, morpheme, syntax, grammar. (Text pages 101-104; television program.)

8. Define and give examples of paralanguage and kinesics. (Text pages 104-108; television program.)

9. Define the following terms found in the field of historical linguistics: language family, glottochronology, core vocabulary. (Text pages 112-113.)

10. Identify the language family which includes English. (Text pages 109-112.)

11. Describe the Whorfian hypothesis about the relationship between language and thought and recognize differing points of view. (Text pages 114-115; television program.)

12. Define and give examples of sociolinguistics, dialects, and code switching. (Text pages 118-124; television program.)

13. Briefly describe Chomsky's theory of transformational grammar, including defining the terms "deep structure" and "surface structure." (Text pages 124-125.)

14. Describe the "gesture theory" of the origins of language. (Text pages 127-129.)

15. Recognize that all known languages are complex, sophisticated, and able to express a wide range of experiences. (Text pages 128-129; television program.)

Assignments For This Lesson

Before Viewing the Program

Read the overview and the learning objectives for this lesson. Use the learning objectives to guide your reading, viewing, and thinking.

Read the preview to Chapter 4 in the text, and look over the topic headings in the chapter.

Read Chapter 4, "Language and Communication," in the text. Also read the "original study" in Chapter 3, "Intelligence in a Captive Gorilla," pages 64-66.

View Program 6, "Language and Communication."

As you view the program, look for:

a contrast of *closed* (animal) communication versus *open* (human) communication and film of the chimpanzee, Lana, who uses language with the aid of a computer device.

discussion on language acquisition.

Professor Keith Kernan's examples of phonemes and morphemes.

some vivid demonstrations of paralanguage and kinesics.

Professor Claudia Kernan in a discussion about "black" English with black students.

discussion of the questions: How does language influence thought, and in what ways does thought influence language? Information comes from the languages of the Iwan, the Hopi, and the Nuer.

After Viewing the Program

Review the terms used in this lesson. In addition to those terms found in the learning objectives, you should be familiar with these:

Indo-European
taboo words
American sign language
displacement

Review the reading assignments for this lesson. A thorough second reading of the text chapter is suggested. Include the summary for Chapter 4 in your study.

Complete each of the study activities and the self-test in this study guide; then check your answers with the answer key at the end of this lesson.

According to your instructor's assignment or your own interests, complete one or more of the suggested activities. You may also be interested in the readings suggested at the end of Chapter 4 in your text.

Study Activities

Vocabulary Check

Check on your understanding of terms by matching those on the left with
the definitions on the right. Check your choices with the answer key at the
end of the lesson.

1. __H__ signal
2. __m__ linguistics
3. __D__ descriptive linguistics
4. __L__ phonetics
5. __N__ phoneme
6. __B__ morphology
7. __P__ syntax
8. __I__ grammar
9. __G__ paralanguage
10. __O__ kinesics
11. __F__ Indo-European
12. __J__ glottochronology
13. __K__ core vocabulary
14. __C__ code switching
15. __E__ dialect
16. __A__ displacement

a. the ability to refer to things
removed in time and space
b. study of meaningful sound
combinations
c. changing from one level of
language to another
d. registers and explains all the
features of a language at one point
in time
e. varying forms of a language,
similar enough to be mutually
intelligible to the various users
f. includes English as one of this
group of languages
g. includes such phenomena as voice
quality and vocalizations
h. sound or gesture that has a natural
or biological meaning
i. includes all rules and principles
governing formation of words and
sentences in a language
j. a method of dating the "branching"
of one language from another
k. includes lower numbers and names
for natural objects
l. study of how speech sounds are
made and heard
m. scientific study of language
n. smallest unit of sound that may
make a difference in meaning
o. communication by body language
p. the rules or principles involved in
making sentences and phrases

Completion

Choose the best word or phrase from the lists provided to fill the blanks in the paragraphs below.

1. Language is a system of communication that uses combinations of sounds as _symbols_ for all kinds of information. In order for communication to take place, there must be general agreement about the _MEANINGS_ of the sounds and the _RULES_ that guide the way the language is expressed. All present societies use language so complex that even the simplest cannot be called "primitive." Cultural patterns and cultural knowledge are so rich and complex that language is essential, not only for transmitting the culture to new generations, but for exchanging information and experiences between members of the culture on a day-to-day basis.

rules
symbols
~~meanings~~

2. _Linguistics_ is the scientific study of language. _hist. linguistics_ is a branch of this science which studies how languages have developed over long periods of time. Studies have found that English is one branch of a language family descended from a single ancestral language called proto _Indo-European_

historical linguistics
linguistics
Indo-European

3. There is evidence that humans are born with a "built-in language acquisition" capability. A linguist named _Noam Chomsky_ has developed a theory which states that a person's innate

surface
Noam Chomsky
transformational-generative
deep structures

knowledge generates underlying forms of sentences retained in the mind, which he calls _deep structure_. These underlying forms, it is theorized, are transformed into actual speech which reveal _surface_ structures. Although both of these structures will vary from language to language, Chomsky theorizes that there should be some general features of language construction common to all languages, reflecting fundamental properties of the mind. Chomsky's theory is termed _transformational-generative_ grammar.

4. Attempts to teach gorillas and chimpanzees to speak like humans have not been successful due to some key differences in their nervous systems and sound-producing mechanisms. However, there have been dramatic examples of success in teaching language to these primates using various kinds of _sign_ languages. It is possible that these animals have ability to use symbolism and language similar to that of young human beings. Some primates have demonstrated ability of _displacement_, the ability to talk about something not present in space and time. Such experiments also suggest that language originated in meaningful _gestures_.

~~displacement~~
~~sign~~
gestures

5. _Sociolinguistics_ is defined as the study of the structure and use of language in relation to its social setting. A major area of interest to sociolinguists is the

dialects
sociolinguistics

study of language uses that reflect particular regions or classes; these forms are called _____ *dialect*. A related concern is whether or not differences in speech among peoples in the same area also reflect other cultural differences. The field of sociolinguistics is proving to be broad and varied, closely related to many other fields of study.

Short-Answer Questions

1. Describe the techniques used by the fieldworker who is gathering information for descriptive linguistics.

2. Explain the terms "paralanguage" and "kinesics," giving two examples of each.

3. Briefly explain and provide examples of the various points of view concerning the influence of language upon perception and perception upon language.

4. Why is it so difficult to gather evidence about the origins of language? What evidence is there that suggests language may have originated in gestures?

Self-Test

(Select the one best answer.)

Objectives 1 and 2
1. From the standpoint of linguistics, what is a symbol?
   a. A sound or gesture that has a natural or biological meaning.
   b. The smallest unit of sound that conveys meaning.
   c. A gesture or sign used as a substitute for a word.
   d. A sound or gesture that has an agreed-on meaning.

Objectives 2 and 7
2. Which of these is the term indicating the rules which a language must follow in word use and sentence construction?
   a. morphology
   b. syntax

c. glottochronology
d. grammar

Objective 3
3. Experiments with chimpanzees and gorillas seem to indicate that these primates have some language ability. Which of these statements best describes the level of ability of Koko and Lana?
   a. ability to vocalize sounds
   b. ability to understand and form sentences
   c. language ability nearly equal to that of adult humans
   d. no ability to think of events separated from them in space and time

Objectives 4 and 15
4. What have anthropologists found in the languages of various isolated societies?
   a. All of them are able to convey complex and subtle messages.
   b. Some small-scale societies have primitive languages involving few sounds and gestures.
   c. All known languages developed from the same primitive language.
   d. Most unwritten languages are restricted to words and gestures that have natural or biological meanings.

Objective 5
5. Which of these would least likely fall within the field of linguistics?
   a. history of languages
   b. tool-making techniques
   c. gesture communications
   d. glottochronology

Objective 6
6. Which of the following divisions would be most concerned with the relationships of older languages to modern ones?
   a. descriptive linguistics
   b. theoretical linguistics
   c. historical linguistics
   d. sociolinguistics

Objective 6
7. Which of the following would be most concerned with the complete system of a single language at one point in time?
   a. descriptive linguistics
   b. theoretical linguistics
   c. historical linguistics
   d. sociolinguistics

8. Which one of the following divisions would be most concerned with the dialects of a particular language?
   a. descriptive linguistics
   b. theoretical linguistics
   c. historical linguistics
   d. sociolinguistics

9. A phoneme is
   a. the smallest unit of sounds that carry meanings.
   b. a combination of sounds in a language.
   c. the smallest class of sounds that may make a difference in meaning.
   d. a chart which indicates written symbols for the sounds produced in a language.

10. In linguistics, the word "syntax" means the
    a. principles governing the production, transmission, and receiving of speech sounds.
    b. rules governing the making of phrases, clauses, and sentences.
    c. rules governing the formation of words and construction of sentences.
    d. study of sounds in combination.

11. To what language family does English belong?
    a. Northern European
    b. Germanic
    c. Latin
    d. Indo-European

12. Why are studies of core vocabulary important in glottochronology?
    a. The rate at which common words change is helpful in determining the date that one language branched off from another.
    b. The number of words in common everyday use is a rough measure of the total vocabulary now used in a language.
    c. It is believed that the names of body parts, small numbers, and similar words change very little over long periods of time.
    d. The knowledge of various dialects reveals the comparative social status of different groups that speak the same language.

13. Which of the following statements represents a viewpoint that is opposite that of the Whorfian hypothesis?
    a. Language limits the kinds of sensations that engage the attention of the mind.

b. Language predisposes a person to see the world in a certain way.
c. Language reflects reality and will change as that reality changes.
d. A language will have more words describing those conditions that are very important to the society.

Objective 11

14. In the Whorfian hypothesis, the phrase "grooves of expression" means that
a. a language influences in specific ways the thinking and behavior of those who use it.
b. a language reflects reality and changes in reality.
c. all languages have certain common ways of expressing concepts.
d. one part of human communication involves sounds that do not necessarily form words.

Objective 12

15. The black students in the television program describe how they could change from one level of English to another called "black" English. The students were demonstrating
a. the use of paralanguage.
b. code switching.
c. the use of kernel sentences.
d. changes in syntax.

Objective 13

16. Identify the concept which is not a central part of the theory of transformational-generative grammar.
a. core vocabulary
b. innate knowledge
c. surface structure
d. deep structure

Objective 14

17. According to the theory which suggests that gestures preceded speech in language development,
a. communication by gesture followed development of the ability to imitate nature sounds, such as animal cries.
b. the earliest types of man (genus *homo*) probably had mouth and throat structures capable of human speech.
c. both "sign" language and spoken language preceded ability to construct tools.
d. human kinesics may be surviving aspects of early sign language.

Suggested Activities

1. Read the article "Conversations with a Gorilla," *National Geographic,*

1978, 154(4): 454-462, and/or "Teaching Language to an Ape," by Ann James Premack and David Premack, *Scientific American,* 1972, 227(4): 92-99. Write a brief review of your reading. In particular, comment on what the articles suggest concerning primate ability to think in symbols and to demonstrate displacement in thought.

2. The *American Heritage Dictionary* of the English Language (Boston: Houghton-Miffin Co., 1978) contains two articles on the proto Indo-European language, which is believed to be the root language of English and related tongues. The articles are "The Indo-European Origin of English" (p. xix) and "Indo-European and the Indo-Europeans" (p. 1496). Read these articles and write a brief summary of the historical linguistic techniques that are mentioned in the articles.

3. A portion of the television program shows Dr. Claudia Kernan and several students in serious discussion of "black" English, and the "original study" in Chapter 4 reports some conversation with a black child. Try to answer these questions:

   a. What are some of the ways that black English differs from white middle-class or "college-accepted" English?

   b. What reasons might there be for black Americans to wish to preserve their own usage of English?

   c. What are some reasons that anthropologists would wish to record and preserve this dialect?

   d. What problems in communication might occur between persons who speak different dialects of the same language?

4. Most people migrating to the United States have to learn to speak and read English. Discuss how the difficulties of learning a "second" language illustrate the close relationship of language and culture and language and thought.

5. Consult the *Oxford Dictionary of English Etymology,* Oxford, England: Oxford University Press, l966, for etymologies of certain categories of words (such as textiles, fruits and vegetables, body parts) and trace their origins and histories. How much selective borrowing from other languages is involved?

Answer Key

Vocabulary Check

1. h	7. p	12. j
2. m	8. i	13. k
3. d	9. g	14. c
4. l	10. o	15. e
5. n	11. f	16. a
6. b		

Completion

1. symbols, meanings, rules

2. linguistics, historical linguistics, Indo-European

3. Noam Chomsky, deep structures, surface, transformational-generative

4. sign, displacement, gestures

5. sociolinguistics, dialects

Short-Answer Questions

1. Describe the techniques used by the fieldworker who is gathering information for descriptive linguistics. Your answer should include:

   The fieldworker gathers all the spoken sounds, or phonemes, that may make a difference to meaning. Usually, one needs special training in phonetics to distinguish sounds adequately.

   Fieldworkers also collect and list morphemes, the smallest units of sound that carry meaning. (Many of these may be words, but some sounds that carry meaning, such as prefixes and suffixes, may be less than words).

   The fieldworker must determine the syntax, or the rules for forming sentences.

   A complete grammar of the language is a major goal of the descriptive linguist. The grammar includes all the rules governing the use of morphemes and construction of sentences.

2. Explain the terms "paralanguage" and "kinesics," giving two examples of each. Your answer should include:

Paralanguage is a term for vocal noises that are "extra-linguistic." It is less developed as a communication system than is language.

Examples of paralanguage might include voice qualities, such as pitch range or articulation control, and vocalizations such as laughing or crying, or a vocal qualifier such as a rapid change in pitch.

Kinesics may be thought of as a communication system using postures, facial expressions, and body motions.

Examples of kinesic communications include facial expressions such as smiling, body movements such as nodding in agreement, or biting one's lip to express doubt.

3. Briefly explain and provide examples of the various points of view concerning the influence of language upon perception and perception upon language. Your answer should include:

Benjamin Lee Whorf has developed a theory that language is a force that guides thought and behavior; that by providing habitual "grooves of expression," people are predisposed to view the world in a certain way.

An opposing point of view is that language *reflects* reality, rather than affecting the way people perceive it.

A third point of view, somewhere between these extremes, was expressed by Peter Woolfson, who suggests that language provides a kind of "filtering system" which selects the sensations to which people will pay attention. Your text points out that a people's language will not stop them from thinking in new and novel ways.

4. Why is it so difficult to gather evidence about the origins of language? What evidence is there that suggests language may have originated in gestures? Your answer should include:

Language has been a key part of human culture for a very long time. It may be surmised that Neanderthals had some type of spoken language perhaps as early as 100,000 years ago.

There are no primitive languages today. Even the smallest-scale societies have developed complex languages.

The ability of primates, such as Koko and Lana, to communicate using sign language suggests that the earliest man-like creatures could have communicated quite a bit of information by gestures. As cultures became more complex, imitating sounds from nature might have helped set the stage for transfer from a gesture-based to a vocal-based language. Kinesic communication might be a remnant of this earlier form of communication.

Self-Test

1. d	7. a	13. c
2. d	8. d	14. a
3. b	9. c	15. b
4. a	10. b	16. a
5. b	11. d	17. d
6. c	12. a	

Culture And Personality

7

Overview

What makes you think of someone as having a pleasing personality? Almost certainly, it is some quality or combination of qualities you have observed in that person's behavior, which is the outward manifestation of personality. Personality itself is defined as those specific physical, mental, and emotional qualities which are characteristic of an individual. Virtually everything we can possibly know about a person comes from our own observations of behavior or the observations of others. How do you know, for example, that your friend is kind, or inquisitive, or humorous? Probably because you have seen acts of kindness, watched expressions of curiosity, or heard your friend tell a funny story or laugh at appropriate times.

In this lesson, you will look beyond behavior to thought and emotion, because one's outward behaviors are determined mostly by the way the individual thinks and feels. The anthropologist is interested in the influence of the culture on individual thinking, feeling, and behavior. You've already learned that culture is transmitted from one generation to the next through symbols, especially through language. Since people express their thoughts in language, you can understand that the culture has a strong influence on the individual's self-image and view of virtually everything else in the environment.

Much of our information on the relationship of personality and culture comes from cross-cultural studies of child-rearing methods. The manner in which a child is cared for and trained both reflects the cultural values of the responsible adults and affects the developing personality of the child.

A second focus of study for this lesson is that of "typical" personalities in a society. Some studies have yielded interesting results concerning the "typical" or "average" personality in some national groups, but both the studies and their findings are still considered controversial.

In Lesson Eight, you will continue your exploration of culture and personality, with a look in some depth at definitions of abnormal personalities.

Learning Objectives

When you have completed all assignments in this lesson, you should be able to:

1. Define personality. (Text page 139.)

2. Define enculturation and give some examples of how it occurs. (Text pages 133, 134, and 142-149; television program.)

3. Recognize that the environment is interpreted (perceived) and organized through a person's culture, especially language. (Text pages 137-139; television program.)

4. Explain why anthropologists are interested in cross-cultural studies of child-rearing techniques. (Text pages 133, 139, and 149-151; television program.)

5. Describe the significance of Margaret Mead's 1920s study of Samoan child-rearing practices. (Text pages 140-141; television program.)

6. Describe Malinowski's study of the Trobriand Islanders as it relates to cross-cultural testing of Freud's Oedipus Complex. (Text pages 141-142.)

7. Contrast cross-cultural child-rearing patterns in terms of dependence and independence training. (Text pages 142-149.)

8. Cite examples of different cultural perceptions regarding time, space, objects, values, ideas, and standards. (Text pages 137-141, and 145-148; television program.)

9. Contrast the conception of the self held by the Penobscot Indians with those of the seventeenth century British settlers in New England. (Text pages 137-139.)

10. Discuss the criticisms of Ruth Benedict's study of culture patterns. (Text pages 150-151.)

11. Define modal personality and indicate some of the difficulties involved in assessing it. (Text pages 151-152.)

12. Describe the studies of the Russians and the Japanese as attempts to delineate "national character." Indicate objections to these studies. (Text pages 152-156; television program.)

Assignments For This Lesson

Before Viewing the Program

Read the overview and the learning objectives for this lesson. Use the learning objectives to guide your reading, viewing, and thinking.

Read the preview to Chapter 5 in the text, and look over the topic headings in the chapter.

Read Chapter 5, "Culture and Personality." You may omit the sections "Abnormal Personality" and "Normal and Abnormal Behavior" (pages 156-158) which will be read for the next lesson.

View Program 7, "Culture and Personality."

As you view the program, look for:

examples of enculturation in various cultures.

Margaret Mead's study of different child-rearing techniques.

stereotypes of national character traits related to studies of the personalities of the Japanese and how post-World War II studies have expanded our understanding of Japanese values and behavior.

comparison of the "core values" of the American and Chinese cultures.

After Viewing the Program

Review the terms used in this lesson. In addition to the terms in the learning objectives, you should be familiar with these terms:

self-awareness
basic personality structures

Review the reading assignments for this lesson. A thorough second reading is suggested. Include the chapter summary in your study.

Complete each of the study activities and the self-test in this study guide; then check your answers with the answer key at the end of this lesson.

According to your instructor's assignment or your own interests, complete one or more of the suggested activities. You may also be interested in some of the readings suggested at the end of Chapter 5 in your text.

Study Activities

Ch. 5

Vocabulary Check

Check on your understanding of terms by matching those on the left with the definitions on the right. Check your choices with the answer key at the end of the lesson.

1. _G_ personality
2. _C_ enculturation
3. _H_ self-awareness
4. _B_ Oedipus Complex
5. _I_ Samoan child-rearing practices
6. _F_ dependence training
7. _D_ nuclear family
8. _A_ modal personality

a. a statistical concept: the central tendency of a defined frequency distribution
b. a theory that a boy feels hostility toward his father and sexual desire for his mother
c. the process by which culture is transmitted from one generation to the next
d. consists of mother, father, and dependent children
e. encourages compliance
f. encourages self-reliance and personal achievement
g. involves behavior, thought, and feelings
h. includes the ability to identify oneself as a distinct object
i. studied by Margaret Mead
j. objects and other features organized by the culture into a "cognitive map"

Completion

Choose the best word or phrase from the lists provided to fill the blanks in the paragraphs below.

1. Enculturation is a term used for the process by which the culture

97

is _transmitted_ from one generation to the next. The first step in enculturation is _self-awareness._ The individual also becomes aware of the world around him; however, the culture defines those parts that are especially significant, and it provides values, ideals, and standards by which the individual will act. The environment as perceived by the individual is therefore termed the _behavioral_ environment. The behavioral environment also includes a temporal orientation, or an understanding of _time & space._

- time and space
- behavioral
- self-awareness
- transmitted

2. Studies have indicated that there is a kind of nonrandom _relationship_ between culture and personality. In particular, there seems to be a relationship between _child-rearing patterns_ and the personalities of adults. However, a cause and effect relationship is not certain.

- child-rearing patterns
- relationship

3. Dependence training of children is more often found in _extended_ families. In this type of society, children learn to subordinate their own desires to that of the group. Independence training is usually found in societies with _nuclear_ families. In contrast with societies which teach dependence, the children are given less attention and indulgence while young. They are taught, however, to be _competitive_ and self-reliant.

- nuclear
- extended
- competitive

4. "Modal personality" is a statistical concept which supposes that there is a hypothetical personality, composed of the personality traits that appear most frequently (the "central tendency") in a large group. Unlike some

- psychological testing
- variation

98

other approaches to identifying group personality, this approach recognizes that there will be considerable _variation_ in the personalities of group members. However, determining modal personalities almost requires _phy. testing_ of a representative sampling of the population, the cooperation of the people being tested, and a minimum of such problems as language barriers or personal conflict between the investigators and the population. In addition, there is not yet general agreement on what personality traits should be identified. All of these factors create special difficulties in determining a true modal personality.

5. Critics of studies that supposedly reveal "national character" point out that social phenomena are complex. It is dangerous to make too many _generalizations_ about the qualities of a nation based on limited data. In any society, there are countless individuals who vary from the "typical," even if it exists. Such studies have ignored the influence on personality of other factors besides membership in a particular country, such as social level and _occupation_.

occupation
generalizations

Short-Answer Questions

1. Summarize the conclusions of Mead's studies in Samoa and Malinowski's study of the Oedipus Complex in the Trobriand Islands.

2. Briefly describe some concepts of self, space, values, and ideas held by the Penobscot Indians in the seventeenth century.

3. What are some criticisms of Ruth Benedict's study of culture patterns?

Self-Test

(Select the one best answer.)

Objective 1

1. Which one of the following is not included in the definition of personality presented in the Haviland text?
   a. behavior
   b. thoughts
   c. feelings
   d. values

Objective 2

2. What change in child-rearing practices takes place relatively early in Western industrialized societies compared to traditional farming societies?
   a. Full responsibility is assumed by the parents.
   b. Much of the task is turned over to specialists.
   c. The process is discontinued.
   d. The child's wishes are followed.

Objective 3

3. The behavioral environment is
   a. organized and perceived through the culture.
   b. identical to the objective environment.
   c. different for the child than for the adult.
   d. similar in all cultures.

Objective 4

4. Anthropologists study cross-cultural child-rearing techniques because those practices
   a. reveal inherited personality traits.
   b. show parenting practices are basically the same everywhere.
   c. reveal cultural values which are enculturated in children.
   d. prove Freud's personality theories are universal.

Objective 5

5. Mead's studies in Samoa
   a. revealed child-rearing practices are similar in all societies.
   b. provided evidence that adolescence is not always accompanied by some degree of stress and conflict.
   c. revealed the Oedipus Complex theory is not valid in all societies.
   d. demonstrated that Western child-rearing techniques are superior.

Objective 6

6. Malinowski successfully challenged a theory by _____ by showing that a Trobriand boy is antagonistic toward his _____.
   a. Benedict; mother

100

b. Freud; father
c. Mead; mother
d. Freud; mother's brother

Objective 7
7. In a(n) _____ society, you would probably find parents spending the least amount of time with young offspring.
   a. industrial
   b. subsistence farming
   c. extended
   d. authoritarian

Objective 8
8. Which of these societies was described as tolerant of premarital sexual activity in older children?
   a. United States
   b. Penobscot
   c. Samoan
   d. Zuni

Objective 9
9. A self-concept that included a physical body and spirit-self was found in
   a. the seventeenth century Penobscot Indian.
   b. seventeenth century British settlers in North America.
   c. both seventeenth century Penobscot Indians and British settlers.
   d. neither of these groups.

Objective 10
10. One criticism of Ruth Benedict's *Patterns of Culture* is that
    a. her theories were based on conflict-inspired prejudices.
    b. she underemphasized the variations of personalities within a culture.
    c. she studied only one cultural group as the basis for her theories.
    d. she did not attempt to show a relationship between culture and personality.

Objective 11
11. What is one difficulty in determining modal personality?
    a. The concept does not recognize variations of personality within a culture.
    b. Studies testing for modal personality could not be duplicated by another researcher.
    c. The measurement techniques for this research are difficult to carry out in the field.
    d. The studies cannot be applied to most societies.

Objective 12

12. What happened after anthropologists studied Japanese "national character" during World War II?
    a. The assumption that Japanese toilet training was extremely strict was proven to be wrong.
    b. The results were applied with success during American occupation of Japan.
    c. Psychological theories developed to explain individual behavior were applied frequently to the behavior of groups.
    d. The "national character" of most countries has been studied and described.

Suggested Activities

1. Margaret Mead's *The Coming of Age in Samoa* has attracted wide attention over the years, but is not without its critics. Read Mead's work, following it with the article "Bursting the South Sea Bubble: An Anthropologist Attacks Margaret Mead's Research in Samoa," *Time*, February 14, 1983 (Volume 121; page 68). The article describes the controversy arising from the publication of a book by Derek Freeman, *Margaret Mead and Samoa: The Making and Unmasking of an Anthropological Myth* (Cambridge, Mass: Harvard University Press, 1983). You may wish to write a brief report emphasizing some difficulties of gathering and interpreting data on psychological aspects of culture from field study.

2. Review two or three current articles or books on the subject of raising young children. What elements do you find in your reading that are consistent with independence training? Do you find any suggestions that seem to go against independence training patterns as described in the text?

3. Have you encountered an example of dependence training in the United States? If possible, do a bit of anthropological fieldwork by interviewing either the parents or the children in such a family. What values and behaviors have been taught to the children? Describe the kind of parent-child contact in this family, the types of duties assigned to children in their early years, and the adult roles which the parents and children believe the children will assume when grown.

Answer Key

Vocabulary Check

1. g
2. c
3. h
4. b

5. i
6. e
7. d
8. a

Completion

1. transmitted, self-awareness, behavioral, time and space

2. relationship, child-rearing patterns

3. extended, nuclear, competitive

4. variation, psychological testing

5. generalizations, occupation

Short-Answer Questions

1. Summarize the conclusions of Mead's studies in Samoa and Malinowski's study of the Oedipus Complex in the Trobriand Islands. Your answer should include:

   Mead found that Samoan children, particularly young girls, grew from childhood to adulthood without the stresses and strains that adolescents go through in Western cultures. Her study suggested that childhood training strongly influences adult personality and showed that different ways of child training are effective in different cultural contexts. Malinowski's study of Trobriand society showed that the Oedipus Complex suggested by Freud is not universal. According to the Oedipus Complex theory, a boy will develop antagonistic feelings toward his father and repress a sexual desire for his mother. In Trobriand society, "family" relationships involve the mother, the mother's brother, and the sister's children, over whom the boy will one day have authority. A male child in Trobriand society directs his antagonism toward the authority figure (his mother's brother) and has an interest in his sister's sexual activity.

2. Briefly describe some concepts of self, space, values, and ideas held by the Penobscot Indians in the seventeenth century. Your answer should include:

   The Penobscot Indians of the 1600s viewed themselves as consisting of both body and "vital self"; the latter was able to leave the body and was vulnerable to attack by others.

   They viewed their space as a flat world, surrounded by saltwater, and centered upon the Penobscot river.

   Some values and ideas held by the Penobscot are closely related to their self-awareness. They were a secretive people, protecting themselves from attacks (especially on the vital self) by distrusting strangers and being cautious in their dealings with living things in the forest (which also were believed to have vital selves).

3. What are some criticisms of Ruth Benedict's study of culture patterns? Your answer should include:

Ruth Benedict's "cultural configuration" approach has been abandoned by anthropologists because it has been judged impressionistic and cannot be duplicated by further studies.

Even the subjects of her study were not consistent in maintaining only one configuration (the "Apollonian" Zunis would sometimes engage in "Dionysian" activities).

Her approach failed to take into account the wide diversity of personalities within any society.

Self-Test

1. d	5. b	9. a
2. b	6. d	10. b
3. a	7. a	11. c
4. c	8. c	12. a

Alejandro Mamani: 8

A Case Study in Culture and Personality

Overview

As you approach this lesson, remember that culture defines appropriate behavior, shapes ideas and values, and orders relationships between individuals. It should not be surprising, then, that *abnormal* behavior is defined by the culture, as well.

The case study which you will explore in this lesson concerns an Aymara man with a mental illness. Anthropologists have gathered evidence indicating that the specific form a mental illness takes is culturally determined. Even if the illness is one which appears in most societies (as the condition suffered by Alejandro Mamani may well be), the Aymara culture strongly affects the way that it is manifested. In the United States, for example, we don't expect to meet a person who is afflicted by evil spirits, as Mamani appears to be. But despondency and despair among the elderly at approaching death is not unique to the Aymara.

The culture also defines and names mental illnesses and determines various treatments with which to "cure" the sufferer. In some cases, a society may class as "honored behavior" what another society condemns as "abnormal," and treatment may be administered or withheld accordingly.

Your challenge in this lesson, particularly while viewing the television program, is to understand the complex system of beliefs and values which underlie the illness of one man. If you can describe the relationship between that culture and the illness, the attempts at cures, and the final resolution of the problem, you will have gained an important anthropological insight into one aspect of mental health and mental illness. You may also gain insight into your own culture's treatment of mental problems and the elderly.

Learning Objectives

When you have completed all assignments in this lesson, you should be able to:

1. Discuss the difficulty of constructing a cross-cultural description of abnormal behavior. (Text pages 156-158; Background Notes.)

2. Describe the types and roles of "spirits" in the Aymara culture and Mamani's interpretation of the spirits that have possessed him. (Television program; Background Notes.)

3. Describe the variety of reactions of members of his family and community to Mamani's illness. (Television program; Background Notes.)

4. Describe the various "cures" tried by Mamani, and explain the cultural interpretation of how they work. (Television program; Background Notes.)

5. Discuss in what ways Mamani's behavior can be seen as a preparation for dying. (Television program.)

Assignments For This Lesson

Before Viewing the Program

Ch.5

Read the overview and the learning objectives for this lesson. Use the learning objectives to guide your reading, viewing, and thinking.

Read the sections on "Abnormal Personality" and "Abnormal and Normal Behavior" beginning on page 156 in text Chapter 5.

View Program 8, "Alejandro Mamani: A Case Study in Culture and Personality."

As you view the program, look for:

Alejandro Mamani's description of the different spirits tormenting him.

reaction of the community and his family to Mamani's illness; and, later, the reaction of his family to the costs of the illness.

the kind of diagnosis made, and the various cures that are attempted. Note how both are based in important Aymara beliefs.

the manner in which Alejandro Mamani resolves two difficult problems for himself: division of his property and final solution to his illness.

After Viewing the Program

Read the background notes for this lesson. Note the location of the Aymara on the map included in the notes.

Review terms used in this lesson.

Review the reading assignments for this lesson. A thorough second reading of the sections in the text and the background notes is suggested.

Complete each of the study activities and the self-test in the study guide; then check your answers with the answer key at the end of this lesson.

According to your instructor's assignment or your own interests, complete one or more of the suggested activities.

Background Notes

Psychological Anthropology and Personality

Some anthropologists consider the name "psychological anthropology" to be a contradiction in terms. Anthropology has traditionally been considered the study of human social behavior. But, early in this century, American anthropologists broke with European traditions, especially the British, by developing an interest in personality. The Haviland text describes some of these early efforts by such pioneers as Ruth Benedict and Margaret Mead. In the past, psychological anthropology has focused on two general issues: (1) enculturation, or how an individual acquires information about and becomes a functioning member of his culture, and (2) "culture types," variations in personality from one culture to another.

These early studies, which came to be generally classified under the heading of "culture and personality," were based on the assumption that personality is a product of one's cultural environment and that, consequently, individual variation within a culture will be minimal. There was a great deal of interest in determining personality types for use in classifying individuals and cultures. Personality, in this context, is generally understood as the set of traits which distinguish an individual and characterize his or her interactions with others.

In the case of Ruth Benedict, the concept of personality was generalized to apply to whole cultures. Even when not carried to this extreme, there were attempts to explain cultural differences in terms of personality traits. Margaret Mead sought to tie variations in child-rearing practices to cultural values. Essentially, she tried to show that certain personality traits are encouraged or inhibited through child-rearing practices that vary from one society to another.

In recent years, interest has shifted to studies of intra-cultural variation, as well as to analyses of cross-cultural differences. This has added a new dimension to psychological anthropology, because it allows researchers to consider the range of variation within a culture and to reexamine the concept of abnormal behavior.

As a social science, anthropology has traditionally focused on normative beliefs and behaviors, that is, those beliefs and behaviors *shared* by most members of the group. But this approach overlooks the range and diversity found in any human group.

All groups have norms, or generally accepted standards of behavior. We are able to live in social groups because we know what to expect from the people with whom we interact. Norms enable us to predict behavior of other people and make it clear what is expected of us as members of social groups. We dress, speak, and make exchanges based on our understanding of norms.

Within these guidelines, however, is a range of acceptable behaviors. Behavior expected of a young unmarried woman is not the same as that expected of a grandmother. Norms vary according to the setting. We behave differently when entertaining business associates at a restaurant than when we are having a family picnic at the beach. Our ability to detect subtle differences in expectations and react appropriately affects our acceptance into our social community.

However, not all people conform to social norms at all times. In fact, most people deviate from the norm at one time or another. Norms are idealized concepts; actual behavior is always subject to negotiation.

But, in any society, some people consistently deviate from the norm. Deviant behavior, if extreme and unchecked, threatens the underlying assumptions on which society is based. But even deviance conforms to normative standards, according to the psychological anthropologist Robert B. Edgerton. Members of gangs in urban United States violate norms of the larger society, but they conform to rigid standards of behavior within their own social groups.

What might be deviant behavior in one society may not be considered deviant in others. Among the Gururumba of Papua New Guinea, one form of greeting is for one man to grab the genitals of another. This custom would be considered deviant in our society, but is well within normative standards of behavior among the Gururumba. However, some types of behavior are considered deviant in all societies. The Haviland text mentions the appearance of schizophrenia in its various manifestations throughout the world. Although it appears in slightly different forms in different cultures, it is recognizable as schizophrenia. It is considered deviant in all societies, even if explanations and forms of treatment for it differ.

There are generally two ways of defining deviant behavior: (1) as an intentional violation of the social code (such as criminality) and (2) as a result of circumstances beyond the individual's control. In most societies, psychological disturbances are viewed as being beyond the individual's control. In our society, these are classified as neuroses (involving a slight degree of disturbance) or psychoses (involving a high degree of disturbance interrupting the individual's ability to function in society).

In other societies, a psychological disturbance may be attributed to witchcraft or to possession by supernatural beings. However, in all cases, including our society, the individual is diagnosed as "ill" or disturbed on the basis of his ability to perform the social duties expected of him.

All societies have methods for treating these disturbances and the treatment is related to the diagnosis. In modern psychiatry, the patient may be treated with drugs, psychodrama, catharsis, and other techniques considered effective in treating psychological disturbances. In cultures which explain psychological disturbance as being due to spirit possession, the patient may be treated with various forms of exorcism. However, anthropologists specializing in cross-cultural psychology have noted that exorcism rituals often use many of the techniques considered effective in modern psychiatry, including psychodrama, catharsis, and drugs.

A Case Study of Abnormality

The television program for this lesson describes a case of psychological disturbance among the Aymara Indians of the Bolivian Andes. In some ways, the illness of Alejandro Mamani is similar to that of people experiencing psychological disturbances in our culture. But its diagnosis and treatment and the circumstances surrounding the illness are rooted in the cultural experiences of the Aymara.

Alejandro Mamani is an old man living in Vitocota, a small village near Lake Titicaca 12,000 feet above sea level. Like his neighbors, he is a peasant farmer relying on his land, where he plants primarily potatoes and raises chickens, goats, and sheep.

The Aymara lack material amenities. Until the Bolivian revolution of 1952, most of them worked as tenant farmers on land owned by the mestizos, the Spanish-speaking middle class. After the revolution, the large landholdings were broken up and distributed to the peasants who worked the land. But the land is not very fertile and hailstorms, wind, and drought are a continual threat to survival.

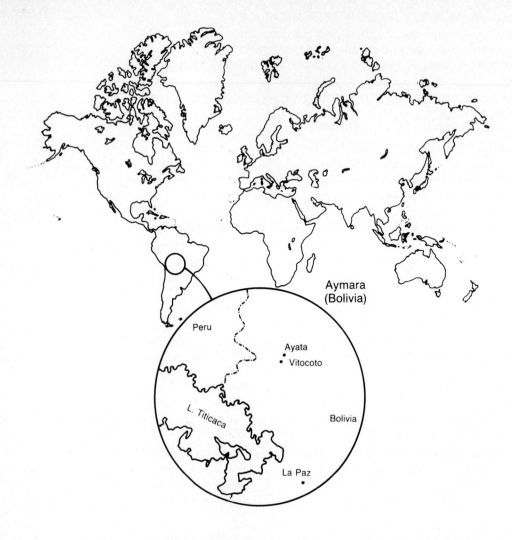

Figure 8.1 The Aymara Indians live and farm in a mountainous region in northern Bolivia bordered by Peru and Lake Titicaca.

By Aymara standards, Alejandro Mamani, the subject of the television program for this lesson, was a wealthy man. Not only did he have sufficient land and animals to make a living, but he was able to secure title to his land for his children in spite of bureaucratic obstruction. He also earned respect by serving in many religious and secular offices and by helping to finance costly religious festivals.

The Aymara commonly get drunk at ceremonies and religious festivals, and this custom provided the occasion for Alejandro Mamani's illness. On the way home from a funeral where he became drunk, Mamani went to sleep at a well-known place where evil spirits dwell. While he was asleep, several spirits took possession of his body. Since then, according to the television program, Mamani cannot sleep at night and when he dozes off, he has nightmares in which the spirits appear as men and women, dancing, talking, and arguing with him. As he becomes increasingly ill, the spirits begin to appear in the daytime as well. One of the spirits appears to be his dead wife. He is attracted to this spirit, because the Aymara believe the spirit of a recently dead person tries to pull others after it. The Aymara also consider dreams as omens and consider them significant both for the person who experiences them and for the community as a whole.

Mamani says the spirits who are possessing him are not Aymara peasants but mestizos. Nevertheless, he undergoes a "divination" ceremony to determine the identity of the spirits. Divination is a ritual means of diagnosis conducted by specially trained diviners. In Mamani's case, curers propose to treat him by transferring his illness into several animals. The curers spend the night with Mamani and the animals—a dog, a rooster, lizards, a piglet, and a chick. At dawn, they take the animals to the place where Mamani became afflicted and set them free. The hope is that the spirits will have entered the body of one of the animals and be unable to find their way back to Mamani.

In another treatment, Mamani fumigates a spirit with some sulfur. The spirit leaves him temporarily, but now demands tribute to stay away.

Mamani and his family also consider seeing a medical doctor for a cure, but they have little faith in his ability. They say the medical doctor cures physical illness, but cannot help with spirit possession. When his family eventually tires of having to pay for his cures, Mamani calls them together and transfers his property to them before committing suicide. Although suicide is disapproved in Aymara culture, Mamani is remembered with respect, and his action is considered logical in view of his afflictions.

Mamani's illness illustrates some general themes in psychological anthropology. The diagnosis of his illness, explanations about how it occurred, and treatment for it are all consistent with the values of Aymara culture. However, the symptoms are recognizable to us and fit within the explanatory framework of modern psychiatry.

All societies have normative standards for behavior. Implicit in these standards are definitions of deviance and limits of acceptable behavior. When individuals fail to conform to these standards, societies have systems for reintegrating individuals into their social group. Divination and other diagnostic methods may serve to uncover social relationships between the patient and other members of his family. When an individual is unable to be reintegrated into the society, his social role will be redefined in such a way as to definitively exclude him from his group.

Study Activities

Vocabulary Check

Check on your understanding of terms by matching those on the left with the definitions on the right. Check your choices with the answer key at the end of the lesson.

1. _D_ ethnic psychosis
2. _G_ windigo
3. _B_ criminality
4. _H_ psychosis
5. _F_ divination
6. _E_ spirit possession

a. a mild degree of mental disturbance

b. abnormal behavior resulting from deliberate violation of the social code

c. a behavior pattern in which a man takes the dress and manners of a woman

d. a mental disorder peculiar to a particular ethnic group

e. a mental experience among the Aymara considered abnormal when occurring frequently and intensely

f. a means of diagnosis and treatment used to cure Mamani

g. a psychosis associated with fear of cannibalism

h. a mental disturbance which severely affects the individual's functioning

Completion

Choose the best word or phrase from the lists provided to fill the blanks in the paragraphs below.

1. The definition for "abnormal behavior" seems to depend on the _culture_ in which it occurs. Some behaviors that are deviant in one society would be considered normal in others. Other conditions would be recognized universally as abnormal, such as schizophrenia. However, the specific _form_ that the mental illness takes may

form
treatment
culture
diagnosis

depend on the culture. Also determined by the culture are both _diagnosis_ and _treatment_

2. Alejandro Mamani's belief in spirits is not considered abnormal in Aymara society. The Aymara religion is a combination of _Roman Catholicism_ and traditional Indian beliefs; both traditions contribute to the idea that much of life is animated by spirits. But the frequency and severity of spirit _possession_ in the case of Alejandro Mamani are taken as indicators of illness, and attempts are made to cure Mamani, using various attempts at divination and driving the spirits away. Mamani's family grows resentful of the mounting _costs_ associated with his illness.

costs
— Roman Catholicism
/ possession

Short-Answer Questions

1. Describe some of the types of spirits which the Aymara believe in. What types of spirits have attacked Alejandro Mamani?

2. Describe the assumptions inherent in the cures attempted for Mamani's illness.

3. In what ways does Mamani's behavior seem to be a preparation for his own death?

Self-Test

(Select the one best answer.)

Objective 1
1. Which of the following behaviors resulted in special honor rather than condemnation in some American Plains Indian tribes?
   a. obsession with cannibalism
   b. demon possession
   c. a man's assuming the dress of a woman
   d. depression

Objective 1
2. Anthropological studies seem to indicate that culture influences
   a. the form a mental illness will take.
   b. the diagnosis of a mental condition.
   c. the treatment of a mental condition.
   d. all of the above.

Objective 2
3. Belief in spirits among the Aymara is
   a. widespread and a part of their religion.
   b. taken as a sign of severe abnormality.
   c. common only among children and the elderly.
   d. unusual, but tolerated by the community.

Objective 3
4. Which of the following was *not* a reaction of Mamani's family and friends to his illness?
   a. sympathy
   b. belief that a cure should be attempted in the community
   c. disbelief
   d. embarrassment

Objective 4
5. Mamani was placed with animals for a night to
   a. attempt a transfer of spirits from him to them.
   b. shame Mamani for his behavior.
   c. bring him back to reason through contact with familiar things.
   d. give him a feeling that something useful was being done.

Objective 5
6. When Mamani decided to will the last of his property, his family
   a. tried to dissuade him from giving in to his illness.
   b. felt he was no longer responsible for his actions.
   c. seemed to consider it appropriate.
   d. was fearful that such action would bring bad luck.

Suggested Activities

1. Make a survey concerning beliefs in spirits in your community. Check newspaper advertisements (especially the "personals" column) for "psychic readers." Determine whether or not there are laws restricting these kinds of practices in your community or state. Write a brief summary of your findings, and defend your opinion as to whether such beliefs should be considered "abnormal" in this society.

2. Do some investigation, including scanning some current "self-help" books and talking with at least one professional, to gather some evidence on whether or not a "midlife crisis" (such as male menopause) is a culturally induced phenomenon. In other words, is it a cultural neurosis or an ethnic psychosis? Or is it a universal response to aging? Speculate on factors in this society which might induce such crises.

3. Read and prepare a brief review of *The Bolivian Aymara*, by Hans C. Buechler and Judith Maria Buechler (Holt, Rinehart and Winston, 1971).

Answer Key

Vocabulary Check

1. d
2. g
3. b
4. h
5. f
6. e

Completion

1. culture, form, diagnosis, treatment

2. Roman Catholicism, possession, costs

Short-Answer Questions

1. Describe some of the types of spirits which the Aymara believed in. What types of spirits have attacked Alejandro Mamani? Your answer should include:

   There are spirits associated with specific places or animals, other spirits associated with natural forces, and some demon spirits, as well as spirits of the dead. Mamani believes that several types of spirits have attacked him, including demons and spirits of the dead such as his wife. The spirit of a dead person may come to a member of the community to lure or entice that person to join the spirit world. Some of the latter include spirits from the mestizo, or upper class of his country.

2. Describe the assumptions inherent in the cures attempted for Mamani's illness. Your answer should include:

   The forms of cures tried on Mamani differed, but all assumed the presence of spirits of various types.

   The purpose of attempted cures was to either drive the spirits and demons away or transfer them to the bodies of animals. The cures also assumed that a person with knowledge or special powers could bring about such cures.

3. In what ways does Mamani's behavior seem to be a preparation for his own death? Your answer should include:

   In the television program for this lesson, Mamani seems preoccupied with death and speaks of suicide as a way out of his problems.

   One of the spirits troubling him is that of his dead wife, who, according to tradition, may be trying to pull his soul after hers.

   In a formal and ceremonial division of property, he finally distributes the last of his possessions to his children and another woman whom he raised from childhood. In Mamani's mind, this leaves him free to end his life.

Self-Test

1. c
2. d
3. a
4. c
5. a
6. c

Marriage And The Family 9

Overview

Marriage and the family evolved long ago as a principal means of solving certain universal problems that confront all human beings, and for this reason, these institutions persist and are universal to all human cultures in one form or another. As social institutions, marriage and the family meet needs for nurturance of offspring, role models for children, cooperation among members of the group, and control of access to sexual relations.

While the needs and the problem-solving mechanism may be universal, however, the forms these customs take and the practices that attend them differ widely. For example, most people in the United States believe in monogamy, or the form of marriage which allows the taking of only one spouse; while the Kaupauku of Western New Guinea practice polygyny, or the practice of marrying more than one wife, or as many as a husband can afford. In our society, most marriageable individuals choose their own spouses; but an Arapesh who has sons of marriageable age picks his sons' brides.

It might seem odd to you, but polygyny, not monogamy, is the most preferred form of marriage among existing societies. For economic reasons, monogamy is more common, however. As you will learn, other current forms include polyandry, the marriage of a woman to more than one man; group marriage, a rare form in which several men and women participate; and serial marriage, in which an individual marries or lives with a series of partners in succession. A variation of serial marriage has become increasingly prevalent in present-day American society.

The form of the family is related to the problems faced by the group, and forms may range from the contemporary nuclear family (father, mother, children) of our own society to the consanguineal family, in which the wife and her children live with her brothers, not her husband.

Studying marriage and the family in the context of different cultures poses a special challenge for you, especially in view of the fact that these customs have in recent years been subjected to severe stress and are undergoing broad changes. In the next two lessons, you will read about and see a variety of marriage patterns and family organizations. Most of them will seem strange, perhaps undesirable, if you view American marriage and family practices as the norm against which all others are measured. As you consider the different forms and practices, ask yourself: What is the cultural value of the practice and how does it contribute to the survival of the society?

A good place to begin your study is with an anthropological definition of marriage. Haviland defines marriage (text page 233) as a contract between a man and woman which provides sexual access to both and makes the wife eligible to bear children. A related but somewhat broader definition includes these points: Marriage is an economic and sexual relationship, socially sanctioned, between two or more individuals, at least one of whom is a different sex than the others. If this definition seems to allow for considerable variation, it is because there *is* much variation in the forms and practices devised by humankind.

Learning Objectives

When you have completed all assignments in this lesson, you should be able to:

1. List and describe the basic functions of the family from a cross-cultural perspective. (Text pages 230-236; television program.)

2. Describe the traditional customs of the Nayar people of India concerning rules of sexual access. (Text pages 233-234.)

3. Define marriage from a cross-cultural perspective. (Text page 233; television program.)

4. Define incest taboo and suggest several explanations for its cultural universality. (Text pages 234-235.)

5. Distinguish between endogamy and exogamy and describe their purposes. (Text pages 235-236; television program.)

6. Define nuclear family. (Text pages 237-239; television program.) ✓

7. Describe the following forms of marriage: monogamy, polygyny, polyandry, group, and serial, and indicate their relative frequency. ✓ Suggest reasons for polygyny. (Text pages 239-240; television program.)

8. Define "levirate" and "sororate" as traditional customs regulating choice ✓ of marriage partner. (Text page 240.)

9. Contrast the mate selection patterns of more traditional societies with ✓ those of modern America. (Text pages 240-245; television program.)

10. Recognize the wide variety of customs and traditions regarding divorce. ✓ (Text pages 245-246.)

11. Define extended family, contrast it with nuclear families, recognize its frequency in traditional societies, and describe the economic functions ✓ served by it. (Text pages 246-249; television program.)

12. Describe conditions in industrial societies that favor the existence of ✓ nuclear families. (Text pages 238-239; television program.)

13. Explain the importance of marital residence patterns, recognize the five patterns, and describe the following three forms: patrilocal, matrilocal, ✓ and neolocal. (Text pages 247-251.)

14. Describe the customs of bride price and bride service. (Text pages ✓ 250-251.)

15. Briefly describe some problems of the nuclear family in modern society. ✓ (Text pages 253-254; television program.)

Assignments For This Lesson

Before Viewing the Program

Read the overview and the learning objectives for this lesson. Use the *Ch. 8* learning objectives to guide your reading, viewing, and thinking.

Read the preview to Chapter 8 in the text.

Read Chapter 8, "Marriage and the Family," in the text.

View Program 9, "Marriage and the Family."

As you view the program, look for:

the importance of the family in the nurturance of children.

a dispute over "bride price" among the Turkana.

the marriage and family customs of the Pygmies, a hunting and gathering people.

an extended family and its functions in India.

the kinds of pressures exerted by present-day industrial society which make it difficult to retain the structure and traditions of extended families. Note the similarities of the problems, whether they occur in India or the Greek community of Baltimore.

After Viewing the Program

Review the terms used in this lesson. In addition to the terms found in the learning objectives, you should be familiar with these terms:

nurturance   consanguineal
affinal   conjugal

Review the reading assignments for this lesson. A thorough second reading is suggested. Include the chapter summary in your study.

Complete each of the study activities and the self-test in this study guide; then check your answers with the answer key at the end of this lesson.

According to your instructor's assignment or your own interests, complete one or more of the suggested activities. You may also be interested in some of the readings suggested at the end of Chapter 8 in your text.

Study Activities

Vocabulary Check

Check on your understanding of terms by matching those on the left with the definitions on the right. Check your choices with the answer key at the end of the lesson.

1. _E_ marriage
2. _a_ incest taboo
3. _I_ nurturance
4. _N_ affinal
5. _B_ endogamy

a. forbids sexual relationships with certain relatives

b. restricts marriage to those within a certain group or category

6. __D__ monogamy
7. __J__ polyandry
8. __M__ nuclear family
9. __L__ patrilocal residence
10. __G__ neolocal residence
11. __O__ bride service
12. __C__ levirate

c. requires that a man marry his deceased brother's wife
d. most common form of marriage today
e. includes economic and sexual relationships
f. requires that a man marry his deceased wife's sister
g. the common residence pattern in the United States
h. prohibits marriage within a certain group
i. refers to taking care of the young; an important function of the family
j. marriage form in which the woman takes more than one husband
k. marriage form in which the man takes more than one wife
l. a married couple living with the husband's relatives
m. a family unit composed of husband, wife, and children
n. related by marriage
o. an obligation undertaken by a husband to the bride's family
p. related by blood

Completion

Choose the best word or phrase from the lists provided to fill the blanks in the paragraphs below.

1. Marriage is a contract between a man and a woman (although arrangements may be made by the _families_) which almost always includes both an _economic_ and a _sexual_ relationship. One of the most unusual marriage patterns is that of the Nayar, in which the man never _lives_ with the woman. However, Haviland states that the most "bizarre and exotic" form of marriage is the serial marriage found in the United States.

lives
families
sexual
economic

2. Other marriage patterns include the most common form, or _monogamy_, a less common form involving more than one wife, or _polygyny_, and two rare forms: more than one husband, or _polyandry_, and _group_ marriage.

\ polygyny
\ group
\ monogamy
\ polyandry

3. Choices of marriage partners are restricted to some degree by all cultures. For example, all cultures have a taboo against _incest_, which has led some observers to believe that this prohibition is ingrained in "human nature." However, the specific category of persons excluded by this taboo varies widely from culture to culture. It virtually always includes the _nuclear_ family, but in some cases the excluded group may be much larger.

\ nuclear
\ incest

4. There are still other marriage choices determined by the culture. In many instances, marriages must be _exogamous_, or outside of a specifically defined group. The opposite cultural requirement is _endogamy_, or marriage within a specific group. One hypothesis for the former is that such marriages help form _alliances_. It is thought that the latter, which is much more rare, is practiced to preserve cultural heritage and to consolidate resources.

\ alliances
\ endogamy
\ exogamous

5. _Industrial_ societies do not lend themselves to maintaining large and stable extended families. As new kinds of jobs become available in new areas, workers

\ isolated
\ Industrial
\ nuclear

move to those jobs, taking their ___nuclear___ families with them. The nuclear family structure poses some problems for members including being ___isolated___ from both sets of kin, thus lacking the psychological and economic support of extended family members.

Short-Answer Questions

1. Summarize the basic functions of the family which are found in virtually all societies.

2. Contrast nuclear and extended families. Briefly summarize the suitability of each in nonindustrial and industrial societies. What special problems does each type encounter in modern industrial societies?

3. In what ways have American patterns of mate selection departed from traditional methods of matchmaking?

4. Briefly define five marital residence patterns.

Self-Test

(Select the one best answer.)

Objective 1
1. One of the basic functions of the family is to
   a. protect property.
   b. equalize labor patterns between the sexes.
   c. nurture children.
   d. provide for mobility of the nuclear family.

Objective 2
2. In the marriage pattern of the Nayar, the
   a. husband resides with the wife's brother.
   b. husband does not reside with the wife.
   c. wife lives with the husband's family.
   d. husband lives with the wife's family.

Objective 3
3. From a cross-cultural standpoint, which of the following is not always true of marriage?

a. It includes an economic relationship.
b. It includes rights of sexual access.
c. It is socially sanctioned.
d. It is a contract between one man and one woman.

Objective 4
4. Of the two statements, (a) some form of the incest taboo is universal, and (b) none of the explanations for the occurrence of the incest taboo is completely satisfactory,
   a. neither one is correct.
   b. both are correct.
   c. a is correct, but b is not.
   d. b is correct, but a is not.

Objective 5
5. A possible explanation for the practice of endogamy is that it
   a. ensures continuation of cultural traditions.
   b. ensures group child-rearing practices.
   c. prevents conflicts over sexual access within the group.
   d. is somehow inherited, a part of "human nature."

Objective 6
6. The nuclear family is typically found in
   a. the Nayar society.
   b. the Pygmy society of Zaire.
   c. the United States.
   d. India.

Objective 7
7. The two most common forms of marriage in the world today are
   a. polygyny and group marriage.
   b. polygyny and monogamy.
   c. polyandry and monogamy.
   d. polyandry and polygyny.

Objective 7
8. Polyandry is a marriage custom in which a
   a. husband has more than one wife.
   b. group of men has sexual access to a group of women.
   c. man or woman may have a series of mates.
   d. wife has more than one husband.

Objective 8
9. Which of the following best describes the marriage custom of levirate?
   a. A woman marries her dead sister's husband.
   b. A man marries his dead wife's sister.
   c. A man marries his dead brother's wife.
   d. A man marries all the sisters in a family.

Objective 9

10. How does the manner in which Americans select their mates differ significantly from mate selection practices in traditional societies?
    a. Americans make selections at a comparatively early age.
    b. Americans select their own mates, rather than allowing their families to make such decisions.
    c. Americans generally base their mate selections on the needs of their family group.
    d. Americans tend to base their evaluation of prospective mates on less emotional and transitory values.

Objective 10

11. Western divorce rates are
    a. considerably lower than those of many matrilineal societies.
    b. higher than those of virtually any traditional society.
    c. lower than those of most traditional societies.
    d. about the same as those in most matrilineal societies.

Objective 11

12. Which of these best explains the organization of extended families in many cultures?
    a. Raising children is more difficult in traditional societies.
    b. Religious beliefs make it difficult for children to leave home.
    c. A lack of money or wealth makes it impossible for family members to leave.
    d. The need for a large labor pool and cooperation in economic activities keeps family members together.

Objective 12

13. An economic environment in which the elderly become a burden rather than an asset favors development of
    a. extended families.
    b. matrilineal families.
    c. nuclear families.
    d. endogamous families.

Objective 13

14. In the _____ residence pattern, a woman leaves her family after marriage to live with the family in which her husband grew up.
    a. patrilocal
    b. neolocal
    c. matrilocal
    d. ambilocal

Objective 14

15. The purpose of *bride service* is to
    a. give the bride an opportunity to prove her worth to the husband's family.

b. enable the bride to remain with her own family after her marriage.
c. allow the man to determine whether or not his prospective wife will be an economic asset.
d. repay the bride's family for the economic loss of losing a daughter.

Objective 15

16. A distinct problem of nuclear families in Western industrialized societies such as the United States is
    a. control of important decisions by relatives.
    b. isolation of husbands and wives in dealing with family responsibilities.
    c. conflict with near relatives such as aunts, cousins, and the like who are outside the nuclear family.
    d. the dependence of children on their parents after they are reared.

Suggested Activities

1. Investigate at least two living patterns for the elderly in or near your community. For example, there may be a "retirement home" under any of several names, such as a "nursing home," and a "retirement community"; or there may be an apartment complex which restricts residents to ages over 55. If possible, visit these residences firsthand, or obtain information from reading articles or promotional brochures. Try to answer these questions: (1) What social advantages do these life-styles have for the residents? (2) What social and economic advantages and disadvantages are realized by the community or by younger members of families of the residents? How do these patterns differ from the position of the elderly in traditional extended families?

2. Assume you are going to debate the proposition that arranged marriages are more stable and long-lasting. Present your arguments in favor of the proposition, using a cross-cultural perspective to prove your points.

Answer Key

Vocabulary Check

1. e	5. b	9. l
2. a	6. d	10. g
3. i	7. j	11. o
4. n	8. m	12. c

Completion

1. families, economic, sexual, lives

2. monogamy, polygyny, polyandry, group

3. incest, nuclear

4. exogamous, endogamy, alliances

5. Industrial, nuclear, isolated

Short-Answer Questions

1. Summarize the basic functions of the family which are found in virtually all societies. Your answer should include:

   The basic functions of the family are the nurturance of children, control of sexual relations (sexual access), and the promotion of economic activity and social status.

   The family also can provide the basis of cooperative alliances between family groups, as well as emotional support and sustenance for its members.

2. Contrast nuclear and extended families. Briefly summarize the suitability of each in nonindustrial and industrial societies. What specific problems does each type encounter in modern industrial societies? Your answer should include:

   The nuclear family consists of mother, father, and dependent children, while the extended family is a much larger group, composed of more than one nuclear family, all related by both conjugal and consanguineal ties.

   The extended family lives and works together in settings, such as farming, that require much cooperative labor. It is especially suited to such environments where "many hands" are needed for a number of tasks. The nuclear family is better suited to the requirement for mobility which is found in industrialized societies.

   Extended families find it difficult to survive as a unit in complex, industrialized societies. Either because of dissatisfaction or economic need, younger members may wish to move away from the family to seek new job opportunities not available in the immediate area.

Nuclear families also face many problems in complex industrialized societies. In a neolocal residence away from kin, the family has no certain support in such matters as childbirth, child rearing, or resolving conflicts between the two adults. Except for raising children, the role of the woman is uncertain. Since the children will also leave home to start their own nuclear families, there is no expectation that anyone will care for the parents when they are old.

3. In what ways have American patterns of mate selection departed from traditional methods of matchmaking? Your answer should include:

In American society, marriage choice and selection of mate have become matters of individual and independent decision, to be made by the individuals themselves. To a great extent, these decisions are influenced by impermanent factors of youth, beauty, and romantic love.

In traditional societies, where the family is a powerful social institution, marriages are most often arranged for the economic and political good of the families and the community.

4. Briefly define five marital residence patterns. Your answer should include:

Patrilocal residence—the married couple lives with the extended family of the husband.

Matrilocal residence—the married couple lives with the extended family of the wife.

Ambilocal or bilocal residence—the married couple can choose to live with either the husband's or the wife's family.

Neolocal residence—the married couple is free to set up a household in an independent location.

Avunculocal residence—the married couple lives with the brother of the husband's mother.

Self-Test

1. c	7. b	12. d
2. b	8. d	13. c
3. d	9. c	14. a
4. b	10. b	15. d
5. a	11. a	16. b
6. c		

The Yucatec Maya: 10
A Case Study in Marriage and the Family

Overview

As you will remember from Lesson Nine, different styles of family organization develop as a means of meeting and solving problems intrinsic to the environment. In other words, structuring the family so that it functions as a group is an ecological adaptation. That sounds pretty simple, doesn't it? In this lesson, though, you will look at more specific details of family adaptation to conditions in a particular region, and it may strike you that in some situations, adaptations are not all that simple. A family sometimes must exercise a number of limited and difficult choices in order to find a suitable adaptation to specific conditions, especially as these conditions change.

Case studies presented in the television program and in the background notes for this lesson affirm once again the lasting importance of the family in human societies. The television program also emphasizes the importance of child nurturance as a function of the family.

In the television program you will observe the field research of Hubert L. Smith, who has spent much time filming a traditional Maya community in the Yucatan region of Mexico over a period of many years. This program profiles a traditional extended family group and another extended family which is attempting to cope with changes from traditional practices. In the background notes you will read a summary of changes that occurred in two other Maya villages during the middle third of this century. These studies document the existence of nuclear as well as extended family arrangements among the Maya during very early periods in their history. Both the television program and your reading illustrate that, no matter what difficulties or enviromental changes may occur, the family is still a most durable and adaptable unit in human society.

Learning Objectives

When you have completed all assignments in this lesson, you should be able to:

1. Describe the slash-and-burn (milpa) agriculture of the Yucatec Maya and explain how the labor pattern of the extended family is appropriate to that process. (Television program; Background Notes.)

2. Describe the characteristics of the extended family of Prudencio Colli Canche as shown in the television program. (Television program.)

3. Describe the changes occurring in the extended family of Reymundo Colli Colli and suggest reasons for those changes. (Television program.)

4. Describe the personality traits prized and fostered by the traditional extended family organization. (Text pages 142-143; television program.)

5. Discuss characteristics of the extended family which make it difficult to adapt to changing economic patterns and other consequences of modernization occurring in the region. (Text pages 251-254; television program.)

6. Describe the changes in family organization which occurred in the Xaibe village and the reasons for those changes. (Background Notes.)

Assignments For This Lesson

Before Viewing the Program

Ch. 8

Read the overview and the learning objectives for this lesson. Use the learning objectives to guide your reading, viewing, and thinking.

Review Chapter 8, "Marriage and the Family," in the text, especially pages 246-249 and 251-254.

Review pages 142-145 in the text on dependence and independence training of children.

Read the background notes, which follow the assignments in this study guide lesson; note the map showing the Yucatec region of Mexico and the state capital, Merida.

View Program 10, "The Yucatec Maya: A Case Study in Marriage and the Family."

As you view the program, look for:

the depiction of slash-and-burn agriculture, and the adaptation of extended family organization to this type of agriculture.

the family of Prudencio Colli Canche, the relationship of this man to others in his family, including his sons Fabian and Daniel, his wife Maria, and his grandchildren.

the pressures exerted upon the family of Reymundo Colli Colli which put stress on this extended family organization. In particular, note the reactions of his sons Audomaro and Romaldo to school experiences and to the traditional life-style of their family. Reymundo's wife is Agrifina, the sick daughter is Margarita, and another son is Bernardino.

After Viewing the Program

Review the terms used in this lesson. In particular, check your understanding of these terms:

patrilocal	extended family
slash-and-burn	nuclear family
milpa	multiple family

Review the reading assignments for this lesson. A thorough second reading of the background notes is suggested.

Complete each of the study activities and the self-test; then check your answers with the answer key at the end of this lesson.

According to your instructor's assignment or your own interests, complete one or more of the suggested activities. You may also be interested in the readings suggested at the end of Chapter 8 in your text.

Background Notes

"Love and marriage, love and marriage go together like a horse and carriage" is a line in a song popular in the United States a number of years ago. But marriage is much more than a culmination of romantic love. In fact, in many societies, romantic love is not considered a significant aspect of marriage. However, marriage is important throughout the world, because it is a key link in that most basic of social institutions, the family. The family is a unit for socialization and economic cooperation.

The various forms of families, such as nuclear, patrilineal, and matrilineal extended families, are described in the text. There is considerable evidence that the structure of families is related to subsistence. The Yucatec Maya are a good example of the way in which family structure varies as a result of economic reality.

The Yucatec Maya

The Yucatec Maya take their designation from the peninsula of Yucatan, a low, level limestone shelf which juts out into the southern part of the Gulf of Mexico. There are no watercourses of any size, because the limestone is too porous to sustain standing bodies of water. The area is diversified only by small hills and depressions. But differences in rainfall produce great changes in vegetation in different parts of the area and, therefore, in the suitability of the land for human occupation. Toward the east and south, scrubby bush gives way to taller bushes which give way to a tropical rain forest.

The Yucatan was the site of a flourishing complex society long before the Spanish arrived in Central America. The Maya built cities, or ceremonial centers, characterized by massive architecture and carved stone monuments. They had developed a writing system, through a system of glyphs, by means of which they could record historical and calendrical events. However, most of the large ceremonial centers were abandoned by the time the Spaniards arrived, a phenomenon which has never been satisfactorily explained.

The Spanish entered the area in 1527, establishing Spanish and Catholic rule by 1545. Following the Spanish Conquest, epidemics of disease greatly reduced the Maya populations and obliterated entire villages. Bloody uprisings of Maya Indians against the Spanish further drastically reduced the Indian population.

As were their ancestors, present-day Mayans are agriculturalists, who practice a form of cultivation known as *milpa*. The soil is made ready for cultivation by cutting and burning the bush. The shallow topsoil makes it impossible to raise corn, their primary crop, on the same plot for more than two or three consecutive years and requires that the land lie uncultivated for many years before it is planted again. The farmer must travel farther and farther from his village in search of good land. At last his cornfields become so remote from his village that he remains at his fields during periods of agricultural labor. As the farmer's family and others from the village join him at the new site, it becomes a *milperia*, or kind of milpa colony. Eventually, it may become a new village. Anthropologist Robert Redfield writes that for the Maya, "To live is to 'make milpa'; there is no other way" (Robert Redfield and Alfonso Villa Rojas, *Chan Kom: A Maya Village*. Chicago: The University of Chicago Press, 1962, p. 32). However, all that may be changing for the Maya, as traditional ways of subsistence give way to "progress."

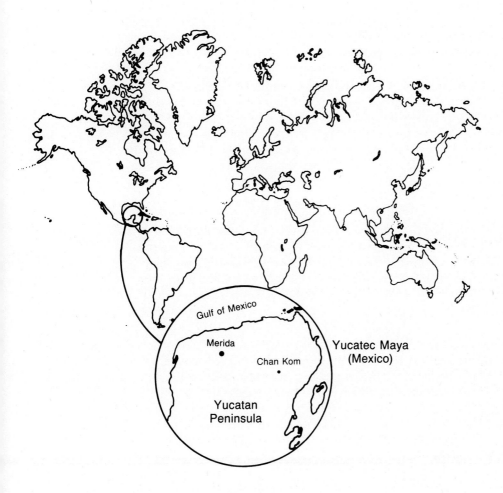

Figure 10.1 Both extended and nuclear family patterns are exhibited in the rural communities of Maya Indians, horticulturalists living in the Yucatan Peninsula of Mexico.

Chan Kom and Xaibe

Two case studies of the Yucatec Maya illustrate how changing subsistence patterns are reflected in alterations in family structure. Redfield worked primarily in the village of Chan Kom in the northeastern part of the Yucatan Peninsula. Most of his fieldwork took place in the early 1930s, but he revisited the village in 1948. When Redfield studied the village in 1931, he noted that "Maize (corn) is the people's food, their work and their prayer—it fills the days and the talk" (p. 51). The people grew twice as much corn as needed for subsistence and the surplus was traded for market goods. Some of the men in Chan Kom also planted beans, sweet potatoes, *jicama* (a root crop similar to a sweet turnip), squashes, and chili peppers. People who did not plant these minor crops bought them from their neighbors. A few of the men owned cattle, but all families raised poultry. Poultry meat was eaten primarily at festivities. Fruit was also grown.

Redfield writes, "In 36 out of 42 cases, milpas were made by individual laborers and the harvests consumed as the individual property of these single agriculturalists in individual small-family households" (p. 56). He adds, "The small family in Chan Kom is much as it is with us, consisting of the mating couple and their children" (nuclear family) (pp. 87-89). According to Redfield, the mating couple recognized kinship ties to both the wife's and husband's relatives. However, "the ties that are emphasized are those between husband and wife" (p. 89).

Redfield further notes that in two cases milpas were made by patrilineal extended families. In the remaining four cases, groups of relatives joined to clear, sow, and harvest a common plot of land. However, within each plot the separate milpas of each laborer were marked off and the harvests were "consumed in the individual small-family households of the separate men" (p. 56).

When Redfield studied the village of Chan Kom in 1931, the villagers went out to markets in surrounding towns when they needed the services of merchants, musicians, or artisans. But when he returned to the village in 1948, Chan Kom had developed its own artisans and merchants as specialists and did not depend very much on other towns for such services. Redfield writes, "The leather workers and the principal baker spend so much time at these maufactures that their work in the milpa is much reduced. . . " (*A Village that Chose Progress: Chan Kom Revisited*. Chicago: The University of Chicago Press, 1964, p. 60).

The nuclear family was the dominant form of family life in 1948, just as it was in 1931. Redfield writes, "The single-family households preponderate as they did before. As before, the family consisting of parents and children is by far the commonest arrangement" (p. 80). However, he notes that the two extended partrilineal families that he studied in 1931 had broken up. Each of the sons had his own milpa and arrangements for meals and many of the sons had their own houses.

Ira R. Abrams studied a Mayan village in northern Belize, which is in the southern part of the Yucatan Peninsula. According to Abrams, the village, Xaibe, is characterized by two developmental periods in this century ("Cash Crop Farming and Social and Economic Change in a Yucatec Maya Community in Northern British Honduras." Ph.D. Dissertation, Harvard University, 1973). Until the 1960s, Xaibe was composed largely of subsistence agriculturalists and part-time wage laborers. In response to efforts by the government and local political forces, a few individuals began to farm sugar cane on a commercial basis after 1950. In 1956, the government purchased the village and most of the land in the district from its single owner and redistributed it to prospective cane farmers, along with cane production licenses and loans to cover the costs of beginning a cane field. By 1963 there was a large-scale shift to cane farming in Xaibe.

The shift from subsistence agriculture combined with wage labor to commercial agriculture was correlated with a change in family structure. Prior to the introduction of sugar cane agriculture, Abrams says there was not one incidence of the patrilineal extended family serving as an economic unit. Forty-four percent of the people lived in what Abrams calls multiple family groups, in which married sons live with the father, but maintain their families as separate economic units. Fifty-four percent were single nuclear families. After the introduction of sugar cane agriculture, extended families made up 4 percent of the households, 47 percent were multiple families and only 12 percent were single families. This represents a clear shift from independent nuclear families to larger cooperating family groups. Abrams suggest that, "In precane days, there was little incentive for a son to form an extended family household with his parents. Part-time wage labor, in which men spent most of their time, was an activity that each man entered into independently" (p. 32).

Abrams says that milpa was not engaged in throughout the year so it did not justify common households or pooled economic resources. "The long duration and large percentage of yearly income derived from commercial agricultural activities could provide more of a basis for making cooperative labor between a father and son a focus for household organization than did small-scale subsistence level milpa agriculture" (p. 36).

Extended families engaged in commercial agriculture could pool credit and earnings to buy a cane truck, which cut down transportation costs and could be hired out to others in the community. Abrams says three extended families engaged in commercial cane agriculture had a "level of material wealth" that was 165 percent over the community average. "There had been only one extended family household in the community that had developed without the aid of cane farming. The members of this household were, however, also commercial agriculturalists; they grew commercial crops of plaintains and oranges" (p. 39). Abrams concludes, "(My data show) with some certainty that the post-cane extended family household represents the addition of a new domestic pattern altogether for Xaibe" (p. 43).

Maya Family Structure

In the television program, filmmaker Hubert Smith compares what he calls a "traditional extended family" with an extended family in which younger sons were sent to school in Merida, the regional capital. During his residence in the region, he observed traditional extended families doing milpa farming as well as a family where children were tempted to reject work in the fields.

The Yucatec Maya are an especially interesting case for anthropologists because their family structures seem to refute the generally accepted wisdom that nuclear family units are a product of modernization. Anthropologist Evon Z. Vogt has suggested that nuclear families among the Maya represent a breakdown of patrilineal extended families (*The Zinacantecos of Mexico: A Modern Maya Way of Life*. New York: Holt, Rinehart and Winston, 1970). However, Joseph J. Gross cites historical sources which indicate that the nuclear family group is a tradition for the Maya. He notes that records of households paying tribute in 1574 indicate that the average-size household was about five members. He adds, "Large extended families could not have been the statistical norm among the Maya of sixteenth century Guatemala" ("Marriage and Family Among the Maya" in Arnaud F. Marks and Rene A. Rooner, eds. *Family and Kinship in Middle America and the Caribbean*. Leiden, The Netherlands: University of the Netherlands Antilles Curacao and the Department of Caribbean Studies of the Royal Institute of Linguistics and Anthropology, 1975, p. 74).

Gross says that anthropologists are making a mistake if they assume that family structure evolves from extended families to nuclear families. He writes, "...those who use the presence of the nuclear family as an indicator of social change or 'modernization,' particularly among the Maya, are holding a false yardstick" (p. 80).

Gross's argument points out the dangers of assuming an evolutionary perspective in evaluating social institutions. Unless we have historical records, we really don't know what was normative before the anthropologist begins observations. And certainly it is risky to assume that all societies everywhere follow the same evolutionary steps. However, the data of Redfield, Abrams, and others suggest that the family, as an economic unit, is responsive to changes in subsistence requirements.

Study Activities

Vocabulary Check

Check on your understanding of terms by matching those on the left with the definitions on the right. Check your choices with the answer key at the end of the lesson.

1. __F__ slash-and-burn
2. __B__ Yucatan
3. __E__ Prudencio
4. __A__ Reymundo
5. __D__ Romaldo
6. __G__ Chan Kom
7. __C__ Xaibe
8. __H__ patrilocal

a. father of an extended family, whose family pattern changes partly because two sons reject work in the cornfields
b. a large region in Southeastern Mexico
c. a Maya village in which families joined together in larger groups to solve the problems of new agricultural practices
d. member of a Maya family who elected to leave the traditional family pattern
e. the elder male of a patrilocal residence
f. agricultural method in which the use of farmed land is rotated
g. a Maya village in which the nuclear family pattern predominates
h. family dwelling pattern based on the father's family

Completion

Choose the best word or phrase from the lists provided to fill the blanks in the paragraphs below.

1. Slash-and-burn agricultural practices are employed where there is sufficient land, usually forest, to allow periodic _cultivation_ of one particular area. For one or two years, the land is farmed, then allowed to return to its _natural state_ to restore fertility. The slash-and-burn agricultural patterns of the Yucatec Maya often encourage formation of extended family groups. For ex-

laborers
natural state
cultivation

137

ample, a larger family group supplies more _laborers_ for the work that needs to be done under this labor-intensive agricultural system. Property such as horses can be owned by the entire group, or several members of the extended family.

2. In other instances, slash-and-burn agriculture may yield such limited returns that it is more economical for a _nuclear_ family to farm a small plot of land, as Abrams concluded from his studies of the Xaibe village. In this village, the arrival of commercial agriculture, in which the cash crop was sugar cane, resulted in the rapid growth of larger family units based on the extended family. In the _multiple families_, married sons continue to live with the father and work cooperatively with him, but maintain their individual families separately.

multiple families
nuclear

3. Both Reymundo and Prudencio head extended families which practice a _patrilocal_ residence pattern. The children of Prudencio and his wife work their land, and some share in the ownership of property. All of them share in the work that needs to be done, and all of them share the benefits of even a small prize. Such sharing serves as a symbol and reminder of the family's _interdependence_

interdependence
patrilocal

4. The major source of income for the family of Reymundo is raising _corn_ , beans, and squash

school
corn

on the various family plots of land in the milpa. Financial pressures on the family's resources occurred when two sons decided to go to _school_ in the nearby city of Merida.

5. In the Maya village of Chan Kom, Redfield found that the nuclear family predominated in 1931. Returning again in 1948, he found that the only two former _extended families_ had disappeared as working units, with each son now working his own milpa and, usually, maintaining his own independent residence. A major change that Redfield noted was that some villagers had developed _specialties_ in various crafts, so that villagers did not have to travel to other communities for such services.

specialties
extended families

Short-Answer Questions

1. Briefly describe the cooperative efforts, interdependence, and personality traits that are illustrated by the family of Prudencio and Maria.

2. What kind of difficulty in adjustment to new conditions can be illustrated by Reymundo's attempt to send two younger boys to school in another city?

3. Why did the family organization patterns change so greatly in the Xaibe village? What does this and other studies suggest about the evolution of extended and nuclear families?

Self-Test

(Select the one best answer.)

Objective 1

1. The kind of agriculture called milpa involves what kind of use of land?
   a. continuous use of land by different family groups
   b. clearing of land for permanent use by a particular settlement
   c. clearing of land and allowing it to return to its natural state after a few years
   d. intensive farming using modern technology

Objective 1

2. Which of these is the greatest advantage that the extended family offers in a milpa agricultural pattern?
   a. a larger work force held together by strong loyalties
   b. more opportunities for supplemental income through part-time work
   c. more freedom for the individual members to determine their own activities
   d. opportunities for younger members to exercise leadership

Objective 2

3. What position does Prudencio hold in his family group?
   a. youngest son in a patrilocal group
   b. family head in a patrilocal group
   c. one of several elders who lead the community
   d. older individual who primarily looks after children

Objective 3

4. Which one of the following is a major change which has occurred in the family of Reymundo?
   a. A crop was lost to drought.
   b. Educational opportunities threaten to break up the family.
   c. Opportunity for city employment threatens to break up the family.
   d. The family was forced to sell the corn supply, animals, and home-woven hammocks.

Objective 4

5. What is the Maya standard for behavior of adults?
   a. fierce and aggressive
   b. even-tempered and considered
   c. independent and competitive
   d. complete lack of emotion

Objective 5

6. What is suggested by Audomaro's and Romaldo's experience with schooling in a strange city?
   a. Maya youth are strongly motivated to leave the family farm for the city.

b. Maya youth usually find it easier to break family ties than do older people.
   c. Rebellion against traditional ways of life is encouraged by the Maya culture.
   d. Even young people find it difficult to leave the traditional family.

Objective 5
7. A characteristic of industrialization which weakens extended family ties and places a demand on individuals is
   a. cooperative work forces.
   b. worker mobility.
   c. literacy.
   d. a heavy workload.

Objective 6
8. In the Chan Kom village, what change occurred between the time of Redfield's two visits?
   a. A large number of extended family groups broke up into nuclear families.
   b. At least one member of each family worked full time for industrial concerns.
   c. Many nuclear families joined in extended family organizations.
   d. Some villagers were becoming craft specialists and devoting less time to milpa.

Objective 7
9. What was the characteristic of the "multiple families" identified by Abrams in the Xaibe village?
   a. several families joined in a patrilocal group
   b. separate nuclear families working a milpa together
   c. sons living with their fathers but maintaining their own families separately
   d. unrelated families joined in a corporate venture

Objective 7
10. The major change in the Xaibe village was
   a. the introduction of commercial farming, which led to an increase in extended families.
   b. the introduction of commercial farming, which led to an increase in nuclear families.
   c. a return to traditional farming, which led to an increase in extended families.
   d. the introduction of new farming techniques, which led many families to leave the village for the city.

Suggested Activities

1. What is suggested in the television program and in the background notes about the adaptability of the family to new circumstances? Does the evidence of any society mentioned in the last two lessons indicate that the family may be disappearing? Use some examples to support your opinion.

2. Using your local library resources, read about developments in the Yucatan Pennisula. What agricultural and economic changes is the Mexican government attempting to introduce into the area? Characterize the relationship between the indigenous Maya and other groups living in the region. What do you think will be the future of the various family patterns of the area?

Answer Key

Vocabulary Check

1. f   5. d
2. b   6. g
3. e   7. c
4. a   8. h

Completion

1. cultivation, natural state, laborers

2. nuclear, multiple families

3. patrilocal, interdependence

4. corn, school

5. extended families, specialties

Short-Answer Questions

1. Briefly describe the cooperative efforts, interdependence, and personality traits that are illustrated by the family of Prudencio and Maria. Your answer should include:

   All members of the family look to Prudencio, the father, for leadership. His authority is not challenged because the wisdom and experience of age is invaluable in this traditional agricultural environment.

All members of the family contribute to the common effort. Sharing is important, not only because it assures that everyone will get his or her necessities, but because sharing symbolizes the interdependence of the family.

The oldest members watch the children, freeing younger members for heavier duties, and providing a role model for the children.

Maya adults strive to maintain a calm, considered, gentle manner in all activities.

2. What kind of difficulty in adjustment to new conditions may be illustrated by Reymundo's attempt to send two younger boys to school in another city? Your answer should include:

Although Reymundo wanted to give his younger sons, Audomaro and Romaldo, the opportunity for schooling, he voiced concern that they were not like his eldest son, who wanted to work in the fields.

The conflict between traditional and new ways became evident when the boys entered school because they did not have the resources (books) nor the sense of independence necessary to adapt to the changes.

After the single attempt at sending the boys to school, Reymundo had them return home. Audomaro eventually resumed farming, although Romaldo later took a job in the city. Breaking free of the traditional ways is difficult, both because new ways are strange, and the family ties are strong.

3. Why did the family organization patterns change so greatly in the Xaibe village? What does this and other studies suggest about the evolution of extended and nuclear families? Your answer should include:

The family organizations in the village of Xaibe changed after the government introduced commercial agriculture with sugar cane crops.

Before sugar cane was farmed, the traditional milpa farming was practiced by individual nuclear families or multiple families, in which the sons lived with the father but maintained separate homes for their families.

After sugar cane was introduced, the multiple family pattern was maintained, and many families joined in extended family organizations. The proportion of nuclear families declined from over 50 percent to only 12 percent.

Abrams believed that milpa, as practiced in Xaibe, did not offer enough incentive for people to join in larger family groups. Individual men could earn more by farming their own plots and working away from the farms part-time. The commercial farming made it possible for larger work forces to gain more income, by combining both their labor and their purchasing power to obtain modern equipment.

The Xaibe experience suggests that families do not simply evolve from extended families to nuclear families as new technology and economic systems are introduced. Families are apparently very adaptable to changing conditions, and may attempt different organizational patterns according to the problems posed by a specific set of conditions. Other studies indicate that extended families may never have been universal in Maya culture, but arose only to solve specific problems.

Self-Test

1. c	6. d
2. a	7. b
3. b	8. d
4. c	9. c
5. b	10. a

Kinship And Descent, Part I 11

Overview

In recent years there has been increasing interest in genealogy throughout the United States, probably stimulated by simple curiosity on the part of some Americans about their "roots." Some people trace their ancestry as a hobby, and, like many hobbies, this one can be expensive. Tracing one's lineage can require correspondence, travel, interviews, and extensive research through libraries and records kept by government agencies, courts, churches, cemeteries, social groups, and ships, which usually carried "manifests" listing all passengers on board. Ship manifests are especially valuable in identifying persons who immigrated to America during the early years of our country.

The novel *Roots* is a famous example of one man's persistent and successful attempts to learn about his forebears. Author Arthur Haley's search for his ancestors began with oral traditions brought from West Africa to America by slaves, handed down through many generations, and persisting despite years of oppression. Haley's account of his search has made gripping reading (and television viewing) for millions of people all over the world. If you could pursue your own roots as Haley did, isn't it possible that you might unearth a story just as interesting?

Most present-day Americans lack knowledge about their ancestry, and little cultural importance is attached to this aspect of kinship. But in the vast majority of societies through human history, kinship and the tracing of lines of descent have played an important role. Knowledge of one's ancestors defined more than family membership.

It confirmed membership within a social group, had strong influence on the status of the individual within the society, determined residence patterns, defined what natural resources were available to the individual, and made available a dependable force of persons under mutual obligation for defense and aid. Many nonindustrial societies still depend today on the kinship ties traced through descent. In those societies, kinship and descent patterns provide the organizational arrangements necessary to handle functions that in more complex societies may be the functions of governments and religious, military, and special interest groups.

In this lesson, the first of two lessons describing the structure and function of kinship in human societies, you will learn about the importance of kinship and descent in shaping the culture. The lesson concentrates on descent as a family bond. In the following lesson, you will explore more fully the structure and functions of kindred relationships.

Learning Objectives

When you have completed all assignments in this lesson, you should be able to:

1. Define kinship and descent groups. (Text pages 259, 260-261; television program.)

2. Identify some of the basic functions of descent groups in nonindustrial societies. (Text pages 259 and 270; television program.)

3. Describe patrilineal descent and organization as one type of a unilineal descent group, and describe the organization and functions of patrilineal descent groups among the Tikopia and among the Yanomamo. (Text pages 262-264; television program.)

4. Describe matrilineal descent and organization as a type of unilineal descent group, and describe the organization and functions of matrilineal descent groups found among the peoples of Truk and of the Trobriand Islands. (Text pages 262, 264-267; television program.)

5. Describe examples showing the connection between patrilineal descent and patrilocal residence, and between matrilineal descent and matrilocal residence. (Text pages 262-264; television program for Lesson 12.)

6. Identify the symbols used by anthropologists in kinship diagrams. (Text pages 262, 264; television program for Lesson 12.)

7. Define double descent and briefly describe how this applies to the Yako of eastern Nigeria. (Text page 267.)

146

8. Define ambilineal descent and briefly describe how this applies to organizations of Jewish families in New York City. (Text pages 267-270.)

9. Distinguish unilineal systems from bilateral systems. (Text pages 262 and 273.)

10. Recoginize that unilineal descent groups are commonly found in horticultural, pastoral, and intensive agricultural societies. (Text pages 262 and 275.)

11. Describe the basic features and characteristics of lineage, clan, phratry, and moiety. (Text pages 270-273; television program.)

Assignments For This Lesson

Before Viewing the Program

Read the overview and the learning objectives for this lesson. Use the learning objectives to guide your reading, viewing, and thinking.

Read the preview to Chapter 9 in the text and look over the topic headings in the chapter.

Read Chapter 9, "Kinship and Descent," in the text and pay particular attention to pages 260-276.

View Program 11, "Kinship and Descent, Part I."

As you view the program, look for:

a fight among members of two descent groups in a Yanomamo village; the fight reveals some of the complexities of kinship obligations in that culture.

the cassowary contest of the Mendi of New Guinea and how it reveals clan alliances as the basis of social organization in that culture.

the economic and political activities of the Trobriand Islanders based on their matrilineal descent patterns.

After Viewing the Program

Review the terms used in this lesson. In addition to those used in the learning objectives for this lesson, you should review the definitions for "consanguineal" and "affinal" (text page 235), and consult a dictionary to clarify the usage of the term "kinship."

Review the reading assignments for this lesson. A thorough second reading of the text chapter is suggested. Include the chapter summary paragraphs related to your reading in this lesson in your study. You may also find that the introduction to Chapters 8, 9, and 10 (pages 226-227) provides a useful perspective on kinship, descent, and other devices for organizing societies.

Complete each of the study activities and the self-test in this study guide; then check your answers with the answer key at the end of the lesson.

According to your instructor's assignment or your own interests, complete one or more of the suggested activities. You may also be interested in the readings suggested at the end of Chapter 9 in your text.

Study Activities

Vocabulary Check

Check on your understanding of terms by matching those on the left with the definitions on the right. Check your choices with the answer key at the end of the lesson.

1. _F_ consanguineal
2. _O_ affinal relationship
3. _P_ patrilineal
4. _L_ matrilineal
5. _B_ patrilocal
6. _N_ triangle
7. _H_ double descent
8. _D_ ambilineal descent
9. _J_ lineage
10. _E_ clan
11. _K_ totem
12. _C_ moiety

a. residing near either groom's or bride's family
b. located or residing in the area of the groom's family
c. one of only two groups in a society that bases membership on descent
d. descent traced through either parent for purposes of group membership
e. claiming relationship to a common unknown ancestor although relationship cannot actually be traced
f. relationships defined by "blood"
g. symbol for female in kinship diagrams
h. descent traced through each parent, each for separate purposes
i. one of several groups that includes two or three clans, in a society, each group claiming relationship to a particular common ancestor
j. claim of relationship to a common known ancestor
k. symbol with religious significance, used as a means of identification by a clan
l. descent traced through females
m. a cousin or uncle

148

n. symbol for male in kinship diagrams
o. relationships defined by marriage
p. descent traced through males

Completion

Choose the best word or phrase from the lists provided to fill the blanks in the paragraphs below.

1. In some societies, the family organization of husband, wife, and children may confront problems that require more than the efforts of a few to resolve. In industrial societies a formal _political_ may be formed to manage these larger social functions. In nonindustrial societies, the _kinship_ group has evolved as a way of handling matters larger than possible for individual families. Such groups have a variety of functions including mutual aid, a means of sharing resources such as land, and cooperative work forces for tasks larger than a single family could undertake.

kinship
political system

2. The study of kinship is the study of the social bonds that are created by birth and marriage. Descent kinship groups form social bonds by tracing kinship relationships to a common _ancestor_. A particular feature of the _descent_ group is that the line of descent can be traced through many generations.

descent
ancestor

3. Groups that trace ancestry through either the male or female line are termed _unilineal_. The Tikopia trace descent only through the male line; thus they are termed _patrilineal_. Residence of a Tikopia nuclear family is almost always near the husband's family. Each family belongs to a larger group, the *paito*, all of whose families trace descent to a common ancestor. The membership of a male

status
unilineal
patrilineal

149

individual within this larger group confers social ___*status*___, as well as a share in land and a site for his house.

4. While patrilineal societies are usually associated with pastoral and ___*agriculturist*___ subsistence patterns, groups that trace descent through matrilineal lines are usually found in ___*horticultural*___ societies where the women perform much of the productive work. In Truk, as in most such societies, power is exercised by ___*men*___ although descent is reckoned through females. Family bonds are formed through the wife's lineage; for example, strong bonds are expected to be maintained throughout life by lineage "brothers" and "sisters"—this includes the children born to sisters of the wife.

horticultural
men
agriculturalist

5. In Truk society, newly married couples actually have some choices as to place of residence. However, living in "isolation" away from *any* extended family is *not* a choice. Usually, the married pair will prefer to live near the ___*wife's*___ mother's lineage, but, if that is undesirable, the next most desirable choice is that of the ___*husband's*___ mother's lineage.

husband's
wife's

6. In a ___*double descent*___ system each line of descent applies to different but definite spheres of the society and culture. For example, a resource such as land might come from the male lineage, while consumable property might come from the female lineage. This descent system is found only rarely. Ambilineal descent differs from double descent because descent through ___*either*___ the male or female lines could determine membership, rather than affecting different aspects of membership.

either
double descent

Short-Answer Questions

1. Explain and cite examples of how the location of postmarital residence (either patrilocal or matrilocal) can be determined or influenced by the descent pattern used by the society.

2. Explain the general purposes of the Jewish "family" circle societies of New York City, and briefly describe how the accepted descent pattern compares with unilineal, double, and ambilineal descent patterns.

3. Define and list some characteristics of lineage, clan, phratry, and moiety.

Self-Test

(Select the one best answer.)

Objective 1
1. Which of the following best describes kinship?
   a. ancestors
   b. descendants
   c. relatives
   d. family

Objective 1
2. Which of these is essential to a descent group?
   a. siblings
   b. clans
   c. an ancestor
   d. a totem

Objective 2
3. The function of descent groups in many nonindustrial societies is best described as
   a. providing for religious and ceremonial observances.
   b. the formation of economic, social, and religious organizations.
   c. encouraging political and defensive alliances.
   d. exercising control of natural resources.

Objective 3
4. A descent group that traces its ancestors through only the male or female line is called a _____ group.
   a. double descent
   b. unilineal
   c. patrilineal
   d. matrilineal

Objective 3
5. In patrilineal descent groups,
   a. the line is traced through male descent for some purposes and through female descent for others.

b. group membership is determined through the male line.

c. group membership is determined through the female line.

d. all children and grandchildren trace descent through the ancestors of both parents.

Objective 3

6. What, in the Tikopia culture, is a *paito*?

    a. a religious celebration held seasonally by the clan

    b. the historical record of a family's descent through the male line

    c. a descent group composed of a number of individual families

    d. the land owned by a particular descent group

Objective 4

7. Which of the following is generally *not* true of matrilineal descent groups?

    a. The brothers of the woman through whom descent is traced exercise authority.

    b. The husband of a woman through whom descent is traced remains a member of his mother's descent group.

    c. Husband-wife bonds are somewhat weaker than other family bonds.

    d. Authority is held primarily by the woman through whom descent is traced.

Objectives 4 and 5

8. In the Truk society described in the text, what are the usual *first* and *second* choices for a dwelling location of a married couple?

    a. wife's mother's lineage; wife's father's lineage

    b. wife's mother's lineage; husband's mother's lineage

    c. wife's mother's lineage; husband's father's lineage

    d. husband's mother's lineage; husband's father's lineage

Objective 5

9. Which of these factors is a strong influence on the choice of residence location for a married couple in Truk society?

    a. It is generally felt that children should be raised in company with "lineage brothers and sisters."

    b. It is generally felt that a man should live close to his father's family.

    c. It is generally felt that the woman should remain close to her mother and sisters in the lineage.

    d. It is generally felt that the married couple should select an available location with good land.

Objective 6

10. In descent group diagrams presented in the text, the triangle is a symbol for _____ and the circle is a symbol for _____.

    a. grandparent; grandchild

    b. female; male

    c. child; parent

    d. male; female

11. A descent system which provides that the matrilineal line confers some rights and the patrilineal line confers others is termed
    a. lineage descent.
    b. unilineal descent.
    c. double descent.
    d. ambilineal descent.

12. Among the Yako people of eastern Nigeria, various types of property are owned by
    a. the matrilineal group.
    b. the patrilineal group.
    c. both groups.
    d. neither group.

13. The "family circles" of Jewish descendants from Eastern European societies are open to membership for anyone who can trace descent from specific ancestors through
    a. male or female lines.
    b. the father's line.
    c. the mother's line.
    d. a friend's ancestors.

14. What is the term for a group which allows membership to anyone who can trace descent through either the father's or mother's line to an ancestor?
    a. lineage descent
    b. unilineal descent
    c. double descent
    d. ambilineal descent

15. Unilineal descent groups are commonly found in
    a. all nonindustrial societies.
    b. agricultural and horticultural societies.
    c. all nonagricultural societies.
    d. hunting and gathering and pastoral societies.

16. Kindred organization is typical of societies which
    a. have large extended families.
    b. hold large tracts of farm land over many generations.
    c. rely largely on the nuclear family.
    d. trace descent for many generations.

17. Which of these is a common feature of lineages?
    a. Marriage within the lineage is usually required.
    b. Marriage with someone from a specific related lineage is usually required.
    c. Marriage with someone from another lineage is usually required.
    d. Marriage choices are usually not restricted by lineages.

18. Which of the following is *not* true of clans?
    a. All members can trace descent from a specific known ancestor.
    b. Totems are frequently used to identify the group and its descent.
    c. Members may gather for ceremonial occasions.
    d. A common descent is claimed.

19. How many moieties may exist in a given society?
    a. two
    b. four
    c. eight
    d. any number

Suggested Activities

1. If you have never charted your own genealogy, prepare a simple chart tracing descent through both your father's male and mother's female lines. While you may include the brothers and sisters of each generation, the key aspect of this descent exercise is to determine how far back (that is, how many generations) you can trace your ancestry. Use the symbols illustrated on text pages 262 and 264 in preparing your chart. If you have previously traced your family's descent, interview a friend and attempt to develop a genealogical chart for that person.

2. Does descent serve any functions in your immediate or larger society? Try to list several specific aspects of life that are influenced by descent. Do you see a relationship between descent groups and nationality groups in the United States such as German-American or Irish-American societies?

Answer Key

Vocabulary Check

1. f	7. h
2. o	8. d
3. p	9. j
4. l	10. e
5. b	11. k
6. n	12. c

Completion

1. political system, kinship

2. ancestor, descent

3. unilineal, patrilineal, status

4. agriculturalist, horticultural, men

5. wife's, husband's

6. double descent, either

Short-Answer Questions

1. Explain and cite examples of how the location of postmarital residence (either patrilocal or matrilocal) can be determined or influenced by the descent pattern used by the society. Your answer should include:

   In a patrilineal society, training children is usually the responsibility of the father or his elder brother; the children will also trace their descent through the father. In Tikopian society, the father's sister has a role as secondary mother.

   In patrilocal residence, a married couple lives in the locality associated with the husband's father's relatives. Although the major determinants of residence are ecological, making the role of the man predominant in subsistence, other factors enter in, such as owning property that can be accumulated, polygyny, warfare, and elaborate political organization. All of these factors necessitate keeping the males of a family together. Thus, where patrilocal residence is practiced, often the bride must move to a different band or community, away from her family. The bride's family is then usually compensated for her loss as a worker and for her potential offspring.

   In a society that traces descent through matrilineal lines, the childen will trace their descent through the mother's line. In the Truk society, for example, it is considered preferable for the childen to be raised near their "lineage brothers and sisters," who will also probably live near the mother's mother; hence, you have matrilocal residence. Yet matrilineal systems actually show a good deal of variation, especially with patrilocal and avunculocal options.

2. Explain the general purposes of the Jewish "family circle" societies of New York City, and briefly describe how the accepted descent pattern compares with unilineal, double, and ambilineal descent patterns. Your answer should include:

   The "family circles" and "cousin clubs" have been organized in New York City and other cities in the twentieth century. They represent an attempt to both preserve and restructure the strong family ties traditional in Jewish cultures from Eastern Europe, and have functioned both to preserve family ties and provide mutual aid.

Membership depends upon descent from an ancestral pair; however, the descent may be traced through either the male or female links, without any set order or pattern. In ambilineal descent, descent through either line is sufficient for the same purpose, that of membership.

This kind of descent reckoning differs from unilineal, which allows tracing of descent only through the father's (male) or mother's (female) line; and from double descent patterns, which trace patrilineal and matrilineal descents, but each for specific purposes.

3. Define and list some characteristics of lineage, clan, phratry, and moiety. Your answer should include:

Lineage: a corporate descent group permitting membership only to those who can trace their genealogical links to a specific known ancestor. In many societies, lineage membership confers status for political and religious purposes. A lineage is a self-perpetuating, usually exogamous, corporate group.

Clan: a descent group claiming descent from a common unknown ancestor without being able to trace the specific genealogical links to the ancestor. Usually, a clan results from the division of a lineage. Clans tend to gather together for ceremonial or similar purposes, identify themselves with totems, offer special hospitality and aid to members of the clan, and are exogamous.

Phratry: a unilineal descent group composed of two or more clans claiming common descent. The feeling of kinship among members of a phratry is generally weaker than that of the clan or lineage. Phratries are useful in controlling marriage (exogamous) and for ceremonial purposes.

Moiety: each of two groups resulting from the division of a society into two parts based on descent.

Self-Test

1. c	8. b	15. b
2. c	9. a	16. c
3. b	10. d	17. c
4. b	11. c	18. a
5. b	12. c	19. a
6. c	13. a	
7. d	14. d	

Kinship And Descent, Part II 12

Overview

Do you know the names of your great-great grandparents? Or, for that matter, can you recall the names of your great grandparents? If so, you probably rank among an exceedingly small percent of the students who are studying "Faces of Culture." Nor is this surprising. Except in the case of a relatively few families distinguished by great wealth or achievement (or both), one's descent does not usually have much significance in the United States today. Does this mean that Western industrial society has, in general, lost interest in relatives? Not really, because, first, the nuclear family is still very important, although its structure and functions may be undergoing stresses, such as those described in earlier lessons. Like most North Americans, you are probably more aware of close relatives, those who are part of your nuclear family and those who have been members of the nuclear families in which your parents were children.

A grouping of relatives such as that described above is called a kindred. As a social organization, kindreds are weaker than descent groups for several reasons, but they are more common than descent groups in industrial societies. And, you may be surprised to learn that kindreds are also preferred in some societies where survival poses a great challenge.

Another interesting aspect of kinship you will explore in this lesson is the pattern by which the kindred names its members, thereby signifying their importance in the group. English names for close relatives (uncle and cousin, for example) do not have universal parallels. In fact, anthropologists have discovered no less than six general patterns for naming the members of one's kindred, and each of these patterns says something about the comparative rank of specific individuals. For example, some societies give the title "mother" to all the sisters of both father and mother as well as to the female parent. What conclusions might you draw about such a society?

After studying these two lessons on kinship and descent, you may find you have a greater appreciation for your own family and relatives and the functions they serve.

Learning Objectives

When you have completed all assignments for this lesson, you should be able to:

1. Define "bilateral kinship." (Text page 273.)

2. Define "kindred" and "ego" as used in studying bilateral systems of descent. (Text pages 273-275; television program.)

3. Explain why kindreds are described as "ego-centered." (Text pages 273-275.)

4. Recognize that bilateral and kindred organizations are commonly found in modern industrial societies as well as in many hunting and gathering societies, where nuclear families are especially important. (Text pages 275 and 277; television program.)

5. Recognize that relatives are categorized differently by different societies and that specialized kinship terminology systems have been developed which reflect these differences. (Text pages 276-280; television program.)

6. Identify which kinship terminology system is most commonly used in the United States. (Text page 277.)

Assignments For This Lesson

Before Viewing the Program   Ch. 9

Read the overview and learning objectives for this lesson. Use the learning objectives to guide your reading, viewing, and thinking.

Read again the preview to Chapter 9 (page 259), and look over the topic headings in the chapter.

Review Chapter 9, paying particular attention to pages 276-282.

View Program 12, "Kinship and Descent, Part II."

As you view the program, look for:

French anthropologist Maurice Gudia trying to learn the kinship terms used by the Baruya of New Guinea. He's speaking a kind of pig latin and works through an interpreter.

the Navajo matrilineal kinship organization and terminology system

the social patterns of men, women, and children of the Greek village of Kypseli reflecting patrilineal *and* matrilineal descent practices.

After Viewing the Program

Review terms used in this lesson. In addition to those terms which appear in the learning objectives, you should understand these:

sibling
bifurcate merging
Eskimo system of kinship terminology

Review the reading assignment for this lesson. A thorough second reading is suggested. Include the chapter summary in your study.

Complete each of the study activities and the self-test in this study guide; then check your answers with the answer key at the end of this lesson.

According to your instructor's assignment or your own interests, complete one or more of the suggested activities. You may also be interested in some of the readings suggested at the end of Chapter 9 in your text.

Study Activities

Vocabulary Check

Check on your understanding of terms by matching those on the left with the definitions on the right. Check your choices with the answer key at the end of the lesson.

1. __C__ bilateral kinship
2. __G__ kindred
3. __B__ ego
4. __E__ nuclear family
5. __A__ kinship terminology
6. __H__ sibling
7. __I__ Eskimo kinship terminology
8. __D__ Omaha kinship terminology
9. __F__ bifurcate merging

a. often identifies the comparative importance of various relatives to an individual
b. the individual at the center of a kindred
c. a system in which an individual feels related equally to all near relatives of both parents
d. a system in which cousins on the mother's side are merged with the mother's generation

e. a kinship unit that may be composed of only a mother, father, and children

f. a system that splits maternal and paternal relatives into two broad groups, one of which is named identically to members of the nuclear family

g. a relatively limited group of people related to one living individual through both parents

h. brothers and sisters

i. a type of group in which kindred relationships may rank more important than descent groups

j. a system used in English-speaking societies

Completion

Choose the best word or phrase from the lists provided to fill the blanks in the paragraph below.

1. The focus of a lineal-descent system of any kind is _an ancestor_, while the "center" of a kindred is a living individual called the _ego_. In a unilineal descent system, the line represented by the _father or mother_ determines which relatives are more important to the individual. In a _bilateral_ system, both descent lines include relatives that are equally important.

bilateral
father or mother
an ancestor
ego

2. In each of the following diagrams, identify each symbol marked with an "X" according to the kinship terminology system at the left. Note: Ego can be represented by a shaded triangle, circle, or square, depending on the sex of the person. Terms can be used more than once.

aunt
brother
cousin
father
father's sister
mother
mother's brother
nephew
niece
sister

ESKIMO

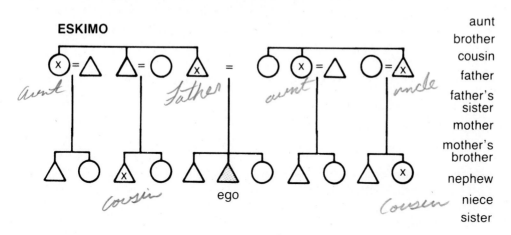

aunt

father

aunt

uncle

cousin

ego

Cousin

IROQUOIS

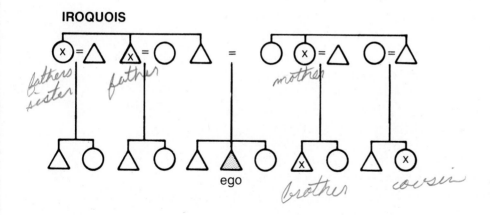

fathers sister

father

mother

ego

brother

cousin

OMAHA

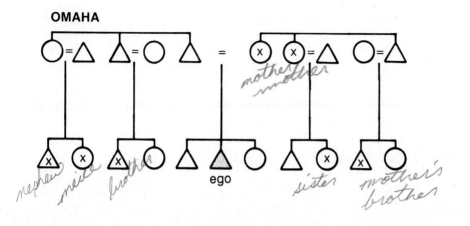

mother mother

nephew

niece

brother

ego

sister

mother's brother

161

Short-Answer Questions

1. In what types of societies are kindred organizations found? Why are they found in these particular societies?

2. Contrast the specific names given some near relatives in the Eskimo and Crow systems of kinship terminology, and explain how each naming system indicates the relative importance of specific relatives.

Self-Test

(Select the one best answer.)

Objective 1
1. In bilateral kinship an individual is
   a. related to the mothers of both parents.
   b. related to his father's relatives for some purposes and his mother's relatives for other purposes.
   c. free to gain membership in either his father's or his mother's descent group.
   d. affiliated with a large number of relatives of both parents.

Objective 1
2. In a unilineal system, descent would be traced through _____ grandparent(s); but in a bilateral system, descent would be traced through _____ grandparent(s).
   a. one, four
   b. four, two
   c. two, four
   d. four, one

Objectives 2 and 3
3. In a bilateral kinship system, the individual from whom relationships to a large number of relatives is traced is called
   a. ancestor.
   b. ego.
   c. kindred.
   d. sibling.

Objective 2
4. "Kindred" includes
   a. all descendants of great grandparents.
   b. descendants of a single significant ancestor.
   c. all near relatives of a living person.
   d. brothers and sisters of the parents.

5. A kindred is ended when
   a. ego dies.
   b. it fissions into two groups.
   c. a child is born to ego.
   d. the grandparent dies.

Objective 2
6. One function performed by kindreds is to
   a. assign unchanging status to individuals.
   b. hold title to property or pass it on.
   c. regulate marriage through exogamy.
   d. continue existence through several generations.

Objective 4
7. Which of the functions listed in Question 6 can be performed by unilineal descent groups?
   a. a, b, and d
   b. b and c
   c. a, b, c, and d
   d. a and d

Objective 4
8. A common factor in societies which recognize bilateral kinship is
   a. advanced technology.
   b. dependence on game and wild food.
   c. intensive agricultural techniques.
   d. mobility.

Objective 4
9. As a social organization, the descent group is _____ the bilateral kinship group.
   a. stronger than
   b. weaker than
   c. about equal in strength to
   d. less well defined

Objective 5
10. Anthropologists have identified _____ different systems of kinship terminology.
   a. three
   b. six
   c. nine
   d. twelve

Objective 5

11. Which of these statements best summarizes the purpose of kinship terminologies?
    a. classification of different kinds of persons into distinct categories
    b. tracing descent from a specific ancestor
    c. categorizing each individual according to his generation
    d. separation of the nuclear family from all other relatives

Objective 5

12. In which system are certain cousins linked with, or given the same names as, the parents' generation?
    a. Omaha system
    b. Iroquois system
    c. neither the Omaha nor Iroquois systems
    d. both the Omaha and Iroquois systems

Objectives 5 and 6

13. The kinship terminology system used in the United States is called the _____ system.
    a. Omaha
    b. Iroquois
    c. Eskimo
    d. unilinear

Objective 6

14. In the Eskimo system of kinship terminology,
    a. only members of the mother's family are specifically recognized.
    b. all relatives of the same sex and generation are referred to by the same term.
    c. no distinction is made between generations among certain kinsmen.
    d. no distinction is made between maternal and paternal sisters and brothers or their children.

Suggested Activities

1. Examine the society sections of your local newspaper for one or two weeks for announcements of weddings, funerals, and other events in which there is some mention of kindred groups or of individuals who are kindred but not immediate family. During this period of time, did you find mention of any kind of activities involving descent—even the meeting of a genealogical society? Write a brief summary of the events you identify, and compare their frequency with events held for other types of groups. What conclusion can you draw about the importance of kinship relationships in your region?

2. William A. Haviland, the author of your text, suggests (page 275) that mobility and individuality weaken kinship ties in Western industrial society. What institutions and organizations have taken over the various functions served by kinship organizations in other societies? In your opinion, are there values which our society has lost as a result of weakened kinship ties?

Answer Key

Vocabulary Check

1. c
2. g
3. b

4. e
5. a
6. h

7. j
8. d
9. f

Completion

1. an ancestor, ego, father or mother, bilateral

2. If you completed the diagrams of the kinship system accurately, the terminology should match that on the charts below.

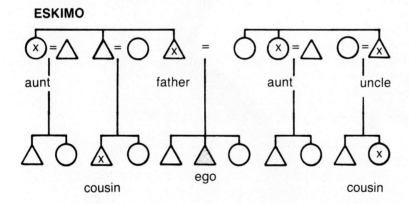

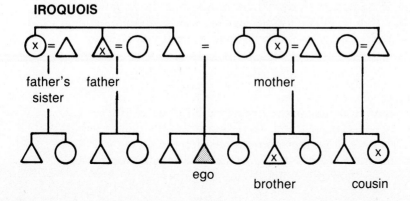

165

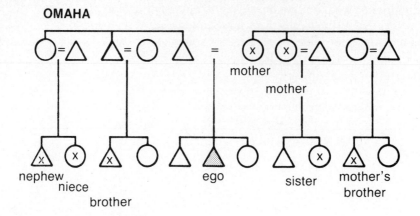

OMAHA

nephew
niece
brother
mother
mother
ego
sister
mother's
brother

Short-Answer Questions

1. In what types of societies are kindred organizations found? Why are they found in these particular societies? Your answer should include:

   Kinship organization is typical of many hunting and gathering societies and industrial societies.

   In both types of societies, the nuclear family is of primary importance. After the nuclear family, a kindred organization of closely related relatives is more likely to rank next in importance.

   A kindred organization is most adaptive under conditions of mobility, where constant ties with a large group of relatives is impractical.

   Descent groups are most adaptive where resources can be treated or exploited by a fairly large group using labor-intensive labor.

   Mobility weakens ties with a large group of relatives; industrial societies tend to encourage a high degree of mobility, making it unlikely that one would remain living in an area with one's lineage. To a lesser extent, the mobility found in hunting and gathering societies is also a deterrent to the formation of descent groups.

2. Contrast the specific names given some near relatives in the Eskimo and Crow systems of kinship terminology, and explain how each naming system indicates the relative importance of specific relatives. Your answer should include:

   In the Eskimo system, brothers and sisters of the father and mother are termed aunts and uncles. In the Crow system, the father and his brother are called by the same term, as are the mother and her sister. In contrasting these two labeling systems, the Eskimo system indicates that the ego's true parents are of greater importance than the parent's brothers and sisters. In the Crow system, on the other hand, the parents' siblings of the same sex rank more nearly equal in importance.

166

In the Eskimo system, all children of the parents' brothers and sisters are labeled with a single term regardless of sex. In the Crow system, such offspring may be termed brother and sister if they are children of any father or mother. Thus, the importance of the father (father's brother) or mother (mother's sister) is emphasized over other children of the same generation. Children of the father's sister are identified with the parent's generation, while children of the mother's brother are identified with the generation of ego's own children (that is, called son and daughter). This serves to identify the importance of the lineage, because the "son and daughter" are, in effect, the product of ego's lineage.

Self-Test

1. d
2. a
3. b
4. c
5. a
6. c

7. c
8. d
9. a
10. b
11. a
12. a

13. c
14. d

Age, Common Interest, And Stratification 13

Overview

Anthropologists have long known that people of all origins, ages, preferences, purposes, and both sexes tend to come together in groups of one kind or another. At this point, midway through your study of "Faces of Culture," you, too, must have noticed that the inclination to "group" together is basic to humankind and is thus universal. Traditional societies have grouped together in family or kinship units for purposes of self-defense, resource-sharing, and pooling of labor. When new problems loom or old ones grow beyond the control of family and kinship units, the society divides its members into structures designed to cope with these problems. In short, the society redefines the bases for status, prestige, and the sharing of resources.

In this lesson, you will be studying three general groupings found in varying degrees in almost all societies, including our own: age-grading, common-interest associations, and stratification (division by social class). Grouping by age is a way of organizing groups to perform specific functions. Common-interest groups have been in existence for thousands of years and are still prominent in industrial societies. Grouping by social class, which is inherently discriminatory in determining one's share of status and resources, occurs in all but hunting and gathering societies in varying degrees.

As you are introduced by your text and the television program to examples of these three types of social organizations, you will find it easy to identify some counterparts of all three in American society, perhaps many in your own community. For example, would you say that the practice of processing all criminal offenders below a certain age through a system of special laws, courts, and detention facilities not available to older offenders is a form of age grading? How would you describe unions, professional associations, the tradition which requires that some young women make their "debut" at a so-called "coming-out" ball? Do you view yourself as a member of some social class? If so, which one?

At the same time you're identifying counterparts, however, you will realize, as you progress through this lesson, that age grouping among the Nuer, common-interest groups among the Crow Indians, and caste systems (which are based on birth and are fixed) don't follow the same patterns or share the same functions as their counterparts in the United States.

Learning Objectives

When you have completed all assignments in this lesson, you should be able to:

1. Define and describe at least three examples of social groupings based on age. (Text pages 286-290; television program.)

2. Describe some functions of age groupings. (Text pages 287-293; television program.)

3. Distinguish between age grade, age class, and age set. (Text pages 287-289.)

4. Define common-interest associations. (Text page 294; television program.)

5. Describe and give the purpose of one common-interest association from a traditional society. (Text page 295.)

6. Suggest reasons why many anthropologists have failed to study women's common-interest associations. (Text pages 296-297.)

7. Describe and give the purpose of one common-interest association from a modern, complex society. (Text pages 297-299; television program.)

8. Compare kinship groups, age groups, and common-interest associations as methods of organizing society. (Text Chapter 9 and pages 286, 287, 289, 293, 294-298; television program.)

9. Define stratification. (Text page 299; television program.)

10. Compare an egalitarian society with a stratified one. (Text page 299.)

11. Define social class and distinguish it from social caste. Give examples of each. (Text pages 299-301.)

12. Cite factors which relate to the degree of mobility in a society. (Text pages 304-305; television program.)

Assignments For This Lesson

Before Viewing the Program

Read the overview and learning objectives for this lesson. Use the learning objectives to guide your reading, viewing, and thinking. Read the preview to Chapter 10 in the text, and look over the topic headings in the chapter.

Read Chapter 10, "Age, Common Interest, and Stratification," in the text.

View Program 13, "Age, Common Interest, and Stratification."

As you view the program, look for:

the comparison of function and types of age groups of the Masai of Africa with age groups such as college fraternities and sororities found in contemporary industrial societies.

the variety of common-interest associations found in pluralistic industrial societies and the various purposes they serve.

the origins and history of the Brotherhood of Sleeping Car Porters, a black labor union in the United States.

After Viewing the Program

Review the terms used in this lesson. In addition to the terms found in the learning objectives, you should be familiar with these:

verbal evaluation
egalitarian society
symbolic indicators
open class society

Review Chapter 9 (especially page 270) in the text to refresh your memory of the functions of kinship organizations.

Review the reading assignments for this lesson. A thorough second reading is suggested. Include the chapter summary in your study.

Complete each of the study activities and the self-test; then check your
answers with the answer key at the end of this lesson.

According to your instructor's assignment or your own interests, try to
complete one or more of the suggested activities. You may also be
interested in the readings suggested at the end of Chapter 10 in your text.

Study Activities

Vocabulary Check

Check on your understanding of terms by matching those on the left with
the definitions on the right. Check your choices with the answer key at the
end of the lesson.

1. _D_ age class
2. _F_ age set
3. _H_ elder warriors
4. _E_ common interest association
5. _A_ Crow Indian
   Tobacco Society
6. _K_ adaptation
7. _J_ stratified society
8. _B_ social class
9. _L_ symbolic indicator
10. _C_ caste
11. _G_ open-class society

a. a common interest association in a
   traditional society
b. a set of families and individuals
   that enjoy nearly equal prestige
c. a kind of social class in which
   membership is determined at birth
d. the people occupying an age grade
e. not based on age, kinship,
   marriage, or territory
f. groups initiated into an age grade
   at the same time
g. permits a great deal of mobility
h. one of the four age grades of the
   Tiriki
i. a category of people based on age
j. has a social structure that involves
   unequal distribution of resources,
   prestige, and influence
k. a major purpose of common
   interest associations in rapidly
   changing societies
l. activity or possession that is
   especially representative of a given
   social class

Completion

Choose the best word or phrase from the lists provided to fill the blanks in
the paragraphs below.

1. Some kind of age grouping is
   nearly _universal_ among

   elderly
   transition

human societies. Different life stages are recognized, and the purposes and resulting organizations vary widely. In some instances, the separation is of the youth, adults, and the *elderly*. In others, there are practices which may teach skills or otherwise aid the *transition* from one stage of life to another. Age groups aid in maintaining social continuity, insuring that important social roles will be filled, and in transmitting the society's cultural heritage.

universal

2. The tribal unions of West Africa are a common interest association whose chief purpose is preservation of *cultural* traditions. A typical characteristic of common interest groups found in traditional cultures is concern for the well-being of the entire *community* not just their own members.

adaptation
cultural
urbanization
community
assistance

Labor unions in the United States arose from movements in the nineteenth and twentieth centuries to improve working conditions and wages. Their efforts are typical of common interest associations in rapidly changing societies that give *assistance* to members through *adaptation* of existing institutions or the development of new ones to meet the challenges posed by industrialization and *urbanization*

3. Social stratification systems are more complex than age or common-interest groupings. Some anthropologists subscribe to the theory that social inequality first

caste
open
privileges
status

arose in food-producing societies when members could accumulate a surplus of goods. This occurrence gave some (those who controlled the surplus) more power than others. Exercise of power led to still greater stratification of societies in terms of _status_, influence, _privileges_, and prohibitions. Other influences, such as political organization beyond the local community, may also have served to intensify the development of a class structure. Social stratification systems range from the most rigidly stratified, such as the _caste_ system of India, to more _open_ class societies where opportunities for mobility between classes exist.

Short-Answer Questions

1. Explain how age classes in Tiriki society may function more effectively than the kinship group by insuring that key social roles are filled.

2. Describe how the functions fulfilled by common-interest associations in rapidly changing societies may differ from those found in traditional societies. Cite an example of traditional and modern common-interest groups having shared functions.

3. Why have women's associations which were established for common interests been generally less noticed until recently?

Self-Test

(Select the one best answer.)

Objective 1
1. The term "senior citizen" is an example of social grouping based on
   a. stratification.
   b. common interests.
   c. age.
   d. urbanization.

2. Which of these statements best summarizes the general purpose of age grouping?
   a. to identify and separate those who are not productive due to age
   b. to identify a number of life stages
   c. to preserve certain privileges for selected groups
   d. to organize those with a specific set of concerns and needs into one organization

3. What is an age set?
   a. a category of people based on age
   b. an organized group of people based on age
   c. a group of people, based on age, who move through a series of stages together for much of their lives
   d. the individuals who actually hold membership in an organization based primarily on age

4. Common-interest associations are found in
   a. advanced industrial societies.
   b. rapidly changing urban societies.
   c. traditional nonindustrial societies.
   d. all of the above.

5. The purpose of the tribal unions of West Africa is
   a. the preservation of cultural heritage.
   b. to provide sufficient members for various social roles.
   c. adaptation to urbanization.
   d. the preservation of stratification systems.

6. Which of the following statements is most true about the participation of women in common-interest associations?
   a. In most traditional societies, women did not develop formal associations.
   b. Women have taken part in formal associations in some societies but not in others.
   c. Women's common-interest associations are a new phenomenon in Western industrial society.
   d. Women have usually had an important role in male common-interest associations.

7. What is usually a major purpose of associations formed in rapidly changing and newly urbanized societies?
   a. preservation of traditions

b. providing members for various social roles
   c. political action
   d. adaptation to new conditions

Objective 8
8. In general, as societies become industrialized and more complex,
   a. both kinship groups and common-interest groups increase in importance.
   b. both kinship groups and common-interest groups decrease in importance.
   c. kinship groups increase in importance.
   d. common-interest groups increase in importance.

Objective 9
9. The term stratification refers to
   a. formation of groups based on age.
   b. a nobility or priesthood class.
   c. ranking of classes based on wealth, power, and prestige.
   d. the existence of a slave class.

Objectives 9 and 10
10. Which of these is true of any stratified society?
   a. It is virtually impossible to move from one social level to another, except possibly by marriage.
   b. Various groups are unequal in resources, power, and prestige.
   c. An individual's position in society depends largely on his own skills.
   d. Social mobility between classes is readily available.

Objective 10
11. In an egalitarian society
   a. there are great differences in rank and privilege.
   b. various groups are unequal in power and prestige.
   c. an individual's position in society depends largely on sex, age, and skills.
   d. an individual's ranking depends upon his birth.

Objective 11
12. The classic example of a system of castes is found in
   a. India.
   b. Canada.
   c. Polynesia.
   d. Western Europe.

Objective 12
13. Social mobility refers to the
   a. breakup of the extended family or kinship group influence.
   b. amount of modern transportation available.

c. ease with which one moves from one common-interest association to another.

d. possibility of changing one's social class membership.

Suggested Activities

1. Analyze some of the factors related to four or five of your closest friendships: In each friendship, what parts do kinship, age, common interests, and social class play? Are you and any of your friends both members of the same common-interest groups, political parties, or groups that indicate social class?

2. Make an anthropological study of a nearby, but fairly large, newsstand or magazine display. How many different common interest groups (even if not formally organized groups) are reflected by the magazine titles? Which of these groups reflect greater than average numbers by having several magazines appealing to their interests? Which of these groups seem to be seeking political or social power, as indicated by a quick check of the titles of articles in the magazines? Categorize the primary function of each group according to the following list: preservation, help members to change and adapt, desire to change some aspect of society.

Answer Key

Vocabulary Check

1. d	7. j
2. f	8. b
3. h	9. l
4. e	10. c
5. a	11. g
6. k	

Completion

1. universal, elderly, transition

2. cultural, community, assistance, adaptation

3. status, privileges (either order), caste, open

Short-Answer Questions

1. Explain how age classes in Tiriki society may function more effectively than the kinship group by insuring that key social roles are filled. Your answer should include:

   Young men in a given age grade are joined in formal association in a grade set, regardless of family. Therefore, there is a social unity, which is community wide, going beyond the family.

   Through the Tiriki system of age grouping, each of four "vital" social positions always has adequate membership. It is possible that individual kinship groups might not supply sufficient numbers at any one time for all four positions. It is also possible that kinship group preparation and training might concentrate on that group rather than the needs of the entire community.

2. Describe how the functions fulfilled by common interest associations in rapidly changing societies may differ from those found in traditional societies. Cite an example of traditional and modern common interest groups having shared functions. Your answer should include:

   Common-interest associations of individuals living in rapidly changing societies serve to help individuals adapt to new conditions in new environments.

   Common-interest associations of individuals living in rapidly changing societies serve to help individuals adapt to new conditions in new environments. Common-interest associations such as political clubs, unions, and women's groups in modern societies may also be a vehicle for introducing change to society. In contrast, common-interest groups in traditional societies tend to preserve the traditional patterns of behavior. However, some contemporary common interest groups may exist to help preserve traditional values and life-styles. These may include ethnic membership clubs, Daughters of the American Revolution, and historical societies.

3. Why have women's associations which were established for common interests been generally less noticed until recently? Your answer should include:

   Until recently, anthropologists have concluded that men's associations tend to have a more public orientation.

   To explain the relatively fewer number of women's groups, it has been suggested that, in some societies, women had much more opportunity to meet informally and visit, so that there may have been less need felt for formal associations.

It has been discovered that women have had groups and have played a part in male associations in some cultures, but the men's role has predominated; perhaps those studying the cultures in which such associations exist tended to assume that the women's role was minor.

Self-Test

1. c	6. b	11. c
2. b	7. d	12. a
3. c	8. d	13. d
4. d	9. c	
5. a	10. b	

The Aymara: *14*
A Case Study in Social Stratification

Overview

Stratification, or division by social class, is most apparent in large societies which have heterogeneous populations and centralized control, including our own society. You probably became aware at a relatively early age that Americans discriminate by social class in the sharing of resources and the bestowing of status and prestige, although some may want to deny this reality. You should know, however, that division or definition by social class is by no means a phenomenon peculiar to Western or industrial societies; social class distinctions also characterized many ancient civilizations. Although the division is not always clear, social classes in stratified societies can be based on birth, wealth, legal status, and other distinctions. Whatever the basis, stratification means that social classes thereby defined will not share equally in status or the resources of the society.

As you first considered social class in Lesson Thirteen, did you realize that class structures are very difficult to change? In this study you will learn how the social class system of northern Bolivia, which has roots dating back more than 400 years, deeply affects the lives of the Aymara Indians living there. Listen to the words spoken by members of the different social classes in the television program for this lesson; note what people say to and about one another, and observe how they interact. You should also be aware that the pattern of stratification is woven into many social institutions of this society, and religious practices perpetuate the social structure.

During the second half of this century, the Bolivian government
has attempted to improve the conditions of the Aymara. But after
viewing the program, you may feel that progress is terribly slow.
Yet, one Aymara says, "But compared to the past we are like free
and radiant doves." While studying this lesson, you may find
yourself reflecting on what it means to be "free," and what it means
to be denied access to social and economic resources.

Learning Objectives

When you have completed all assignments in this lesson, you should be able
to:

1. Briefly describe the origins of the stratification system of the Aymara
   and the mestizos in Bolivia. (Television program; Background Notes.)

2. Describe the indicators of the power and influence of the mestizos. (Text
   pages 303-304; television program; Background Notes.)

3. Describe indicators of Aymara lower class status. (Text pages 303-304;
   television program; Background Notes.)

4. Describe indicators of mobility in the stratification system of the
   Aymara. (Background Notes.)

5. Identify in what ways the Aymara and mestizos are mutually
   interdependent. (Television program; Background Notes.)

6. Describe how the Bolivian Revolution of 1952 has changed the
   relationship between the Aymara and the mestizos. (Background Notes.)

7. Discuss indications of class attitudes and economic conditions present in
   scenes of the Aymara and mestizo children. (Television program.)

Assignments For This Lesson

Before Viewing the Program

Read the overview and the learning objectives for this lesson. Use the
learning objectives to guide your reading, viewing, and thinking.

Review Chapter 10 in the text, "Age, Common Interest, and Stratification," especially page 285 and pages 299-306.

Read background notes for this lesson.

View Program 14, "The Aymara: A Case Study in Social Stratification."

As you view the program, look for:

the attitudes shown by the *mestizo* (the Spanish-speaking landholders) toward the Aymara throughout the program.

the educational, economic, social, and other differences between the mestizo town of Ayata and the Aymara village of Vitocota.

evidence of the limited resources available to the Aymara such as educational opportunity, medical care, and political and economic opportunities.

the evidence of class distinctions shown in the Flag Day celebration near the end of the program.

After Viewing the Program

Look at the map of Bolivia in Lesson 8 in this study guide.

Check your understanding of these names and terms:

mestizo	Vitocota
social stratification	class
Aymara	symbolic indicators
sharecroppers	mobility
Viracocha	Movimiento Nacional Revolucionario (MNR)
Ayata	

Review the reading assignments for this lesson. A thorough second reading of the background notes is suggested.

Complete each of the study activities and the self-test in this study guide; then check your answers with the answer key at the end of this lesson.

According to your instructor's assignment or your own interests, complete one or more of the suggested activities.

Background Notes

The Aymara

The Aymara are agriculturalists who live in the Andes in Bolivia. The television program focuses on a village and a town, Vitocota and Ayata, which are located near Lake Titicaca 12,000 feet above sea level. Because of the altitude, it is often cloudy and frost at night is common. The Aymara are dependent on the weather for survival. The ground they farm is not very fertile and they are sometimes plagued by hail, winds, and drought. Due to the short growing season and infertile soil, they can produce only one crop a year.

The Aymara farm much as they did before the Spanish conquered the area in the sixteenth century. Men break up the sun-hardened ground with a wooden foot-plow, and both women and men use stones to break up the soil even more.

Land is now individually owned and the Aymara try to have plots of land at various altitudes. This dispersed pattern of landownership allows the Aymara a greater chance for growing enough food. If frost damages the crop in a plot of land higher up the mountain, the yield from a lower-lying plot might prevent them from going hungry. If too much rain destroys the lower crop, the crop on higher terrain might still be available for harvest. Multiple plots give them access to crops from a variety of weather zones. The Aymara enhance the fertility of the soil by adding manure and by using a sophisticated eight-year cycle of crop rotation.

Potatoes are the primary crop for the Aymara. Up to 300 varieties are grown, and a single family may grow as many as forty varieties, some for their taste and some because they are frost-resistant. Potatoes provide about two-thirds of the Aymara diet. They are consumed principally in the form of *chuno*, which are potatoes preserved by alternately freezing and sun-drying. Prepared in this way, the potatoes last almost indefinitely.

The Aymara also grow other tuber crops and grain. They raise guinea pigs and sheep, but they usually trade or sell the meat and do not consume it themselves (they eat only the edible intestines). Consequently, the Aymara diet is low in protein.

The Aymara live in close-knit extended family groups headed by an elder male. All children, male and female, inherit land equally. There is sexual division of labor in most agricultural tasks. Women select the seed and prepare manure to use as fertilizer. They decide how much seed will be sown, how much chuno will be prepared, and which potatoes will be sold. Women dominate most matters having to do with livestock and control the family finances. Men do the heavier plowing tasks and help with the planting and harvesting. They are also in charge of conducting rituals associated with planting and harvesting.

Harvests are often carried out as a community effort, and become a time of social interaction and merriment. The Aymara also exchange labor and hire themselves out as labor. Successful Aymara are expected to sponsor religious festivals and other ritual events. Sponsoring a fiesta involves them in a series of gift exchanges—in the form of food, alcohol, and coca leaves—and enhances their prestige. For the Aymara, coca serves much the same social and stimulant functions that coffee does in our society; it is also important in rituals.

Although the Aymara use many of the same planting and harvesting techniques they did before they were conquered by the Spanish, their social, political, and economic role has changed considerably. The Spanish established a system of feudal landownership and forced labor in the tin and silver mines. When Bolivia achieved independence from Spain in 1825, forced labor in the mines was abolished, but the system of landownership remained essentially unchanged. As late as 1950, 90 percent of the land was owned by fewer than 5 percent of the people. This meant that most of the farmers were tenants who were bound to the land and could legally be bought and sold with the land they worked.

The Mestizos

Many of the landowners were *mestizos. Mestizo* is a Spanish word meaning "mixed" and usually refers to racially mixed people. But, in Bolivia, the mestizos are distinguished from the Aymara not so much by race as by language, occupation, residence, culture, and style of living. Mestizos speak Spanish, the official language of the country, and wear Western dress. The Aymara speak their own language, one of two major native language groups in the area, and wear handwoven clothing. Mestizos are largely urban, the Aymara are rural peasants. Mestizos have access to Western medicine; the Aymara, as a rule, do not. Mestizos control certain ritual duties needed by the Aymara. For example, most doctors are mestizo, and the Aymara must hire mestizos to conduct parts of religious festivals in Latin.

Mestizos and Aymara are educated differently. Mestizo children are taught in combined primary-secondary schools, which can prepare them for professional training. Aymara children may attend the first few grades in a peasant school. If they seek further schooling, they are sent to a "central" school, perhaps in another community, where they can complete the primary grades. Few continue with secondary or professional education.

Salaries and working conditions for teachers who work in rural schools are inferior to those in urban schools. The curriculum for peasant children is aimed at teaching Spanish, reading, writing, arithmetic, and a few vocational skills. This education is mostly irrelevant for one who stays in a rural community, but also inadequate preparation for further study. The inadequacy of peasant education is reflected in Bolivia's illiteracy rate, which is 17 percent for urban dwellers over the age of fifteen and 85 percent for the rural population over fifteen.

There is much distrust between the mestizos and the Aymara. In the television program, Aymara boys talking on the soccer field are convinced that food is available to the school, but it is not being distributed equally to the mestizo and the Aymara children. On the other hand, mestizos living in town fear the growing power of the rural areas, a power which was sparked by the "great revolution" of 1952.

The Bolivian Government

The peasants did not start the 1952 revolution. It was brought about by the Nationalist Revolutionary Movement (Movimiento Nacional Revolucionario or MNR), a loose coalition representing a variety of interests, including miners, factory workers, and intellectuals. About the only thing the 1952 revolutionists had in common was their opposition to the tiny urban elite which had previously taken turns occupying seats of power through a series of "revolutions" that had little effect on the vast majority of the populace.

The Nationalist Revolutionary Movement came to power in 1952 after brief but bloody fighting. The movement immediately initiated sweeping changes, some of which were aimed at securing the support of the peasants. Education for rural children was assigned to the Ministry of Peasant Affairs and extended into some of the most remote areas of the country. The present form of rural education exists primarily because of the revolution.

The MNR also instituted major agrarian reforms. Large landholdings were broken up and the land redistributed to the peasants who had been farming it. They were faced with a limited amount of tillable land in the highlands, where the Aymara live, to be divided among a vast number of people. Thus, the MNR began resettlement of people into less populated and more tropical areas in the eastern lowlands. However, in the mountainous region, the fact that Aymara became landholders was an important change in the stratification patterns relating Aymara and mestizo. They also tried to set up an internal transportation system and improve roads. This proved more difficult because of the mountainous terrain of the Andes. The MNR also nationalized Bolivia's tin mines and extended the vote to greater numbers of people.

Since 1952, inflation and mismanagement have led to new concentrations of power in Bolivia's central government. Some political scientists speak of Bolivia's present political system as "internal colonialism." Wealth and power remain concentrated in the capital, which drains off the economic resources of the rest of the country.

But the changes brought about by the revolution of 1952 were too far-reaching to be erased. The Aymara are beginning to demand a greater voice in determining their social and economic roles. And they are seeking better educational opportunities for their children. Limited land combined with a rapidly expanding population means that future generations cannot hope to keep dividing the family plot among siblings, so they must find jobs away from the land. For the Aymara, education may be the key to a better economic future and a way to break down barriers between them and the mestizos. Anthropologist William E. Carter writes, "Their sons, they claim, also want to be doctors." (*The Children Know,* film essay from the series *Faces of Change,* produced by The American University's Field Staff, 1976, page 5.)

Study Activities

Vocabulary Check

Check on your understanding of terms by matching those on the left with the definitions on the right. Check your choices with the answer key at the end of the lesson.

1. _C_ Andes
2. _A_ feudal
3. _I_ Viracocha
4. _D_ mestizo
5. _E_ Vitocota
6. _H_ language
7. _I_ Ayata
8. _F_ MNR

a. system in which owning the land involves virtual ownership of those who work the land
b. vegetable grown by Aymara
c. mountain region in which the Aymara live
d. literally means "mixture"
e. Aymara village
f. "revolutionary" government which has instituted some land and education reforms
g. church official
h. one of the symbolic indicators of social position in Bolivia
i. a god of the indigenous religion in Bolivia
j. mestizo town

Completion

Choose the best word or phrase from the lists provided to fill the blanks in the paragraphs below.

1. The Spanish conquest of Bolivia imposed many changes on the Aymara-speaking Indians in the region, although some aspects of their life remain largely

religious
forced
language
feudal
agricultural

unchanged. For example, the Aymara still use the same *language*, and *agricultural* practices remain largely as before the conquest. Some aspects of the older *religious* beliefs still survive, although these are now blended with Roman Catholic ritual. However, the Spanish imposed a *feudal* pattern of landownership and *forced* labor in the mines.

2. The mestizos are the class of *middle-class* landowners which resulted from Spanish rule. Generally, they live in *urban* areas, speak Spanish, and have an *educational* system which can lead to *professional* training. The Aymara, in contrast, are rural people, habitually speak their own language, and have been provided limited formal education only in this century.

educational
middle-class
professional
urban

3. Reforms instituted in the 1952 Revolution which have affected the Aymara include *landownership* and *education*. The Aymara and mestizos *distrust* each other, and the contrast in opportunities for such services as medical care is still great. According to the television program, mestizos view the Aymara as *lazy* and given to drinking too much. In the television program, one Aymara views his fellow villagers as spending too much effort and money on *fiestas*.

distrust
landownership
fiestas
lazy
education

Short-Answer Questions

1. Are there any indications in this lesson that Aymara can change their class status? What are the conditions that block upward mobility?

2. In the portrayal of a National Flag Day celebration in the television program, there are a number of examples of class attitudes. What are some of these attitudes? How do they ignore the dependence of each group on the other?

Self-Test

(Select the one best answer.)

Objective 1
1. The term "mestizo" identifies a group in Bolivia that is primarily
   a. the aristocracy of La Paz.
   b. a Spanish nobility class.
   c. small-town landowners.
   d. tenant farmers and laborers.

Objective 1
2. The present stratification system of the Aymara and mestizos in Bolivia has its origins in
   a. the feudal landholding patterns established by the Spanish.
   b. the need for laborers to work the farms.
   c. linquistic, educational, and ethnic differences between the mestizos and the Aymara.
   d. all of the above sources.

Objective 2
3. Which of the following reflects the status of the mestizo?
   a. rural residence patterns
   b. religious preference
   c. education and wealth
   d. political party

Objectives 2 and 3
4. Which of the following was still true at the time the television program for this lesson was filmed?
   a. Landowners used Aymara labor to work the farms.
   b. Aymara are required to work in mines.
   c. No educational opportunities are provided for the lower class.
   d. All farming land is owned by individual farmers.

Objective 3

5. A criticism frequently leveled against the Aymara by the mestizos is that
   the Aymara
   a. do menial work.
   b. are ignorant.
   c. do not take part in politics.
   d. drink too much.

Objective 3

6. The language of the Aymara affects their status because it is
   a. the official language of the nation.
   b. difficult to understand.
   c. not the official language of the nation.
   d. now spoken by very few residents.

Objective 4

7. What obstacle makes it difficult for the Aymara to receive professional
   education?
   a. They are prohibited by law from entering most professions.
   b. The elementary education available to them does not adequately
      prepare them for further schooling.
   c. Values derived from their old religion prevent young Aymara from
      seeking education.
   d. No professional education is available in Bolivia.

Objective 4

8. Which of the following is *not* true of elementary education in Aymara
   communities?
   a. All instruction is in Aymara.
   b. Teachers in rural schools are paid less than those in urban schools.
   c. All instruction is in Spanish.
   d. Students may have to leave their community for upper-grade
      education.

Objective 5

9. Many Bolivian Indians depend upon mestizo society for their religious
   practices because
   a. all churches are located in mestizo cities.
   b. the Aymara still follow the older worship of Viracocha.
   c. religious clergy are supported by the government.
   d. the clergy are from the mestizo society.

Objective 5

10. The Aymara of Vitocota primarily provide _____ for the
    mestizos.
    a. household servants
    b. field labor

188

    c. teachers, police, and similar work

    d. office and shop workers

Objective 6

11. What land reforms were instituted by the Bolivian revolutionary government after 1952?

    a. All farm land was nationalized.

    b. Peasant farmers began owning land.

    c. Landownership was taken over by mestizos.

    d. Modern farm methods were introduced widely.

Objective 6

12. Since the Nationalist Revolutionary Movement came to power,

    a. educational opportunities have decreased greatly due to closing of many schools.

    b. the native languages, as well as Spanish, are now used in primary school instruction.

    c. peasant schools have been established in Aymara villages.

    d. comprehensive high schools teach vocational skills important to rural communities.

Objective 6

13. For what reason(s) does the mestizo population distrust the rural Aymara population?

    a. Some of the revolutionary government's reforms were designed to gain peasant support, and the Aymara are beginning to demand a larger voice in government.

    b. The peasants led the 1952 revolution, causing the mestizo to fear further political changes.

    c. Due to changes in education, the rural populations are not as literate as those of the cities and thus have become a strong political force.

    d. The Aymara are moving rapidly into the cities and threatening to disrupt city life.

Objective 7

14. The Flag Day celebration shown in the television program suggests that Aymara and mestizo children

    a. are able to ignore the social barriers and play together.

    b. have habitually played together in the past.

    c. do not mix or play together.

    d. play together now, as they did in the past.

Objective 7

15. The scenes of the Aymara school in the television program reveal that it has

    a. glass in the windows and central heating.

    b. poor lighting, seating, and educational curriculum.

c. modern desks and schoolbooks.

d. a mestizo teacher who is harsh with the children.

Suggested Activities

1. Read and prepare a brief review of *The Bolivian Aymara,* by Hans C. Buechler and Judith-Maria Buechler, New York: Holt, Rinehart and Winston, 1971.

2. What similarities do you see in the situation of the Aymara as presented in the television program and the situations of one or more of the minority groups in the United States? Use your local library resources to compare, in particular, the literacy levels of various minority groups in the United States with those for the two Bolivian social groups as reported in the background notes.

3. The Bolivian revolution of 1952 inaugurated extensive land reforms that changed a feudal ownership system extending back more than 400 years. However, the changes made after the revolution have not had a great effect on the social stratification of the Aymara. Read additional information on the revolution and evaluate its effect on opportunities for social mobility for the Aymara.

Answer Key

Vocabulary Check

1. c
2. a
3. i
4. d

5. e
6. h
7. j
8. f

Completion

1. language, agricultural, religious, feudal, forced

2. middle-class, urban, educational, professional

3. landownership, education, distrust, lazy, fiestas

Short-Answer Questions

1. Are there any indications in this lesson that Aymara can change their class status? What are the conditions that block upward mobility? Your

answer should include:

Two examples of possible upward mobility are shown in the program: the police chief of Ayata, the mestizo city, is an Aymara, as is Hugo, the schoolteacher. In both cases, it is the fact that they are professionally educated which has allowed the two men to assume higher class jobs.

However, both these examples are *limited* in that they are exceptions to the common pattern.

Some of the serious obstacles to upward mobility facing the Aymara include: poverty, poor health, limited access to education, a high illiteracy rate, primitive farming techniques. There are no indications of other economic potential for the Aymara, and opportunities for work other than farming in a rural area are limited.

2. In the portrayal of a National Flag Day celebration in the television program, there are a number of examples of class attitudes. What are some of these attitudes? How do they ignore the dependence of each group on the other? Your answer should include:

All participants seem aware of the differences in status reflected by clothing and appearance.

The members of each group do not really "mix"; the mestizo children play separately from the Aymara.

Attitudes of the mestizo adults toward the Aymara seem condescending; expressions of resentment are heard from the Aymara.

The mestizos appear to ignore the extent to which they depend on the Aymara for labor and the performance of menial tasks, as well as for agricultural products.

The Aymara resent the mestizos, yet they depend on them for employment, for certain religious services, and for professional services such as health care. They also depend on the government, which actually arises from groups identified with the mestizos.

Self-Test

1. c	6. c	11. b
2. d	7. b	12. c
3. c	8. a	13. a
4. a	9. d	14. c
5. d	10. b	15. b

Economic Anthropology 15

Overview

If you were asked to define the term "economics" without reference to a dictionary or economics text, what would you say? Your definition might well sound something like this: "Economics is the study of money and the principles and rules that govern its use." And you wouldn't be entirely wrong; your definition would be partly true in the sense that money *is* one aspect of the study of economics in our modern industrialized society.

But of course, it is not that simple. Economics—even in highly industrialized Western societies—is much more than merely the study of money. But the main problem with the "Westernized" interpretation is that the use of money, or currency, is a rather recent development in the history of world cultures, and many nonindustrial, non-Western cultures do not use either money or profit as bases for their economies. These cultures do not encourage the accumulation of material goods for personal wealth, and they often do not permit private ownership of property or land. Such economies cannot, therefore, be interpreted in light of either our own money-based system or the technologies and values governing work and property in our society.

For these reasons, many anthropologists believe that principles which are used to study Western economies are not applicable to nonindustrialized, non-Western economies. You might then well ask the obvious question: "How do economic systems fit into the study of anthropology?" Simply put, economics is the study, description, and analysis of the production, distribution, and consumption of goods and services, whatever the motive or form of exchange. And, by this definition, *all* societies have some kind of economic system, since to subsist, all must produce, share, and consume available resources. It is also true that some aspects of economic systems are universal. Each society has resources which are more or less limited; people work to make use of the resources; some kind of technology (even if it is only knowledge) makes possible the use of resources; there is a division of labor based on age and sex; cooperation is required; some specialization is evident; and rules for controlling allocation of resources exist. Economic activity, then, is a form of adaptation which contributes to the health and survival of the society.

Many anthropologists feel that economic systems must be studied in the context of the cultures in which they flourish; therefore, this lesson will give you glimpses of some striking contrasts between the values and practices of Western and non-Western cultures. You will see some seemingly *opposite* economic practices used effectively to satisfy similar needs of both Western and non-Western cultures, while practices which otherwise are quite similar in both cultures are being used to satisfy quite *different* motives and purposes.

As you progress through this lesson, it will interest (and perhaps amuse) you to reflect on the motives and the contrasting outcomes of the "conspicuous consumption" practices typical of many wealthy and acquisitive Americans and the motives and outcomes of the "potlatch" staged by the Kwakiutl Indians of British Columbia. Kwakiutl leaders give away, throw away, and sometimes destroy their most prized objects of value for the same reason some Westerners acquire and display them. Note, too, the interesting differences between the concepts of "market" and "marketplace."

Learning Objectives

When you have completed all assignments in this lesson, you should be able to:

1. Define economic system. (Text page 200; television program.)

2. Recognize natural resources, labor, and technology as essential ingredients for the production of goods and services. (Text pages 201, 205-208, and review pages 164-175.)

3. Describe common sex and age patterns for the division of labor. Discuss conditions in modern industrial societies that have begun to alter these patterns. (Text pages 201-203.)

4. Describe various patterns of the way in which land as a natural resource is allocated for purposes of economic production. (Text pages 205-206.)

5. Define capital and explain how both tools or money could serve as capital in various societies. (Text pages 206-207; television program.)

6. Define technology and describe two examples of technological knowledge in nonindustrial societies. (Text pages 207-208.)

7. Define and describe three systems of distributing goods in nonindustrial societies: reciprocity, redistribution, and market exchange. (Text pages 209-210, 214-215, and 220-222; television program.)

8. Describe barter (including silent trade) as a form of negative reciprocity. (Text pages 211-213; television program.)

9. Describe the conditions necessary for redistribution to emerge as a system of economic distribution. (Text pages 214-215; television program.)

10. Describe how the potlatch of the Kwakiutl Indians serves as a "leveling mechanism" in the distribution of wealth. (Text pages 216-219.)

11. Describe the functions of the marketplace in nonindustrial societies. (Text pages 220-222; television program.)

Assignments For This Lesson

Before Viewing the Program

Read the overview and the learning objectives for this lesson. Use the learning objectives to guide your reading, viewing, and thinking.

Read the preview to Chapter 7 in your text, and look over the topic headings in the chapter.

Read Chapter 7, "Economic Systems."

Review the material in Chapter 6 (text pages 164-175) on adaptation, evolutionary adaptation, culture areas, and culture core for information on the relationship of natural resources to culture.

View Program 15, "Economic Anthropology."

As you view the program, look for:

examples of generalized reciprocity among hunter-gatherers and horticultural societies.

scenes of the Kula trade of the Trobriand Islanders.

the Mendi of New Guinea negotiating a bride price and the cassowary contest.

an Afghan marketplace, an example of redistribution.

the variety of modern economic practices, based on money and wage labor, and accumulations of wealth and displays of affluence.

After Viewing the Program

Review the terms used in this lesson. In addition to those in the learning objectives, you should be familiar with these:

conspicuous consumption   balanced reciprocity
craft specialization   Kula ring
generalized reciprocity

Review the reading assignments for this lesson. A thorough second reading is suggested. Include the chapter summary in your study.

Complete each of the study activities and the self-test in this study guide; then check your answers with the answer key at the end of this lesson.

According to your instructor's assignment or your own interests, complete one or more of the suggested activities. You may also be interested in some of the readings suggested at the end of Chapter 7 in your text.

Study Activities

Vocabulary Check

Check on your understanding of terms by matching those on the left with the definitions on the right. Check your choices with the answer key at the end of the lesson.

1. _E_ economic system
2. _I_ craft specialization
3. _M_ feudal system
4. _C_ tools
5. _G_ reciprocity
6. _I_ generalized reciprocity
7. _L_ leveling mechanism

a. requires production of a surplus and the existence of government
b. a form of barter without verbal communication
c. one kind of capital found in nonindustrial societies
d. a term for displaying wealth to gain prestige

195

8. _K_ barter
9. _H_ necklaces and armshells
10. _A_ redistribution
11. _D_ conspicuous consumption

e. the overall pattern through which goods are produced, distributed, and consumed in a society

f. the value and times of items exchanged are fairly specific

g. exchange of goods of about equal value

h. products of symbolic value which have great importance in the Kula trading system

i. one type of division of labor found in more complex societies

j. an exchange where neither the value of what was given is calculated nor the time of repayment specified

k. one type of exchange in which each participant tries to get better value

l. social obligations which function so that no one person tends to accumulate more wealth than another in a society

m. a pattern of landownership in which all land ultimately belongs to a single leader

Completion

Choose the best word or phrase from the lists provided to fill the blanks in the paragraphs below.

1. An economic system involves goods in three ways: _production_, _distribution_ and _consumption_. Economic systems are studied by anthropologists because culture defines the wants or demands of people in a society, dictates how and when available goods will be distributed, and establishes the division of labor—all needed for an economic system. The culture also determines the society's _adaption_ to the environment and supplies the technologies that will be used to exploit natural _resources_.

distribution
adaptation
production
consumption
resources

2. All societies assign certain tasks to members of each _sex_, although in modern industrial societies, the importance of this kind of division of labor is diminishing. People of various ages also have different roles. The exact pattern for all division of labor is established by the culture. Land-owner-ship patterns also vary among nonindustrial societies—in one common pattern, the land is owned by a _kinship_ group. In some societies, however, there is a feudal pattern in which land ultimately belongs to the _chief_. Individuals who work the land have some "ownership rights," but cannot sell or give their land away without approval. Individual ownership of land is rare in nonindustrial societies.

kinship
chief or king
sex

3. Taxes and government expenditures in the United States are a form of _redistribution_. In nonindustrial societies, a similar pattern can be part of the economic system. Some of the goods go to the government, which in turn distributes them according to its needs, thus replacing one-to-one exchange. In order for this process to exist, there must be a fairly substantial _surplus_ of goods, combined with a complex _political_ organization.

political
surplus
redistribution

4. The "market principle" applied in modern industrial societies refers to the methods by which price is established through the balancing of _supply_

demand
themselves
social
supply

and _demand_. In non-industrial societies, the market principle is applied in an actual marketplace. In these market-places, people exchange goods grown, raised, or made by _themselves_. The market-places in these societies also have _social_ functions which are as important as economic functions.

Short-Answer Questions

1. Define each of these terms in relation to *nonindustrial* societies: capital, technology, balanced reciprocity, generalized reciprocity, negative reciprocity.

2. What are the social and economic aspects of barter and silent trade?

3. In what ways does generalized reciprocity resemble the potlatch, and how do these two practices differ?

Self-Test

(Select the one best answer.)

Objective 1
1. Of the following processes, which is not essential to an economic system?
   a. production
   b. taxation
   c. distribution
   d. consumption

Objective 2
2. The ownership of land and resources is
   a. necessary to the sexual division of labor.
   b. a form of technology in market economies.
   c. common to all subsistence patterns.
   d. rare in nonindustrial societies.

Objectives 2 and 3
3. Which of the following societies has comparatively little place for aged people in its division of labor?
   a. Ihalmuit

b. Vietnamese
c. Kwakiutl
d. Kogi

Objective 3
4. According to Haviland, the main factor in the sexual division of labor in traditional societies is
   a. the environment.
   b. technology.
   c. cultural patterns.
   d. biology.

Objective 4
5. A _____ pattern of landownership is practiced by the Tiwi.
   a. feudal
   b. individual
   c. band
   d. society

Objective 5
6. Which of the following is an example of capital in a hunting-gathering society?
   a. an arrow
   b. a digging hoe
   c. territory
   d. game animals

Objectives 2 and 6
7. Which of these skills is the best example of technological knowledge in a nonindustrial society?
   a. knowing how to conduct a seasonal ritual
   b. identifying land belonging to a kin group
   c. observance of rights of chiefs
   d. identifying edible plants

Objective 7
8. A system of reciprocity where neither the value of what is given is calculated nor the time of repayment specified is called
   a. balanced.
   b. open ended.
   c. generalized.
   d. negative.

Objectives 7 and 8
9. The Kula ring involves what two systems of exchange?
   a. barter and balanced reciprocity

b. barter and generalized reciprocity
c. barter and negative reciprocity
d. barter and silent trade

Objectives 7 and 9

10. Which of the following societies developed a sophisticated redistribution system?
    a. Trobriand Islanders
    b. Kwakiutl
    c. Kota
    d. Inca

Objective 9

11. What conditions are essential for the establishment of a system of redistribution?
    a. conspicuous consumption, surplus
    b. leveling mechanism, surplus
    c. central administration, surplus
    d. central administration, leveling mechanism

Objective 10

12. The potlatch is considered a leveling mechanism because it
    a. is also an occasion to renew friendships and exchange gossip.
    b. tends to distribute goods so that no one retains more than anyone else.
    c. is a procedure that involves balanced reciprocity.
    d. involves conspicuous consumption of wealth.

Objective 11

13. Which of the following is *not* a function of a nonindustrial marketplace?
    a. the display of wealth for social prestige
    b. the display and sale of goods produced or grown by the people
    c. the opportunity for social exchanges
    d. a location for the exchange of goods produced in a region

Objective 11

14. Which of these is similar to a nonindustrial marketplace?
    a. New Orleans cotton exchange
    b. New York stock exchange
    c. a flea market
    d. a potlatch

Suggested Activities

1. Haviland has listed several advances and trends in industrial societies which tend to reduce division of labor by sex. From your own observations or additional reading, what evidence is there that roles

200

assigned due to sex are disappearing in the United States? Do you see indications that some such roles are remaining firmly entrenched? You may wish to read the article "Society and Sex Roles," by Ernestine Friedl, in *Human Nature*, Vol. 1, April 1978, pp. 68-75.

2. Carefully observe exchanges in some of the following situations: birthday parties, weddings, holiday gifts, and in bar gatherings. Then make a report on the exchange patterns. Can you describe these patterns in terms of balanced, generalized, and negative reciprocity?

3. The "profit motive" has generally been cited as the driving force behind successful industrial enterprise and much individual achievement. Many have considered it "universal." Based on the information in this lesson, would you agree or disagree with the concept of a "prestige motive"? In North American society, are "profit" and "prestige" identical? How do they differ?

Answer Key

Vocabulary Check

1. e	5. g	9. h
2. i	6. j	10. a
3. m	7. l	11. d
4. c	8. k	

Completion

1. production, distribution, consumption, adaptation, resources

2. sex, kinship, chief or king

3. redistribution, surplus, political

4. supply, demand, themselves, social

Short-Answer Questions

1. Define each of these terms in relation to *nonindustrial* societies: capital, technology, balanced reciprocity, generalized reciprocity, negative reciprocity. Your answer should include:

Capital: resources such as tools that are not depleted in the production of goods in nonindustrial societies.

Technology is the capability to apply knowledge for practical purposes. Examples could include ability to make tools and weapons or identify plants that can be used as food.

Balanced reciprocity: an exchange of goods or services of about equal value with agreement about both relative values and the times for exchange to take place.

Generalized reciprocity: a system of exchange in which neither the value of goods given is calculated nor a time of repayment specified. For example, general distribution of food to group members from a hunt is considered generalized reciprocity.

Negative reciprocity: exchanges in which one party tries to obtain the better value in the trade. This type of exchange may involve deceit or even use of force.

2. What are the social and economic aspects of barter and silent trade? Your answer should include:

Barter is a type of exchange that usually takes place between people from different groups.

To minimize negative reciprocity and help insure a balance, much bargaining may take place in the calculation of relative value.

Barter allows exchange to take place despite the likelihood of some hostility and competition between the respective groups.

Silent trade is a form of barter without any verbal communication. For example, goods offered for trade are displayed, and the opposite group in turn displays what it offers in exchange. Acceptance may be shown when the first group takes possession of the traded goods.

Silent trade makes exchange possible when the groups are prohibited from openly communicating with each other, when verbal communication might lead to hostility, or when there is no common language.

3. In what ways does generalized reciprocity resemble the potlatch, and in what ways do these two practices differ? Your answer should include:

Generalized reciprocity and the potlatch both serve as leveling mechanisms: They tend to prevent great accumulation of wealth and encourage distribution of wealth throughout the group.

They also resemble each other in that both are viewed as social obligations within the group.

They are different in several respects. The potlatch is an elaborate celebration with ceremonial features; reciprocity need not be an elaborate occasion. The potential for prestige is probably much greater in the potlatch than in most instances of generalized reciprocity. As described in the text, generalized reciprocity usually does not involve the extensive accumulation of surpluses necessary for a potlatch.

Self-Test

1. b	6. a	11. c
2. d	7. d	12. b
3. a	8. c	13. a
4. d	9. a	14. c
5. c	10. d	

The Highland Maya: 16
A Case Study in Economic Anthropology

Overview

Are you somewhat uncomfortable with the idea of people in some societies giving economic surplus away in order to gain honor and prestige, even at the risk of rendering themselves destitute? When you learned about the Kwakiutl Indians of British Columbia and their intricate and colorful ceremony of the potlatch in Lesson Fifteen, you may have felt that such a philosophy is quite alien to your own life-style. And, in truth, the practice of giving away valued possessions, rather than accumulating them, *is* quite foreign to most people living in industrial societies. It is not so unusual, though, in modern *nonindustrial* societies, and the Kwakiutl Indians are not the only society in the Western Hemisphere which bases its economic system on the practice of divesting its members of their wealth.

After studying the "cargo system" of the Highland Maya of Mexico in this lesson, you may not find the idea of giving wealth away so strange. The Highland Maya have institutionalized the practice of exchanging their surplus goods solely for the rewards of social approval. In their system, a Maya male may become destitute and fall deeply in debt, but he has won prestige and the respect of his society. And it is well to remember that to the Maya the reward is greater than simple "approval." He who gives is taking the major available pathway for advancing his status and prestige in the society. Attaining status and prestige in turn binds him to specific civic and religious responsibilities important to the Highland Maya society.

The economic practices of the Highland Maya are called a "cargo system." Cargo, in this case, does not refer to "goods" but to a "burden." The cargo holder carries out civil and religious "burdens," or responsibilities, for an entire year, receiving no payment from the community, although there are costs, and sometimes sizable ones, involved in performing these duties.

A culture is, of course, integrated; each part of the pattern reinforces other parts of the culture. At times, as you watch the television program, it may seem to you that the cargo system is, more than anything else, religious in nature. While it is true that the cargo system gives essential support to religious observances and other Highland Maya community interests, the system also is important politically and economically. One economic effect of the cargo system is to prevent individuals from accumulating more wealth than others in the society. The system keeps surplus money and goods in circulation throughout the region. It is also the means by which the financing essential for religious and social activities is made available, and these activities help to maintain the Maya sense of identity and community. Just as important perhaps, is the fact that the system guarantees that men will devote their time and efforts to the community.

Learning Objectives

When you have completed all assignments in this lesson, you should be able to:

1. Describe the subsistence pattern of the Highland Maya of Mexico. (Television program; Background Notes.)

2. Describe the functions and importance of cargo positions in the Maya society. (Television program; Background Notes.)

3. Explain in what ways the cargo system serves as a leveling mechanism among the Maya. (Television program; Background Notes.)

4. Discuss how the cargo system contributes to a feeling of community and regional solidarity and the importance of such solidarity. (Television program; Background Notes.)

5. Explain how the cargo system of the Maya helps to maintain inequalities between the Maya Indians and the mestizos. (Television program; Background Notes.)

Assignments For This Lesson

Before Viewing the Program

Read the overview and the learning objectives for this lesson. Use the learning objectives to guide your reading, viewing, and thinking.

Read the background notes for this lesson.

Review Chapter 7, "Economic Systems," in the text, and give special attention to the section "Distribution and Exchange" (page 209), and the discussion of leveling mechanism (pages 210-211).

View Program 16, "The Highland Maya: A Case Study in Economic Anthropology."

As you view the program, look for:

the meaning and significance of the cargo system.

Augustin Gomez, his life-style and his position in the community.

the close relationship between civil and religious functions, unlike custom in the United States, where there is a separation of church and state.

the hierarchy of the cargo system; the roles of the mayordomo and the alferez.

the descriptions of the duties undertaken by various cargo holders.

After Viewing the Program

Review the terms used in this lesson. In particular, make certain that you understand these terms:

cargo	stratified system
leveling mechanism	mestizo
milpa	

You should also locate the state of Chiapas, the home of the Highland Maya, on the map of Mexico. (See Figure 16.1.)

Review the reading assignments for this lesson. A thorough second reading of the text chapter and the background notes is suggested.

Complete each of the study activities and the self-test in this study guide; then check your answers with the answer key at the end of this lesson.

According to your instructor's assignment or your own interests, complete one or more of the suggested activities. You may also be interested in reading *The Zinacantecos of Mexico: The Modern Way of Life* by Evon Z. Vogt (Holt, Rinehart & Winston, 1970) for a more detailed picture of the life and culture of the Highland Maya.

Background Notes

The Highland Maya

The Maya Indians shown in the television program live in the highlands of southern Mexico. They are farmers, and corn is their primary crop. Because of the altitude, which is often more than 6,000 feet, the weather is too cold to grow much of a surplus crop for selling, for corn is particularly vulnerable to frosts. The Maya diet consists mainly of corn tortillas, beans, and a variety of green vegetables; meat and poultry are eaten only on ceremonial occasions.

Nuclear families live in one-room adobe houses on lands owned by the extended family. The highland Maya use an intensive form of shifting agriculture called slash-and-burn, or "milpa" farming. They cut forest and undergrowth from a plot of land, burn it, and plant corn with a digging stick. After four or five years, the yield declines and the plot is allowed to reforest.

Social organization of the Highland Maya is shaped by the cargo system. (The name "cargo" comes from the Spanish word for "burden.") Males gain prestige in a community by undertaking periods of service to the community. The period of service, or cargo, lasts for one year. Types of services performed are ranked, so that a man works his way up through a series of graded steps, like rungs on a ladder, alternating between civil and religious offices.

Young men enter the system by doing menial tasks, such as running errands for older men. As they grow older, they hold political offices, equivalent to mayor, council member, or sheriff. Cargo holders on the first level of religious office may sweep the floors or change the flowers in the church. As they progress they sponsor religious festivals. This includes providing food and liquor, as well as paying for church services, musicians, dancers, and bullfighters.

Taking part in the cargo (or burden) is time-consuming and expensive. Young men may be reluctant to enter a cargo, but they can be coerced into it by social pressure. When they enter the cargo, they are expected to perform their duties joyfully and give most of their financial resources, so that they are in debt at the end of their cargo term. Anthropologist Frank Cancian says, "The cargo must be a financial

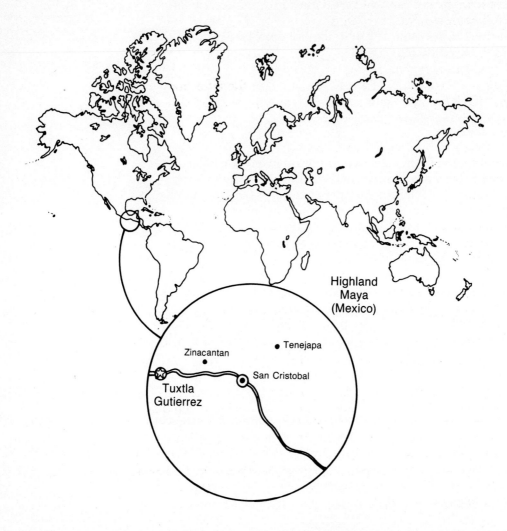

Figure 16.1 The economy of the Highland Maya, who live at a high altitude in southern Mexico, is based on the growing of corn by the slash-and-burn system, or milpa.

burden to the cargo holder, and he must accept this burden in good spirits, happy that he is sacrificing for the gods and the saints" *(Economics and Prestige in a Maya Community: The Religious Cargo System in Zinacantan.* Stanford: Stanford University Press, 1965, p. 97).

However, the cargo holder gains in prestige what he loses in time and money. A senior cargo holder always has authority over a junior cargo holder. On ceremonial occasions, cargo holders address each other by the names of their cargos, rather than their personal names. If two men meet on a path, the junior stops to let the senior pass, and if they are walking together, the senior walks ahead. Cancian writes, "Who is senior and who is junior is almost always a question of great importance in Zinacantan [the town he studied], whatever the situation" (p. 32). He describes the following drinking behavior:

> When drinking formally, the older person is served first and is bowed to as he toasts the younger. He extends his hand touching the younger's forehead, and thus indicates that the latter may raise his head. When the younger person is served, he bows to the older as he speaks the words of toast (p. 32).

In the hierarchy the ranking applies to the cargos and not to the ages of the men.

Some anthropologists have suggested that the cargo system is a leveling device which redistributes resources in the society. According to this theory, the cargo prevents individuals from accumulating wealth. Since each man participating in the cargo system must "give until it hurts," the rich give more than the poor.

However, Cancian feels that the cargo system may, in fact, maintain stratification, since the cargo hierarchy has many positions at the bottom and very few at the top. Thus, few males are able to occupy the top positions. He adds that cargos in Zinacantan involve expenditures ranging from 50 to 14,000 pesos in a community where the average man is fortunate to clear 1,000 pesos a year. Thus, poor men can afford only the less expensive cargos, while the rich take the more expensive cargos. He writes, "This is leveling in some sense, but in fact the rich seem to be so rich that they do not lose their relative standing" (p. 292). Thus, the rich are able to maintain their standard of living and gain prestige through the cargo system. Also, prestige afforded by the more expensive cargos gives them an advantage, such as arranging favorable marriages, in community exchange.

The Maya are descendants of Maya Indians who lived in the area prior to the Spanish conquest of Central America. Today the Indians coexist with mestizos living in the region. As you learned in Lesson 14, the word mestizo is derived from the Spanish word for "mixed," but the difference between Indians and mestizos is more cultural than biological. Indians speak a Maya dialect, wear Indian clothes, and take part in the cargo system. Mestizos speak Spanish, wear modern dress, and consider themselves aligned with the nation's elite.

Mestizos don't take part in the cargo system, but they benefit from it. The cargo system reinforces economic differences between Indians and mestizos which keep the Indians subordinate to mestizos. The merchants and shopkeepers who sell supplies for religious festivals are mestizos. Also, the fiestas require large expenditures of cash. Since the Maya are able to grow only enough for their subsistence needs, with very little left over to sell, they have little cash. When they complete their cargo service, they have accumulated prestige, but are destitute and in debt. One way of acquiring cash to pay their debts is to sign on as cheap labor for mestizos.

As the Maya example illustrates, the economic system of a society is far more complex than a balance sheet or bank statement. Cash may not even be the most important commodity exchanged. In the cargo system, goods, services, and prestige are all important considerations. Success in the economic arena may not be determined simply by accumulations of wealth and goods, but is related to the role of each individual in the community.

Frank Cancian says the cargo system helps to integrate the community by coercing members into reinvesting their resources in the community, rather than spending it on non-Indian goods and activities. Individuals are forced to commit themselves to the Maya way of life by participation in the cargo system for which they receive more intangible rewards. Also, the rich are required to invest time and money in community service. Thus, the cargo system represents more than just economic activity; it integrates the economic arena with social and religious traditions.

Study Activities

Vocabulary Check

Check on your understanding of terms by matching those on the left with the definitions on the right. Check your choices with the answer key at the end of the lesson.

1. _D_ cargo
2. _G_ alcalde
3. _E_ milpa
4. _H_ mayordomo
5. _B_ leveling mechanism
6. _J_ stratified system
7. _C_ mestizos

a. encourages accumulation of wealth
b. discourages accumulation of wealth
c. Spanish-speaking people living in the highlands with the Maya
d. derived from the Spanish word for burden
e. "slash-and-burn" corn farming
f. religious leader of the community
g. highest rank in the cargo hierarchy
h. cargo position with the largest number of "openings" each year
i. second rank in civil-religious hierarchy
j. encouraged by scarcity of upper-level positions in the hierarchy

Completion

Choose the best word or phrase from the lists provided to fill the blanks in the paragraphs below.

1. The Maya Indians of the highlands of southern Mexico are agriculturalists, producing _corn_ as their primary crop to meet their needs, but little in the way of a surplus. They practice a _slash & burn_ system of agriculture, in which the fields of an individual family are allowed to return to forest after about five years. The towns used by the Highland Maya for ceremonial occasions are left _vacant_ most of the time.

   slash-and-burn
   vacant
   corn

2. Taking part in the cargo system is called a _burden_, yet most men do so, for this is an important, socially accepted pathway to _status_ and _prestige_ in the community. A young man begins in one of the lower positions in the hierarchy, serving in this position for a full year, and performing mostly menial tasks. Later, the man may advance through the hierarchy, taking more important positions. All of this work might be described as volunteer labor, for the men receive no compensation. Instead, they are required to spend money out of their own assets and frequently go into debt. Through the cargo system, important _civil_ and _religious_ offices are filled without any kind of redistribution system such as taxation.

   prestige
   religious
   status
   civil
   burden

3. An important function of the town is to provide a center for _festival_ organized and carried out by members of the cargo hierarchy, who also bear all costs. The festivals are essentially _religious_ in nature, and the ceremonies have roots both in Roman Catholic and the traditional _Maya_ religions. Taking care of the religious materials, such as statues of the _saints_, is one of the responsibilities of those who have taken on cargo burdens.

Maya
saints
religious
festivals

4. Other residents of the area, mestizos, benefit in several ways from the cargo system, although they do not take part in it and are not part of the Highland Maya subculture. Mestizo merchants sell the wine and other goods necessary for the festival celebrations. They also provide work, at _menial_ wages, for the Maya. Such work is virtually the only way the Maya can obtain sufficient money to pay the _debts_ he has contracted as a result of his _year_ of cargo service.

debts
menial
year

Short-Answer Questions

1. Explain how the cargo system serves as a leveling mechanism for the Highland Maya, but at the same time does not create an egalitarian society.

2. In what ways do the offices and the festivals which are part of the cargo system serve to knit the Maya society together?

Self-Test

(Select the one best answer.)

Objective 1
1. What is the chief product of Highland Maya subsistence activities?
   a. poultry
   b. beans and grains
   c. cattle
   d. corn

Objective 1
2. What level of surplus do the Highland Maya typically produce?
   a. sufficient to cover the costs of social obligations, such as festivals
   b. almost none, chiefly because of the climate
   c. often less than enough for family survival, which makes work in the cities necessary
   d. sizable surpluses are possible in good years with fertile ground

Objective 2
3. Augustin Gomez has achieved the prestige he enjoys in his society because he has
   a. reached the level of mayordomo.
   b. reached the level of alcalde.
   c. accumulated sufficient wealth to discontinue farming.
   d. mestizo ancestors.

Objective 2
4. The cargo holder might best be described as
   a. a volunteer.
   b. a paid civil servant.
   c. part of the priesthood.
   d. an elected official.

Objective 2
5. How do cargo holders receive their positions?
   a. Ranks are based on kinship status.
   b. In effect, they purchase the rank they hold.
   c. They must work their way up through a hierarchy of positions.
   d. Positions are assigned based on consensus of the elders of the community.

Objective 3
6. The estimated expenses of the highest-ranking cargo holder during his term of service totalled
   a. 50 pesos.
   b. 400 pesos.

c. 2,000 pesos.
d. 14,000 pesos.

Objective 3
7. The cargo system tends to affect distribution of wealth because
    a. money tends to be held by the wealthiest farmers.
    b. those who are wealthiest tend to contribute more to the community activities.
    c. those who are cargo holders tend to hold the concentration of wealth.
    d. cargo holders cannot retain any money or economic resources.

Objective 4
8. Which of the following is *not* an effect of the cargo system?
    a. Cargo holders have an opportunity to gain prestige in the community.
    b. Cargo holders are required to commit themselves to their society.
    c. Cargo holders carry out the duties of both civic and religious offices.
    d. Cargo holders generally gain economic advantage from participation.

Objective 4
9. To the Highland Maya, the chief contribution of the festivals is that they
    a. provide a time when all the families join together as a community.
    b. provide a socially accepted means for contact with the mestizo subculture.
    c. are a time for rewarding the cargo holders for their service.
    d. provide a time when the oldest members of the community are honored.

Objective 4
10. "Vacant towns" are
    a. villages that are abandoned due to loss of fertility in the land.
    b. mock villages that have been constructed to be dwellings for ancient Maya gods.
    c. towns that are largely inhabited on special ceremonial occasions.
    d. towns that are avoided because of traditional taboos.

Objective 5
11. In what way are the Highland Maya dependent upon mestizo communities?
    a. Mestizo cities provide most of their food, as well as other goods.
    b. Employment by mestizos is virtually the only way to gain cash.
    c. The mestizo leadership controls the cargo system.
    d. The mestizo perform menial labor for the Maya.

Objective 5

12. The effect of cargo responsibilities upon most participating Maya is
a tendency to
   a. lose prestige.
   b. go into debt.
   c. leave Indian society.
   d. acquire better farm holdings.

Suggested Activities

1. In a brief essay, compare and contrast the cargo system with the potlatch ceremony as leveling mechanisms.

2. In what ways is the cargo system and its obligations similar to those of American civic-service organizations such as Kiwanis and Lions? In what ways is it similar to government-sponsored programs such as Vista and Peace Corps? or the military service?

3. Read and write a brief report on *Economics and Prestige in a Maya Community: The Religious Cargo System in Zinacantan*, by Frank Cancian, Stanford University Press, 1965. This book is a thorough analysis of the cargo system in and around the town of Zinacantan, a Highland Maya community.

4. What would be the impact on the cargo system if the Highland Maya were faced with any of the following problems: increase in wealth, increase in population, or increase in access to Western goods?

Answer Key

Vocabulary Check

1. d   5. b
2. g   6. j
3. e   7. c
4. h

Completion

1. corn, slash-and-burn, vacant

2. burden, status, prestige, civil, religious

3. festivals, religious, Maya, saints

4. menial, debts, year

Short-Answer Questions

1. Explain how the cargo system serves as a leveling mechanism for the Highland Maya but at the same time does not create an egalitarian society. Your answer should include:

   The cargo system tends to prevent individuals from accumulating wealth; those with more money are expected to donate more during cargo service.

   Since prestige and status result from cargo activities, and not from wealth, simply holding wealth is not encouraged.

   The system does not create an egalitarian society in practice. Instead, the society is stratified, and the richer members seem to have enough wealth that cargo obligations do not adversely affect them.

   The rich are better able to afford the more expensive offices in the cargo hierarchy. Thus, they tend to have more prestige, which gives them social advantages. These, in turn, may give them economic advantages.

2. In what ways do the offices and the festivals which are part of the cargo system serve to knit the Maya society together? Your answer should include:

   Highland Maya society may especially need some kind of mechanism to knit it together, because Maya normally live and work in isolated areas, away from each other.

   The festivals, which are managed by the cargo holders, give the larger community a time to be together in celebration.

   The religious celebrations, and especially the statues of saints, may add to the sense of continuity, since the Maya identify the saints with the ancient gods.

   The cargo holders commit themselves to the continuation of the community by their service and their economic contributions.

Self-Test

1. d	5. c	9. a
2. b	6. d	10. c
3. b	7. b	11. b
4. a	8. d	12. b

Political 17 Organization

Overview

Anyone who has ever attended a political convention or—more likely—followed on television the hoopla, impassioned speechmaking, and flinging of charges and countercharges by candidates during an important election campaign might well believe that politics is a peculiarly American cultural phenomenon.

Not so. *All* societies have some form of political organization and leaders or persons of recognized authority who have titles or names that are appropriate to their status in the organization. The types of political organizations developed by societies vary greatly, of course, as do the means of selecting leaders and the privileges or authority accorded these leaders. For example, the process of selecting a "president" of the United States, which includes the color and frenzy of multimillion-dollar television campaigns and national elections, is vastly different from the way in which the !Kung Bushmen of the Kalahari Desert select their "headman," or *kxau*. !Kung bands designate as "headman" one member who has demonstrated leadership and ability to make the "right" decisions but members of the band follow the headman only so long as he continues to display these qualities.

You may doubt it, but for all their differences, there are some basic similarities among political organizations in all societies. First, political systems have leaders who have special names or titles, as noted above. Second, political organizations exist for a common purpose: They provide the mechanism by which societies maintain internal social order, cope with public affairs, and manage relations with external groups, such as other political organizations or other societies. Third, all political systems employ some method of social control, which may be as informal as gossip or as formal as force and rigid codes of law.

Political organizations usually take one of four general forms, which are distinguished by their complexity. These forms are identified as bands, tribes, chiefdoms, or states. As you may suspect, a more complex society gives rise to a more complex form of political organization. Thus, it's not surprising that there is a relationship between a society's patterns of subsistence, stratification, and economics on the one hand, and political systems on the other. After all, you learned at the beginning of this course that cultures are integrated, and that each specific feature of a culture complements and supports many of its other facets. Thus, family organizations, social organizations, economic systems, and political organizations tend to be mutually supportive. You will find it valuable, then, to be alert to these relationships of political systems to other aspects of the cultures in which they function.

In this lesson, you will explore the four kinds of political organizations societies have developed to meet their basic social needs, and in Lesson Eighteen you will learn more about the methods of social control employed by political organizations. One additional thought is suggested for this lesson: While studying the cultural examples presented here, you should be alert to any hints about those qualities of personality and character which society expects of its "politicians," whether they be high officials in a complex governmental system or informal leaders in a village or camp. What traits do these politicians have in common? How do they differ?

Learning Objectives

When you have completed all assignments in this lesson, you should be able to:

1. Recognize that all societies have some form of political organization. (Text page 316; television program.)

2. Describe the basic functions of political organizations. (Text page 316; television program.)

3. Identify the four basic kinds of political systems (bands, tribes, chiefdoms, and states) presented in your text. (Text page 316; television program.)

4. Describe the general features of band organization, including a description of the !Kung as an example. (Text pages 316-318; television program.)

5. Describe the general features of tribal organization and discuss how the following societies have achieved political integration:

   Nuer (kinship-lineage)
   Kipsigis (age-grade)
   Cheyenne (common-interest associations)
   Kapauku ("Big Man")
   (Text pages 318-322.)

6. Describe the general features of a chiefdom, including description of *traditional* Hawaiian society as an example. (Text pages 323-324; television program.)

7. Describe the general features of a state society including a description of the Swazi as an example. (Text pages 324-326; television program.)

8. Identify the similarities and differences between band and tribal political systems. (Text pages 316-322; television program.)

9. Identify the similarities and differences between chiefdom and state political systems. (Text pages 322-326; television program.)

10. Explain the concept of "legitimacy" and its role in maintaining political power. (Text pages 340-342.)

11. Explain how religion may be used to legitimize political power and cite examples. (Text pages 342-343; television program.)

Assignments For This Lesson

Before Viewing the Program

Read the overview and the learning objectives for this lesson. Use the learning objectives to guide your reading, viewing, and thinking.

Read the preview to Chapter 11 in the text, and look over the topic headings in the chapter.

Read Chapter 11, "Political Organization and Social Control," pages 314-326 and 340-345 in the text. The remaining pages in this chapter will be studied in connection with the next lesson.

View Program 17, "Political Organization."

As you view the program, look for:

societies which exemplify the four types of political organization: bands, tribes, chiefdoms, and states.

the democratic nature of the political organization among !Kung bands.

scenes of the Mendi of New Guinea, a flourishing tribal society.

the close relationship between religious beliefs, politics, and social order among Tibetan people supporting their traditional theocratic government in exile in India.

After Viewing the Program

Review the terms used in this lesson. In addition to those terms used in the learning objectives, you should be familiar with centralized and decentralized systems, age-grade organizations, common-interest association organization, and the designations for leaders in various societies described in the text.

Review the reading assignments for this lesson. A thorough second reading is suggested. Include the chapter summary in your study.

Complete each of the study activities and the self-test in this study guide; then check your answers with the answer key at the end of this lesson.

According to your instructor's assignment or your own interests, complete one or more of the suggested activities. You may also be interested in some of the readings suggested at the end of Chapter 11 in your text.

Study Activities

Vocabulary Check

Check on your understanding of terms by matching those on the left with the definitions on the right. Check your choices with the answer key at the end of the lesson.

1. _C_ political organization
2. _J_ band
3. _H_ tribe
4. _D_ age-grade organization
5. _A_ centralized political systems
6. _B_ chiefdom
7. _G_ state
8. _E_ legitimacy

a. found in societies with specialization of labor and surplus of production
b. centralized society in which every member has a unique rank in the hierarchy
c. a system that provides for the coordination and regulation of behavior

d. political organization which cuts across family lines
e. support for the political system based on important values of the society
f. political organization in which a clan is subdivided along family descent lines
g. combines centralized power with delegation of authority
h. any type of society in which the leader does not have real authority for final decisions
i. a group of bands that speak a common language and share a common culture and region
j. a small, autonomous group of related people

Completion

Fill in the blank squares with information from your Haviland text.

Comparison Of Four Political Organizations

POLITICAL ORGANIZATIONS (LISTED FROM SIMPLEST TO MOST COMPLEX)	DEGREE OF CENTRALIZATION	DESCRIPTION OF REGION OCCUPIED (SIZE)	DEGREE OF STRATIFICATION	SUBSISTENCE PATTERN	EXAMPLE OF LEADERSHIP
band	decentralized	single region	egalitarian	hunter gatherer	headman
tribe	decentralized	specific region	little or none	horticulture pastoral	Big Man
chiefdom	centralized	any size	ranked society	horticulture or intensive agriculture	chief
state	centralized	large	social class or caste	market economy	king

222

Short-Answer Questions

1. Briefly describe the functions of these four organizational systems to achieve a political integration of their respective societies: (a) segmented lineage in the Nuer; (b) age-grade organization for the Kipsigis; (c) common interest associations for the Cheyenne; (d) and the "Big Man" for the Kapauku.

2. How do the political organizations of the band and the tribe differ?

3. How do the political organizations of the chiefdom and the state differ?

4. Why is it an oversimplification to state that the legitimacy of a government is based on religious values and beliefs?

Self-Test

(Select the one best answer.)

Objective 1
1. Political organizations are found in
   a. hunting-gathering bands.
   b. tribes organized around descent groups.
   c. societies encompassing many clans.
   d. all of the above groups.

Objective 2
2. The fundamental means by which societies maintain social order and reduce disorder is by
   a. political organization.
   b. military and police power.
   c. coercion.
   d. religious belief.

Objective 3
3. Which of the following is an anthropologist's term for one type of political system?
   a. lineage
   b. clan
   c. tribe
   d. centralized system

Objective 4
4. The band represents
   a. probably the oldest form of political organization.
   b. the simplest centralized type of political organization.

c. the political integration of several clans.

d. delegation of authority.

Objective 4

5. Among the !Kung of the Kalahari, the kxau or headman
   a. owns the land settled by his people.
   b. holds authority by descent.
   c. controls the surplus grown by his group.
   d. loses his position if he leaves the territory.

Objective 5

6. The Kipsigis political system features
   a. a series of common interest groups.
   b. a king and nobility.
   c. age classes that advance through warrior and elder positions.
   d. a chief and several high-ranking persons who have authority over specific territories.

Objective 5

7. The leader of the Kapauku tribe of West New Guinea acquires his status by
   a. oratorical ability.
   b. obligating people to him through loans.
   c. obtaining a second wife.
   d. giving many gifts.

Objective 6

8. Which of the following is characteristic of a chiefdom?
   a. Each male member of the society is basically equal.
   b. Each kinship group is basically equal.
   c. The leaders are considered one class, the rest of the population another class.
   d. Every member of the society has a unique position in the hierarchy.

Objective 6

9. What pattern of political organization developed in traditional Hawaiian society?
   a. chiefdom system with hereditary ranking
   b. chiefdom system with rank determined by wealth and courage
   c. tribal system with hereditary ranking
   d. tribal system with rank determined by wealth and courage

Objective 7

10. Which of the following is *not* characteristic of the state pattern of political organization?
    a. a bureaucracy
    b. social classes

224

c. rigid hierarchy
d. market economy

Objective 7
11. The highest official position in the government of the Swazi is
    a. the council of elders.
    b. the king.
    c. the *libanda,* or council of state.
    d. a hereditary chief.

Objective 8
12. Which of the following is usually found in both band and tribal political organization?
    a. informally selected leaders
    b. area confined to a single, limited region
    c. organized around a single kinship group
    d. an intensive agriculture subsistence pattern

Objective 9
13. Which of the following is characteristic *only* of state systems?
    a. military
    b. warrior class
    c. formal police
    d. unequal ranking of members

Objective 10
14. The concept of legitimacy is an important aspect of
    a. ownership of land.
    b. support for the political system.
    c. coercion.
    d. hereditary ranking.

Objective 11
15. Religious values and beliefs may be employed to support claims of legitimacy in
    a. societies with tribal and chiefdom systems.
    b. societies with band and tribal systems.
    c. societies with centralized political systems.
    d. all types of political systems.

Suggested Activities

1. The Haviland text suggests some of the characteristics of personality and character which are required of leaders in societies that select those leaders informally. What similarities and differences do you see in the traits desired of a leader in band and tribal societies and the traits often desired in a complex political system, such as that of the United States?

2. Review Haviland's definition of political systems. Then relate this to the smallest unit of general government which affects you (such as a city, town, or county, rather than a specialized unit such as a school or sanitation district). Review the activities of the governing body through the minutes, agenda, or other summary of its last three or four meetings, and explain how each of the expressed concerns relates to "social order and disorder."

3. Investigate the conditions "prompting" change from one type of system to another (such as band to tribe to chiefdom to state).

Answer Key

Vocabulary Check

1. c	5. a
2. j	6. b
3. i	7. g
4. d	8. e

Completion

Comparison Of Four Political Organizations

POLITICAL ORGANIZATIONS (LISTED FROM SIMPLEST TO MOST COMPLEX)	DEGREE OF CENTRALIZATION	DESCRIPTION OF REGION OCCUPIED (SIZE)	DEGREE OF STRATIFICATION	SUBSISTENCE PATTERN	EXAMPLE OF LEADERSHIP
band	decentralized	single religion	society of equals (egalitarian)	hunting-gathering	"headman" (!Kung)
tribe	decentralized	a specific region	little or none; varies depending on leadership and subsistence pattern	horticulture or pastoralism	"Big Man" (Kapauku) "Leopard Skin Chief" (Nuer)
chiefdom	centralized	any size	ranked society	horticulture or intensive agriculture; produces a surplus	chief
state	centralized	large enough to hold a heterogeneous society and have a market economy	social classes or castes	market economy; intensive agriculture; produces a surplus	king (Swazi); delegated authority

Short-Answer Questions

1. Briefly describe the functions of these four organizational systems in achieving a political integration of their respective societies: (a) segmented lineage in the Nuer; (b) age-grade organization for the Kipsigis; (c) common interest associations for the Cheyenne; (d) and the "Big Man" for the Kapauku.

   Your answer should include:

   The segmented lineages of the Nuer serve as links with other groups in their own major and maximal lineages, the clans which join lineages, and the tribe. The relationships are better described as alliances which become active only during times of conflict between minimal lineage segments.

   The age-grade system of the Kipsigis groups men into categories according to successive fulfillment of key functions in the society, such as warriors and elders. The elders hold a certain amount of political authority.

   In the Cheyenne society, a young man might have been invited to join one of seven military societies. These societies had a variety of military, ceremonial, and social roles. Identical societies with identical names existed within each band, so that membership cut across band lines and helped to integrate the entire society.

   The "Big Man" of the Kapauku achieves his leadership status through wealth, generosity, and other desirable traits. He is thus "accepted" rather than elected, and may lose his position through, for example, loss of wealth. As "Big Man," however, he is recognized as a negotiator, judge, and leader in a variety of social situations. Hence, he is a "focus" for social integration.

2. How do the political organizations of the band and the tribe differ? Your answer should include:

   Many tribal systems involve significantly larger numbers of people than bands; they typically involve more than one band.

   The band itself is adequate organization for its political system. Decisions are usually made on the basis of a democratic consensus. Tribes often contain organizations of other groups smaller than the tribe, such as age-grade or common interest organizations, and these organizations can serve political functions.

Bands usually recognize the leadership of one individual, such as the !Kung headman, who has no permanent authority. Some tribes also have such leaders without authority, although others, such as the Kipsigis and the Kapauku, seem to exercise authority to make decisions in conflicts.

3. How do the political organizations of the chiefdom and the state differ? Your answer should include:

In a chiefdom, the chief is the greatest and final authority in all political and economic matters. In turn, there are lesser authorities who control major and minor subdivisions of the chiefdom in a kind of chain-of-command structure. In the Hawaiian traditional society, the chief had absolute power over the life and property of his subjects.

The state involves the idea of a permanent government, a "central power," rather than just a single individual. The state also has a formal legal code. Organization is more complex than in the chiefdom; power is delegated for specific functions, such as police and foreign ministries, rather than over territorial subdivisions of the state. Various significant organizations in the Swazi society, for example, include the king's advisors, two councils at the state level, councils at district levels, and homesteads.

4. Why is it an oversimplification to state that the "legitimacy of a government is based on religious values and beliefs"? Your answer should include:

Many governments rely on religious belief to some extent, however limited, in making claim to legitimacy.

However, claim to legitimacy is also based on other important values of the society. Age is an important aspect of legitimacy in cultures such as Dahomey. The expectations of the people also define legitimacy. A government which meets the expectations of its subjects will be relatively more secure than a government that fails to do so. This is a cultural basis.

Self-Test

1. d	9. a
2. a	10. c
3. c	11. b
4. a	12. a
5. d	13. c
6. c	14. b
7. b	15. d
8. d	

Social Control *18*

Overview

Did you know that gossip is a form of social control—and a very effective one at that in some societies, including our own? Gossip is, of course, an expression of public opinion, and public opinion can and does exert a powerful influence upon the behavior of individuals in the society. Ridicule and embarrassment are similarly effective as mechanisms for encouraging conformity in behavior.

You will remember from your study of political organizations in Lesson Seventeen that all societies have political systems and that one important function of such systems is to maintain order and promote conformity to accepted norms and standards of behavior. For this, the society must exert some form of social control. If you've thought about this term at all before, your impressions may be that it usually means "laws, police, and courts," or even "force." In reality, social controls can be as informal as gossip or as formal as rigid laws.

However, in most societies, social controls are, in fact, frequently *not* based on laws or rules, in the sense that an impersonal standard is clearly established and penalties for violation are clearly defined and applied. Social controls are usually present in every society even without stated rules. Even in our own society, controls are quite strong in matters where the rule of law doesn't apply. For an example, do you generally cover your mouth if you cough or yawn when someone else is nearby? Do you eat with silverware, not your hands? Do you wear a dress or suit to church instead of a swimsuit? Do you usually wear colors and designs that match or coordinate? Two socks of the same color? You wouldn't be arrested or sued for doing or not doing any of these things, but when you behave in these ways you're responding to a very real kind of social control.

This lesson discusses methods of social control which range from gossip to warfare. Some of them are nearly universal, while others appear only in more complex societies with centralization of power. Many have a long history.

Learning Objectives

When you have completed all assignments in this lesson, you should be able to:

1. Recognize that one of the basic functions of any political system is to maintain social order. (Text page 326; television program.)

2. Distinguish between internalized and externalized controls as methods of maintaining social order. (Text pages 330-331; television program.)

3. Describe the use of internalized controls by the traditional Wape culture of New Guinea. (Text pages 326-330.)

4. Define positive and negative and formal and informal sanctions as forms of externalized control. (Text pages 331-333; television program.)

5. Identify E. A. Hoebel's definition of law. (Text page 334.)

6. List the three basic functions of law. (Text pages 335-336.)

7. Recognize that one way to understand the nature of "law" and "crime" in non-Western societies is to analyze the ways in which disputes are settled. (Text pages 337-338; television program.)

8. Explain the difference between negotiation, mediation, and adjudication. (Text pages 337-338; television program.)

9. Recognize the use of "trial by ordeal" as an example of adjudication in some traditional societies. Briefly describe the use of ordeal by the Kpelle in Liberia. (Text page 338; television program.)

10. Describe some of the reasons why warfare is not very practical among most hunting-gathering societies. (Text pages 338-339; television program.)

11. Describe some of the reasons why warfare is more prominent among farming and pastoral populations. (Text page 340; television program.)

12. Define "world view" and explain in what sense food-gathering and food-producing populations may have differing world views. (Text page 340; television program.)

Assignments For This Lesson

Before Viewing the Program

Read the overview and the learning objectives for this lesson. Use the learning objectives to guide your reading, viewing, and thinking.

Read the preview to Chapter 11 in the text, and look over the topic headings in the chapter.

Read pages 326-330 in Chapter 11, "Political Organization and Social Control."

View Program 18, "Social Control."

As you view the program, look for:

scenes of Amish society in the United States. Identify the kind of social control illustrated by this subculture.

several examples of various forms of dispute settlements including song duels among the Eskimos, negotiation among the Nuer, mediation among the Nundewalas of India, adjudication among the Barabaig tribe of Tanzania, and trial by ordeal of the Kpelle of Liberia.

scenes of warfare among Masai tribes in Africa and modern technological warfare illustrating the near universality of conflict between peoples.

After Viewing the Program

Review the terms used in this lesson. In addition to the terms used in the learning objectives, you should be familiar with:

the distinction between crime and tort
naturalistic world view
exploitive world view

Review the reading assignment for this lesson. A thorough second reading is suggested. Include the chapter summary in your study.

Complete each of the study activities and the self-test in this study guide; then check your answers with the answer key at the end of this lesson.

According to your instructor's assignment or your own interests, complete one or more of the suggested activities. You may also be interested in some of the readings suggested at the end of Chapter 11 in your text.

Study Activities

Vocabulary Check

Check on your understanding of terms by matching those on the left with the definitions on the right. Check your choices with the answer key at the end of the lesson.

1. __D__ social control
2. __K__ internalized controls
3. __A__ negative sanctions
4. __J__ formal sanctions
5. __B__ law
6. __E__ tort
7. __I__ mediation
8. __F__ adjudication
9. __G__ naturalistic
10. __C__ exploitive

a. form of externalized control that discourages certain behaviors
b. an external sanction that requires the threat or application of physical force and one or more persons having the social privilege of applying force
c. a world view involving a belief that nature will yield rewards only after great effort and labor
d. the methods employed to ensure acceptable behavior by members of a society
e. a wrongful act or injury of an individual
f. requires a third party who does have the power to render decisions
g. a world view often found among hunting-gathering cultures which includes respect for and dependence on nature
h. decisions made voluntarily by the parties involved
i. requires a third party, who does not have power to enforce decisions
j. organized and precise agents of social control
k. exemplified by fear of revenge by ghosts

Completion

Choose the best word or phrase from the lists provided to fill the blanks in the paragraphs on the following page.

1. _Sanctions_ are external social controls developed by a society to encourage desirable behaviors. _positive_ sanctions include everything from specific awards to a simple smile of approval from a neighbor. _Negative_ sanctions involve the threat of something unpleasant if the person does not conform to social _norms_.

positive
norms
sanctions
negative

2. The forms of social control called sanctions may be either formal or informal. Informal sanctions are _spontaneous_ expressions by members of the community. They have a powerful effect, because most people want to be _accepted_ in their community. Formal sanctions are _organized_, quite specific and exact. Both formal and informal sanctions may be either positive or negative.

organized
accepted
spontaneous

3. Many societies do not have formal laws. The Haviland text suggests that a worthwhile approach to understanding the nature of law is to study the way in which _disputes_ are settled in the absence of formal legal systems. Negotiation involves argument and _compromise_ between the parties involved. Mediation brings in a _third_ party, who can assist in settling the problem, but does not have authority to enforce a decision. _Adjudication_ differs from this because the third party is authorized to make a decision to which the parties in the dispute are bound. Not all societies utilize this last method of settling disputes; the "judge" may involve appeal to supernatural forces, such as the employment of trial by ordeal by the Kpelle of Liberia.

compromise
adjudication
disputes
third

4. Law is described as having three primary functions: Law defines the _relationships_ among members of the society and proper behavior under specific circumstances; it grants authority to individuals or organizations to use _coercion_ to enforce the law; and it redefines social relations and ensures social _flexibility_

relationships
flexibility
coercion

Short-Answer Questions

1. Explain why the beliefs and behaviors of the Wape shotgun cult illustrate the power of internalized controls.

2. What are the essential components of Hoebel's definition of law?

3. Contrast the hunting-gathering bands and pastoral-agricultural tribes and chieftains and identify those factors which may contribute to their different attitudes toward warfare.

Self-Test

(Select the one best answer.)

Objective 1
1. One of the most important basic functions of a political system is to
   a. set up a system of laws for its subjects to follow.
   b. maintain social order and prevent disorder.
   c. oppose threats to its territorial sovereignty.
   d. insure that the values and beliefs of the society are passed on to succeeding generations.

Objective 2
2. Which of the following best describes internalized controls?
   a. values and beliefs which the individual subscribes to in his or her own mind
   b. formal methods used by society to insure an acceptable behavior pattern among its members
   c. methods of control which involve rewards or approval
   d. sanctions which are spontaneous

Objective 3
3. The Wape society of New Guinea seeks to avoid or settle quarrels for what reason?
   a. Quarrels are severely punished by community leaders.
   b. They fear that quarrels will lead to warfare.
   c. They believe quarrels adversely affect their supply of game.
   d. Any quarrel brings rapid individual retaliation.

234

Objective 4
4. "Sanction" is best defined as a(n)
   a. externalized control.
   b. formal control.
   c. negative control.
   d. internalized control.

Objective 4
5. A formal sanction is always
   a. spontaneous.
   b. organized.
   c. in the form of punishment or threat.
   d. written in law.

Objective 4
6. Would approval of a marriage arrangement by neighbors be classed as
   (1) a positive, (2) a negative, (3) a formal, or (4) an informal sanction?
   a. both 1 and 3
   b. both 2 and 3
   c. both 2 and 4
   d. both 1 and 4

Objective 5
7. E. A. Hoebel's definition of law requires which one of the following?
   a. a formal process involving a court or judge
   b. the threat or actual use of physical force
   c. a general acceptance of an act as "right" or "wrong"
   d. a written code of behavior covering the legal or illegal act

Objective 6
8. Which of the following is *not* a basic function of law?
   a. defining relationships among members of society
   b. redefining social relations and ensuring social flexibility
   c. protection of land or territory from misappropriation
   d. defining who has authority to enforce the law through coercion

Objective 7
9. Why does the term "crime" have different meanings in state and non-state societies?
   a. In nonstate societies, all offenses are considered to be against individuals.
   b. In most nonstate societies, a careful distinction is made between offenses against individuals and crimes against the social order.
   c. Some nonstate cultures do not make any attempt to maintain social control.
   d. The kinds of punishments applied vary from one society to another.

Objective 8

10. The Nuer bride price dispute shown in the television program is an example of
    a. mediation.
    b. negotiation.
    c. trial by ordeal.
    d. adjudication.

Objective 9

11. What assumption is basic to the concept of "trial by ordeal"?
    a. The stronger person deserves the support of the community.
    b. Fear of punishment will prevent most offenses.
    c. Supernatural forces will protect the innocent and punish the guilty.
    d. A guilty person will be afraid to undergo any kind of test.

Objectives 10 and 11

12. Which of these differences between hunter-gatherers and agricultural or pastoral peoples may account for different attitudes of these groups toward warfare?
    a. size of individual families
    b. the precision with which territories are defined
    c. manner in which children are nurtured
    d. quality of food consumed by the various societies

Objective 12

13. The world view of farming and pastoral societies tends to be
    a. naturalistic.
    b. legalistic.
    c. cooperative.
    d. exploitive.

Objective 12

14. A naturalistic world view is best summed up as a
    a. tendency to live in close harmony with nature.
    b. tendency to extract what is needed from the environment as one's "right."
    c. tendency to desire combat with one's neighbors.
    d. belief that all living things are controlled by spirits.

Suggested Activities

1. For further reading and the basis for a written report, you may be interested in one of the following books. They deal with topics covered in Lessons Seventeen and Eighteen.

    Marvin Harris, *Cannibals and Kings,* New York: Random House, 1977 (ecological consideration of warfare and state development of control over resources and population).

Hilda Kuper, *The Swazi: A South African Kingdom,* New York: Holt, Rinehart and Winston, 1963 (an ethnographic study of a nation with a state system of political organization).

E. A. Hoebel, *The Cheyennes: Indians of the Great Plains,* 2nd edition, New York: Holt, Rinehart and Winston, 1978 (a classic ethnographic study of a society with a tribal system of political organization).

Eugene V. Walter, *Terror and Resistance: A Study of Political Violence,* London: Oxford University Press, 1972 (an intensive study of internal conflict and efforts to control it).

2. For one day, try to keep track of all the behaviors you engage in which result from strictly informal sanctions. Refer again to suggestions made in the overview for this lesson and the reading assignment in the Haviland text.

3. Discuss the implications of Hoebel's definition of law in relation to organizations other than government which establish written rules or "laws," whether it be an institution such as a bank or a "social" organization such as the Elks. Do the constitution and bylaws of such entities qualify as "law," according to Haviland's definition?

Answer Key

Vocabulary Check

1. d	5. b	8. f
2. k	6. e	9. g
3. a	7. i	10. c
4. j		

Completion

1. sanctions, positive, negative, norms

2. spontaneous, accepted, organized

3. disputes, compromise, third, adjudication

4. relationships, coercion, flexibility

Short-Answer Questions

1. Explain why the beliefs and behaviors of the Wape shotgun cult illustrate the power of internalized controls. Your answer should include:

   The Wape believe that their gunman's lack of success is due to intervention of ancestral ghosts, who can adversely affect the supply of game and the gunman's aim. These ghosts will act, they believe, if their specific (living) descendants have a quarrel with the gunman.

This belief that a quarrel or resentment leads to poor success in hunting serves to minimize quarrels in the community.

This is a deeply ingrained belief shared by the Wape, and it strongly influences their behavior, both encouraging the avoidance of quarrels and the settling of differences when they occur. This is a good example of internalized control.

2. What are the essential components of Hoebel's definition of law? Your answer should include:

Hoebel sought to make a definition of law that would apply to the widest possible range of human societies. There are societies which have laws that do not use a system of courts to enforce them, and there are those that do have such enforcement systems.

Hoebel defined a law as, in effect, a "legal social norm."

The definition states that law is a legal social norm regularly enforced by the threat or application of physical force; this force can be applied by an individual or group that has the recognized privilege of performing this function.

3. Contrast the hunting-gathering bands and pastoral-agricultural tribes and chieftains and identify those factors which may contribute to their different attitudes toward warfare. Your answer should include:

In general, hunting-gathering societies do not have centralized political systems. Their territories are not well defined, bands may range over wide, vaguely defined areas, and members may move individually from one band to another. Marriage patterns increase the likelihood that kinfolk may live in nearby bands, thereby reducing possibilities for conflict. Populations in hunting-gathering societies tend to remain relatively small.

The world view of hunting-gathering societies frequently is naturalistic; these societies view themselves as a part of nature, working in cooperation with nature.

Farming and pastoral societies with tribal and chiefdom forms of organization are more likely to develop centralized government. Often, individual or family ownership of property is common. Their territories are not flexible, and expansion may be limited by the presence of neighboring territories. Agricultural production may permit growth in population, which leads to a need for more land and conflict with neighbors over land and resources.

The world view of food-producing societies may be more exploitive: an attitude that one must take from nature, and that nature exists to be used.

On the one hand, the pressures which may develop in farming-pastoral societies may account for the tendency of such societies to engage in wars. On the other hand, the world view typical of such societies lends itself to taking what is needed or wanted, rather than find ways to live in harmonious balance with the environment.

Self-Test

1. b	6. d	11. c
2. a	7. b	12. b
3. c	8. c	13. d
4. a	9. a	14. a
5. b	10. b	

Religion And Magic 19

Overview

In December 1968, Apollo VIII made man's first journey to the moon. Apollo VIII did not land on the moon's surface, but a television broadcast was beamed back to earth as the craft orbited the moon. During the broadcast, the three astronauts aboard Apollo VIII took turns reading the Creation myth from the Book of Genesis. It was a moment that joined one of America's most visionary technical achievements with religious traditions originating many thousands of years ago. To many people in our modern society, this combination of science and religion was logical and appropriate. To others it was startling and thought-provoking, because our society, like most modern industrialized societies, has separated religious activities from everyday life.

In both modern and traditional cultures, religion seeks to deal with ultimate questions of human purpose and meaning. As Haviland points out in your text, religion embodies many "truths" about humanity, its cultures, and its social practices. Religion meets important needs for both individuals and society. Just how important these needs are is dramatically illustrated by the fact that every society known to have existed has engaged in some form of religious activity. However, among cultures around the world there is enormous diversity in religious practices and beliefs and in the functions these religions serve.

One of the major questions you will explore in this lesson deals with the many important social and psychological functions religion serves. It's important to keep in mind, however, that neither this course nor the field of anthropology can draw conclusions regarding the existence of supernatural forces. Nor does anthropology attempt to judge whether or not metaphysical "truths" are indeed true.

Why study religion, then? The answer is that, as noted earlier, every culture practices some form of religion because it serves needs critical to the culture. Thus, religious practices can be seen as another form of adaptive behavior. And anthropology is, of course, interested in *all* human behavior.

In this lesson you will also examine the meaning and practice of magic and recognize the similarities and differences between magic and religion. As you read the text chapter and view the television program, see if you can distinguish clearly between religion and magic. Where do they overlap? In what ways are they different?

Learning Objectives

When you have completed all assignments in this lesson, you should be able to:

1. Define religion from the viewpoint of anthropologists. (Text pages 349-351; television program.)

2. Recognize that some form of religion is found in all human cultures. (Text pages 351-353; television program.)

3. Describe at least five psychological and social functions of religion. (Text pages 349, 371-372, 376; television program.)

4. Explain the difference between "gods and goddesses" and "ancestral spirits." (Text pages 353-354.)

5. Explain the difference between animism and animatism. (Text pages 354-355; television program.)

6. Define and indicate the importance of *mana*. (Text pages 355-356.)

7. Define and describe the differences between priests and priestesses and shamans. (Text pages 356-360; television program.)

8. Discuss the factors which contribute to the power held by shamans in the Ona culture. (Text pages 360-361, 364.)

9. Identify two general purposes of religious rituals. (Text page 364; television program.)

10. Define rite of passage and briefly describe the male initiation rites of Australian aborigines as an example. (Text page 364-365.)

11. Define rite of intensification and describe at least two kinds of intensification rites. (Text pages 365-367.)

12. Define magic and identify the relationship between religion and magic from the point of view of anthropology. (Text pages 367-368; television program.)

13. Define witchcraft; describe the psychological functions of witchcraft among the Navajo and the social function of witchcraft among the Ndembu. (Text pages 368-371.)

14. Define divination. (Text page 370-371; television program.)

15. Define and cite examples of revitalization movements. (Text pages 373-375; television program.)

Assignments For This Lesson

Before Viewing the Program

Read the overview and the learning objectives for this lesson.

Use the learning objectives to guide your reading, viewing, and thinking.

Read the preview to Chapter 12 in the text and look over the topic headings in the chapter.

Read Chapter 12, "Religion and Magic."

View Program 19, "Religion and Magic."

As you view the program, look for:

an explanation of American Indian belief in the spirits of nature.

Maya religion today, a mixture of Roman Catholic and traditional Maya. In particular, take note of the role of the shaman and the employment of magic.

the purposes of the *Eka Dasa Rudra* ceremony of the Balinese people, and the extent of participation in these rites.

the contrast in outcomes of two revitalization movements: Jonestown and Mormonism.

After Viewing the Program

Review the terms used in this lesson. In particular, check your understanding of these:

religion   priest and priestess
ritual   shaman
supernatural   rite of passage
gods and goddesses   rite of intensification
ancestral spirits   magic
nature spirits   witchcraft
animism   revitalization movements
animatism   divination

Review the reading assignments for this lesson. A thorough second reading is suggested. Include the chapter summary in your study.

Complete each of the study activities and the self-test in this study guide; then check your answers with the answer key at the end of this lesson.

According to your instructor's assignment or your own interests, complete one or more of the suggested activities. You may also be interested in some of the readings suggested at the end of Chapter 12 in your text.

Study Activities

Vocabulary Check

Check on your understanding of terms by matching those on the left with the definitions on the right. Check your choices with the answer key at the end of the lesson.

1. _D_ religion
2. _G_ magic
3. _M_ ritual
4. _C_ pantheon
5. _J_ ancestral spirits
6. _A_ animism
7. _H_ shaman
8. _E_ Bali
9. _B_ rite of passage
10. _N_ funeral rites
11. _K_ witchcraft

a. a belief in nature spirits or impersonal spiritual powers
b. rituals marking important stages in the life of an individual
c. the group of rather remote supernatural beings in which a particular society believes
d. an approach to influencing or controlling the powers of supernatural beings or forces
e. dwellers in Central America who have combined animism with Roman Catholicism
f. an especially remote being, viewed as ultimate creator of the world

g. compelling supernatural powers to act in certain ways through the exercise of precise rituals and formulas

h. one who develops special religious powers through his or her own initiative

i. religious specialist usually found in more complex societies

j. reflect a belief that people are formed by both physical and nonphysical elements

k. actions undertaken to cause harm

l. island in Indonesia

m. "religion in action"; the means through which an individual relates to the sacred

n. one of the rites of intensification

Completion

Choose the best word or phrase from the lists provided to fill the blanks in the paragraphs below.

1. From an anthropological view, religion is an attempt to deal with serious problems by calling on _supernatural_ beings and powers, especially in those areas where technology or social organizations cannot solve such problems. There is much variation in religious practices and beliefs among societies, but some form of religion is found in _all_ known cultures. In traditional societies whose members tend to see themselves as part of nature, religious activity is likely to be a part of _daily life_; while in modern industrial societies, such activity tends to be limited to _special occasions_. In societies that do not have occupational specialization, the religious practitioners are usually _shamans_. In contrast, those societies which

special occasions
daily life
all
priest and priestess
supernatural
shamans

244

have developed specializations usually have religious specialists formally inducted into the offices of *priests & priestesses*.

2. Rituals are described as "religion in *action*," religious activities which mark important events. One type of ceremony, illustrated by the Australian aborigine initiation into manhood, is called a "rite of *passage*." Such rites deal with crucial times in the life of individuals, and usually involve three stages, *separation*, *transition*, and *incorporation*. Other rites, such as the Eka Dasa Rudra of Bali, are called "rites of *intensific*," and are practical at times of crisis for the society as a whole.

passage
transition
action
intensification
separation
incorporation

3. Several factors seem to contribute to the strength of a society's belief in supernatural beings and powers. One important factor in maintaining belief is the "manifestation of *power*," by which is meant that people may see success or failure resulting not so much from their own efforts and skills as from the supernatural influences that aided or hindered them. Still another factor which maintains belief in the supernatural is that supernatural beings tend to have *attributes* that are familiar to the believers. A third is the role of *mythology*, the stories which rationalize religious beliefs and practices. Belief in the supernatural does not necessarily decline as science

mythology
attributes
grown
power

advances. Both "mainline" and "fundamentalist" religions attract new believers in Western societies, and the number of newspapers carrying astrology columns has _grown_ over the past thirty years.

4. Revitalization movements might be defined as an attempt to _reform_ a society through a new religious movement. Many of these movements, such as the Jonestown cult in Guyana, are so removed from reality that they fail. Other movements meet such basic social needs that they survive and flourish. An example is _Mormonism_ a movement which began in the 1840s in New England, spread west, and has experienced continuous growth ever since.

Mormonism
reform

5. Sir James George Frazier drew a contrast between religion, which he defined as "propitiation or conciliation" of supernatural powers, and magic, which he saw as an attempt to manipulate supposed _natural_ laws. Magic involves attempts to _control_ supernatural forces by employing specified _formulas_. Witchcraft and sorcery involve the capability and skills to do _harm_ through supernatural means. Witchcraft provides a number of functions to both individual and group, as examples of the Navajo and Ndembu illustrate. Belief in witchcraft may provide

formulas
relief
control (or compel)
natural
harm

relief _____ from tensions;
it may also provide the society
with a convenient rationale for
maintaining its present organizational structure.

Short-Answer Questions

1. How does religion differ from magic, according to anthropologists?

2. Describe the categories of supernatural beings and powers that are
   discussed in text Chapter 12 and the television program for this lesson.

3. Summarize the significant social and psychological functions of religion.

Self-Test

(Select the one best answer.)

Objective 1
1. According to anthropological definition, religion involves
   a. the use of known technology to solve problems.
   b. the influence of supernatural forces to solve problems.
   c. employment of specific formulas to compel desired actions.
   d. any kind of gathering that promotes social solidarity.

Objective 2
2. Which of these most accurately contrasts a hunting-gathering society
   with specialized Western society?
   a. Western societies are more likely to include religious activity in their
      daily routine.
   b. Hunting-gathering societies are more likely to include little or no
      religious activities.
   c. Western societies are more likely to experience decreasing
      observance of religious activities.
   d. Hunting-gathering societies are more likely to include religious
      activity in their daily routine.

Objective 3
3. According to the Haviland text, which of the following is not a
   psychological function of religion?
   a. validating the political and social organization of a culture
   b. reducing anxiety by explaining the unknown
   c. promise of supernatural aid
   d. transferring responsibility for decision making from the individual to
      the supernatural

Objective 3

4. According to the Haviland text, which of the following is not a *social* function of religion?
   a. sets precedents for acceptable behavior
   b. sanctions a certain range of conduct
   c. aids in maintaining social solidarity
   d. provides an outlet for unstable personalities

Objective 4

5. Supernatural beings, often with human-like qualities, who seem rather remote, yet control the universe and take an interest in human affairs, are called
   a. gods and goddesses.
   b. ancestral spirits.
   c. nature spirits.
   d. mana.

Objective 5

6. Animism refers to belief in
   a. gods with animal shapes.
   b. gods and goddesses.
   c. spirits identified with nature.
   d. impersonal supernatural forces.

Objectives 5 and 6

7. Mana is a name given to _____ and is an example of _____.
   a. an impersonal supernatural force; animatism
   b. pantheons; animism
   c. nature spirits; animism
   d. ancestral spirits; animatism

Objective 7

8. A _____ undergoes formal initiation into a religious role and holds a socially recognized office.
   a. witch
   b. shaman
   c. priest or priestess
   d. sorcerer

Objectives 7 and 8

9. Which of the following does *not* contribute to the prestige of the shaman in the Ona culture?
   a. skills at sleight-of-hand tricks
   b. traditions learned from predecessors in the office
   c. providing assurance of protection from the supernatural
   d. serving as a focus of religious attention for the group

248

Objective 9

10. Which of the statements listed in this paragraph best describe the general function of religious rituals? Religious rituals function generally as (1) a means of strengthening the social bond, (2) a reaffirmation of the status of the priest or shaman, (3) support at times of individual or group crisis, (4) a way of employing formulas to control supernatural forces.
    a. All are correct.
    b. Statements 1 and 4 are correct.
    c. Statements 3 and 4 are correct.
    d. Statements 1 and 3 are correct.

Objective 10

11. A ceremony marking a crucial point in the life of an individual is called a rite of
    a. passage.
    b. intensification.
    c. transition.
    d. incorporation.

Objective 10

12. Among the Australian aborigines, one stage of a young man's initiation into adult life could be termed "transition." What is the principal activity or event that takes place during this stage?
    a. removal of the young man from his mother
    b. introduction of a new adult into society
    c. oral instruction in tribal traditions
    d. a physical operation

Objective 11

13. Funeral rites are classified as rites of
    a. intensification.
    b. incorporation.
    c. reversal.
    d. separation.

Objective 11

14. The Eka Dasa Rudra of the Balinese is best described as which kind of rite?
    a. funeral rite
    b. seasonal rite
    c. rite of passage
    d. rite of incorporation

Objective 12

15. What is magic, from the viewpoint of anthropology?
    a. belief in any supernatural power or force
    b. belief in any ancestral or nature spirit

c. use of supernatural means to cause harm or injury

d. use of specific formulas to control or compel supernatural forces

Objective 13

16. Haviland suggests that the Navajo belief in witchcraft serves the psychological function of providing
    a. a means for the ordinary person to gain control over difficult problems.
    b. an acceptable outlet for feelings of hostility that are otherwise suppressed.
    c. a means for making the preferred personal and social decisions.
    d. status for the witch and a convenient means of expression for unstable personalities.

Objective 14

17. Divination is defined as
    a. determination of the cause of an event by magical means.
    b. the study of spirits associated with objects and living things.
    c. the entire group of gods and goddesses recognized by a particular society.
    d. the cause of harm, such as illness, through the use of magical formulas.

Objective 15

18. According to anthropologist Anthony Wallace, all religions began as
    a. a type of animism.
    b. pantheons.
    c. attempts to apply magical formulas.
    d. revitalization movements.

Suggested Activities

1. Read accounts of some of the contemporary religious movements, such as the Unification Church, the cult of the Reverend Jim Jones, Scientology, EST, and UFO groups. In reporting on your reading, identify some needs of individuals and groups which are met by such movements.

2. Many cultures have complex mythologies regarding the creation of the universe and the relationship between humans and the supernatural. Choose a culture and study its mythology, and describe how that mythology relates to and reinforces the religious beliefs of that culture.

3. Attend a religious service as if you were an anthropologist studying a culture about which you have little previous knowledge. Write a summary of what you see and hear. Include the details of the ceremony

itself, the structure and layout of the place of worship, visible symbols and artifacts employed in the service, and descriptions of worshipers, especially those performing rituals or leading the service.

Answer Key

Vocabulary Check

1. d	7. h
2. g	8. l
3. m	9. b
4. c	10. n
5. j	11. k
6. a	

Completion

1. supernatural, all, daily life, special occasions, shamans, priest and priestess

2. action, passage, separation, transition, incorporation, intensification

3. power, attributes, mythology, grown

4. reform, Mormonism

5. natural, control (or compel), formulas, harm, relief

Short-Answer Questions

1. How does religion differ from magic, according to anthropologists? Your answer should include:

   The classical definition of magic is the use of specified formulas for the purpose of *compelling* supernatural powers to act in specified ways. In contrast, religious rituals are done with the goal of *entreating* supernatural powers to act in specific ways.

   Sir James Mazer further defined magic, in contrast to religion, as an attempt to manipulate certain laws of nature. From this perspective, magic beliefs and practices are a kind of pseudoscience.

2. Describe the categories of supernatural beings and powers that are discussed in the text and television program. Your answer should include:

Gods and goddesses—rather remote beings, usually with many familiar (human) characteristics, who are believed to take interest in and influence human affairs. They are believed to have the power to control the universe.

Ancestral spirits—believed to be the still-living vital spirits of those who have died physically. Frequently, such spirits are believed to retain an interest in society and most of the personality and character traits of living humans.

Nature spirits (animism)—those spirits associated with animals, plants, or inanimate objects such as mountains and springs. They are usually believed to be involved in daily affairs and may have any of a wide range of attitudes toward human activities.

Impersonal spiritual power (animatism)—such as *mana* of the Melanesians, or the Iroquois *orenda*. Though not associated with a personality, like gods or spirits, animatism is responsible for good fortune, luck, success, or failure.

3. Summarize the significant social and psychological functions of religion. Your answer should include:

Social functions: Religion sanctions a wide range of conduct by prescribing "right" and "wrong." It sets precedents for acceptable behavior. It aids in maintaining social solidarity through the sharing of common beliefs and rituals. It serves education, particularly in transmitting oral traditions.

Psychological functions: Religion reduces anxiety by explaining the unknown. It promises supernatural aid. It transfers the burden and responsibility for certain decisions from the individual to the supernatural.

Self-Test

1. b	7. a	13. a
2. d	8. c	14. b
3. a	9. b	15. d
4. d	10. d	16. b
5. a	11. a	17. a
6. c	12. c	18. d

The Asmat Of New Guinea: 20
A Case Study in Religion and Magic

Overview

Where do we—and everything else—come from? What binds and holds us together in groups? What are our responsibilities as members of our societies and which of these responsibilities are most vital? Finally, what happens after we die?

As children, we ask questions like these time and again, but answers don't usually come that easily; we generally learn the answers we seek as we grow up, learning the values and beliefs of the cultures and subcultures to which we belong. Human societies attempt to answer many such questions through religious beliefs and practices, and some also turn to the practice of magic. As you will remember from Lesson Nineteen, in all cultures, religion is used to meet many social and psychological needs.

In this lesson, you will see how religion and the practice of magic can become a very effective survival mechanism for a culture which believes itself to be surrounded by danger and death. You will take a detailed look at the religious beliefs and customs of the Asmat, a society which, until recently, has been isolated from the influence of other cultures. The Asmat's strange forest-mudflat environment and subsistence pattern have had strong influence on the development of their religious and magic practices. The Asmat perceive their world as being hostile, made dangerous by nature, physical enemies, and ancestral spirits. Their religious beliefs respond to the hostility which they perceive in nature and in other humans. And their perception of nature includes much more than meets the eye.

Be prepared for some surprises at your first introduction to the Asmat. For example, violence against an enemy is a part of a religious rite, as well as a form of magic; trees and plants are powerful in their own right; and the dead, though honored, remain as spirits that cause problems for the living. But as strange as the Asmat religious beliefs and practices may seem at first, you will come to see how consistent and functional these beliefs and practices are within the Asmat culture.

Learning Objectives

When you have completed all assignments in this lesson, you should be able to:

1. Describe how the Asmat beliefs in ancestral spirits and nature spirits are a form of belief in supernatural beings and powers. (Text pages 353-356; television program; Background Notes.)

2. Explain the relationship between revenge killing, ancestral spirits, and ancestor poles. (Television program.)

3. Describe the Asmat myth of creation and its justification of revenge killings. (Text page 356; television program.)

4. Cite two examples of the Asmat use of magic. (Text pages 367-368; television program; Background Notes.)

5. Describe the significance of trees, especially the sago palm, to the Asmat. (Television program; Background Notes.)

6. Describe the carver's role and authority in Asmat society. (Television program; Background Notes.)

7. Describe some of the religious symbols seen in Asmat society and explain their significance and function. (Television program; Background Notes.)

Assignments For This Lesson

Before Viewing the Program

Read the overview and the learning objectives for this lesson. Use the learning objectives to guide your reading, viewing, and thinking.

Review Chapter 12, "Religion and Magic," in the text.

254

View Program 20, "The Asmat of New Guinea: A Case Study in Religion and Magic."

As you view the program, look for:

the brief descriptions of creation myths concerning *Neso-ipitj*, "the man of the wound"; and *Fumerew-ipitj*, "the carver of wood."

the *Bis* ceremony, its elaborate preparations, and the religious and magical beliefs which underlie it.

the practical and symbolic importance of trees, particularly the sago palm and the mangrove tree.

the Asmat beliefs which give special meaning to the ancestor poles, dancing, coconuts, and the praying mantis.

After Viewing the Program

Read the background notes for this lesson.

Review the terms used in this lesson. In addition to the Asmat names mentioned in the television program, you should be familiar with these:

shaman	ritual
magic	myth
animism	

Review the reading assignments for this lesson. A thorough second reading of the background notes is suggested.

Complete each of the study activities and the self-test in this study guide; then check your answers with the answer key at the end of this lesson.

According to your instructor's assignment or your own interests, complete one or more of the suggested activities.

Background Notes

The Hostile World of the Asmat

The Asmat live in a world dominated by the ebb and flow of the tides and by a tropical rain forest. The territory inhabited by the Asmat is located in the western half of New Guinea in an area now controlled by Indonesia. It is a wide mud flat which is crisscrossed by many rivers and is actually divided into two distinct environmental zones. Near the ocean, at high tide, the rivers can become very broad and the area covered with water. At low tide, the rivers may dry out completely, but further inland the land is a swampy forest. The Asmat, who are headhunters by tradition, perceive their unusual environment as a hostile one, made even more hostile by the threat of attack from neighboring villages.

There are two general subsistence areas for the two environmental zones. Saltwater swamps near the ocean are rich in marine protein, while upstream, in the fresh water swamps, grow the sago palms which the Asmat need for other food and materials. According to anthropologist David Eyde, the fierce warfare associated with headhunting and cannibalism, which is characteristic of traditional Asmat society, is related to the way resources are distributed in the two zones. People living upstream needed access to the animal protein in the form of marine resources near the ocean, and people near the ocean needed the starches and carbohydrates of the sago palm which grew upstream.

Many Asmat, who are probably closely related to the aborigines of Australia, are quite blond when young and have a variety of skin tones. They live in wooden houses built on low piles in villages of about 400 people. The dwelling houses are made up of thatched sections, each with its own doorway and fireplace or hearth. Each doorway usually corresponds to a family grouping of husband, wife, and children. The Asmat travel from place to place by dugout canoes that are tied in front of the houses when not in use. When walking through the forest, the people use footpaths of fallen trees and loose branches to keep from sinking into the mud. Each village considers the surrounding forest its own, although territorial limits really are determined by the ability of each village to assert control over its territory against the claims of a neighboring village.

The sago palm is the most important item in the Asmat diet. It is gathered in expeditions away from the village, when people stay in temporary shelters. The tree is chopped open and the pith is chopped up. Traditionally, women chop up the pith while men stand guard by forming a circle around them. The pith is rinsed with water and the sago starch settles to the bottom of the hollowed-out trunk. The congealed starch is cut into sections and roasted before eating. For ritual feasts, an especially fine sago tree is dressed in a skirt of sago leaves. Then it is chopped down and left to lie so the capricorn beetle will lay eggs in it. The larvae of the capricorn beetle are a great delicacy that is a basis for ritual feasting.

Fish or shrimp are caught by the women who use small hand nets or, in groups, stretch nets across the rivers. The men sometimes kill a wild pig with their bows and arrows. The Asmat grow a few crops around their houses, including coconut and sago palms, breadfruit (a tropical fruit that looks and tastes like bread when baked), and yams. But they depend mainly on hunting and gathering.

256

The Asmat rely on wood for building houses and canoes, making weapons, and as fuel for fire. Since there is no stone in the area, the Asmat trade for stone axes. Since the introduction of metal tools, stone axes are now used primarily for ritual purposes. The Asmat do not use pottery for cooking but roast their food over an open fire.

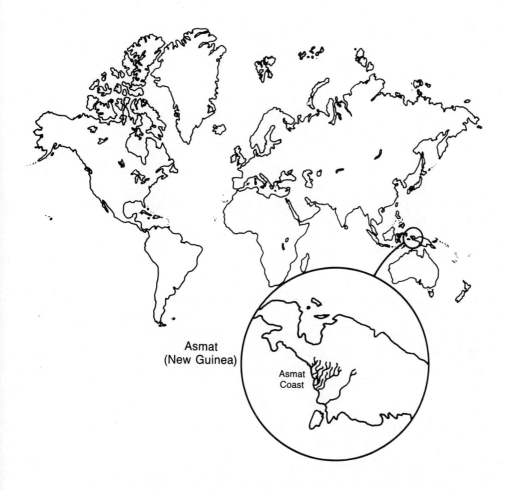

Figure 20.1 The Asmat of western New Guinea live in a hostile world, a wide mudflat dominated by the tides and a tropical rain forest.

Unmarried men live in men's houses, large rectangular houses built on pilings about six yards high. The houses are built facing the rivers and serve as guard houses in case of attack. Since the Asmat travel primarily by boat, attacks are most likely to come by way of the rivers. Each men's house has an upstream and a downstream half, marked by the central hearth. A men's house contains a number of other hearths, each belonging to a patrilineal family group. Thus, membership in the men's house is determined patrilineally. This hearth group is also related to the maintenance of cutting rights, or family "plots," in the sago forest. Family plots are, in turn, divided among individual members of the group. Each individual knows the plants in his area and gives a name to each young sago palm as he finds it. Paths through the forest are known by the name of the owner.

Each hearth consists of a rectangular mud slab baked by the fire, with a post at each corner. A drying rack is fastened between the posts. One post is associated with an ancestor figure. It may be carved in the form of a human figure and be given that ancestor's name.

In front of the men's house is a space cleared of vegetation where the men carve their canoes, hold dances, and bury their dead. The men's house is a ceremonial center and women never enter it except on important ceremonial occasions.

The men's house is also a kind of community center, serving as a focus for patrilineal groups, and a training center for young men, where they learn Asmat customs. They are taught to drum, to dance, and to sing and they learn which sacred songs go with particular ceremonial feasts. Young men are initiated into headhunting and cannibalism customs in the men's house and learn about the distribution of power, both within the village and in relation to neighboring villages. Leadership among the Asmat is not hereditary, but is related to superiority in warfare and economic life.

In the men's house, the young men listen to legends about early heroes, like those described in the television program. Through interaction with lineage leaders and village elders in the men's house, adolescent males learn what will be expected of them as fully participating adults.

The Significance of Woodcarving

The Asmat are skilled woodcarvers, and woodcarving is associated with important ceremonial occasions. Woodcarving is usually done by specialists, who learn by observing and helping established woodcarvers. Selection of the young men to be trained as woodcarvers appears to be based on both skill and desire to learn, rather than on descent.

The woodcarver is not released from regular subsistence duties, except when he has been commissioned to do a carving for a major ceremonial event. His employer then takes over his subsistence duties, such as pounding sago, hunting, or fishing. The carver may also receive extra delicacies from the ceremonial feast, but he receives no other compensation for this work. The woodcarving becomes the property of the man who commissioned it. However, a respected woodcarver shares the status of a successful headhunter.

Ancestral poles are important objects of the woodcarver's art. These poles are very tall, with one human figure carved on top of another. The bottoms of the poles usually end in boats. All of them have a large, open-work, pennant-shaped projection at the top. The Asmat also carve the prows of their canoes, paddles, spears, shields, and a wide variety of human figures.

Headhunting As Religious Ritual

Until headhunting was outlawed by the Dutch colonial government, almost all major rituals or public ceremonies were associated with headhunting raids. The initiation of a young male into adulthood was marked by the preparation of a newly taken human head. During the initiation rite, the young man was smeared with the burnt hair and blood of the victim and given the dead man's name. This established a kin tie between the initiate and relatives of the dead man. When he later met these relatives, they called him by the name of their dead kin, gave him presents, and protected him during his stay in their village. The Reverend Gerard A. Zegwaard, who lived among the Asmat for some time, writes, "It is strictly forbidden to kill people from other villages who, because of their ritual names, are related to one's village" ("Headhunting Practices of the Asmat of Netherlands New Guinea." *American Anthropologist.* 1959, Vol. 61:1027.)

An object of most Asmat rituals, including headhunting, was to drive away the spirits of the dead, especially the decapitated dead. On the one hand, the deceased was replaced by assigning his name either to someone else or to an object. Zegwaard writes, "The names of these spirits are passed on to other persons who will take over their duties and functions, and thus it is made quite clear to them that they are no longer needed" (p. 1029). New canoes, houses, spears, paddles, and other objects are named after the dead.

But the spirits are also driven away, by rituals and ceremonies such as those shown in the television program. Spirits are allowed to remain in the village for only a limited time. When faced with a new, frightening, or potentially dangerous situation, the Asmat cope by boasting about their exploits. So, in order to drive away the spirits of the dead, the Asmat boast about the deeds of the living headhunters.

Headhunting is related to safeguarding the territory and therefore the food supply, according to Zegwaard. Since the Asmat do not cultivate extensively, they are entirely dependent on the forest resources surrounding the village and their territorial rights over it. Zegwaard writes, ". . . according to the origin myths, the prime function of the ancestors is the protection of the tribe's economic prerogatives . . . they . . . emphasize the fact that the ancestor selected a definite territory for himself and his progeny" (p. 1032). For the Asmat, headhunting is consistent with their "charter" handed down in the legends of great heroes. Headhunting is also a means by which young men gain status and open their way to becoming respected elders.

As with other religious systems, Asmat religion frames a coherent explanation for their experience of the world. To the Asmat, death is always very near in the form of ancestor spirits and headhunting. The ancestor spirits must be driven away by threats and intimidation. If a man is to survive the onslaught of ancestors and headhunting, he must constantly show that he is very fierce. When the Asmat man dies and rejoins his ancestors, they will demand to know how he has died. He will respond with stories about men he has killed and heads he has taken in battle. He will show them his scars and tell them how he acquired each one. His status in the afterworld will be determined by how well he conveys a sense of his own ferocity and valor. For the Asmat, life with the ancestors, as with life on earth, demands courage. Their religious and magic practices promote such courage as well as provide protection from the spririts.

Study Activities

Vocabulary Check

Check on your understanding of terms by matching those on the left with the definitions on the right. Check your choices with the answer key at the end of the lesson.

1. __E__ Neso-ipitj
2. __I__ Fumerew-ipitj
3. __K__ Bis
4. __H__ sago
5. __C__ mantis
6. __G__ magic
7. __D__ Asmat
8. __F__ animism
9. __A__ ancestral spirits

a. these have supernatural powers for the Asmat
b. beliefs and patterns of behavior by which people try to control the area of the universe that is beyond control
c. symbol for the life force of plants and the power which comes from ritual headhunting
d. "tree people"
e. mythical figure from whose severed head the stars and universe came
f. belief that spirits are responsible for the life seen in nature
g. practice of using specified formulas to compel certain acts by supernatural powers
h. member of the palm family that provides much of the Asmat diet
i. mythical figure of the great carver who made humanity
j. take place at important stages in the lives of individuals

k. ceremony by which Asmat drive
   off threatening ancestral spirits

Completion

Choose the best word or phrase from the lists provided to fill the blanks in the
paragraphs below.

1. To the Asmat, both the visible
   and invisible worlds are extremely hostile. Other villages
   are considered enemies; there
   are also _spirit_ of their
   own, ancestors waiting for an
   opportunity to create mischief;
   and there are still other evil
   spirits in the _plants_.
   The Asmat make efforts to calm
   some of the plant spirits with
   offerings left in the forest, but
   more often, the spirits must be
   frightened off. In the television
   program, the men _sing_
   and the women attack with
   spears to frighten
   spirits away.

   spears
   plants
   sing (or chant)
   spirits

2. According to traditional Asmat
   belief, the spirit of a dead person
   remains on earth for a time.
   There are several practices designed to make the spirit leave.
   For example, the dead man's
   name is taken by the one who
   killed him; the name
   may be given to inanimate objects as well. The _Bis_
   ceremony is performed to chase
   these spirits away and to build
   fervor for _headhunting_. To
   free the spirit, however, his death
   must be _avenged_.

   headhunting
   avenged
   Bis
   killed

3. The universe was created, according to Asmat myth, from the
   severed of Neso-ipitj.
   The human race was formed by
   Fumerew-ipitj, who carved human figures from _trees_

   trees
   creation
   severed head

and gave them life. By beheading an enemy, the Asmat reenact the _creation_ of the universe.

4. The woodcarver also participates in a mythological event
   when he carves _ancestor poles_
   for the Bis ceremony. His skills
   and artistry make it possible for
   the village to _honor_ the
   spirits, for each figure represents
   someone who has recently died.

     honor

     ancestor poles

Short-Answer Questions

1. Why do certain practices of the Asmat fall into the category of magic rather than religion?

2. In what ways are trees an important environmental resource to the Asmat? How is this related to the role that trees play in their religion?

3. Explain the religious significance of dancing, the ancestor pole, the mantis, and the coconut.

Self-Test

(Select the one best answer.)

Objectives 1 and 2
1. What is the Asmat belief concerning life after death?
   a. Souls are reborn into another body.
   b. The spirit goes immediately to Safan.
   c. The spirits of the dead inhabit trees.
   d. Spirits of the dead may remain and cause trouble.

Objectives 2 and 7
2. The religious function of the ancestor poles is to
   a. provide a temporary dwelling place for spirits of the dead.
   b. serve as a pictorial history of the patrilineal descent.
   c. decorate the hearth in the men's lodge.
   d. record the names of enemies who have been beheaded.

Objective 2

3. Why is revenge killing an important Asmat religious belief?
   a. Killing an enemy is supposed to strengthen defenses against nature spirits.
   b. A young man is not given a name until he has killed someone.
   c. The spirit of someone killed by an enemy is earthbound until an enemy is killed.
   d. Important trees will cease to grow if attacks on the village are not punished.

Objectives 1 and 2

4. Dances are performed at the climax of the Bis ceremony to
   a. drive away ancestral spirits, and to build courage for headhunting.
   b. gain the aid of ancestral spirits as the men prepare to go on a raid.
   c. frighten the spirits of trees that have been cut down.
   d. recount the brave deeds of those who have died.

Objective 3

5. According to Asmat religious belief, the universe was created
   a. by a great woodcarver, who designed all the world.
   b. from the severed head of an ancient mythical figure.
   c. from the first sago palm, whose edible parts became the material of the universe.
   d. from a great flood that had covered the entire world.

Objective 3

6. In what way do the Asmat identify revenge killings with their myth of creation?
   a. The enemy represents dark forces that opposed and almost prevented creation.
   b. Creation, according to the Asmat myth, was an act of revenge.
   c. The killings are demanded by the gods responsible for the creation.
   d. The killings are reenactments of the creation myth.

Objectives 3 and 6

7. According to the Asmat myth, the earth was populated from the
   a. original sago palm.
   b. severed head of a mythical figure.
   c. figures done by a woodcarver.
   d. nature spirits.

Objectives 4, 6, and 7

8. Which one of the following is not an example of magic as practiced by the Asmat?
   a. assigning a slain enemy's name to a member of the village
   b. beheading an enemy to revenge a villager's death
   c. growing crops in the village area
   d. carving the ancestor poles

9. Which of the following statements does not explain why trees are so important to the Asmat?
    a. Trees provide most of the environmental resources used by the Asmat.
    b. Trees are regarded as important religious symbols by the Asmat.
    c. Trees are used as a major export product.
    d. Trees contain spirits and therefore are protected, not used.

10. The sago palm plays such an important part in the life of the Asmat because it(s)
    a. fronds are an important religious symbol.
    b. fruit is eaten at important feasts.
    c. contributes the major part of their regular diet.
    d. wood is used for carving religious symbols.

11. A chief responsibility of the woodcarver is to
    a. be the shaman for the village.
    b. carve important religious symbols, as well as other objects.
    c. preserve the history of the village in pictorial form.
    d. carve decorations for the lodges, as well as for festivals.

12. A woodcarver in the Asmat village is
    a. equivalent to that of the village chief, although he does not lead headhunting raids.
    b. equivalent to that of a successful headhunter, although he does not take part in raids.
    c. equal to that of a successful headhunter, although he must also prove himself as a headhunter.
    d. equal to that of the women of the village.

13. Which of these symbols is related to Asmat beliefs about both plants and headhunting?
    a. the new moon
    b. the mantis
    c. facial details in the ancestor pole
    d. the boat-likeness on the ancestor pole

Suggested Activities

1. From what you have learned about Asmat practices and belief, it should be apparent that there is a basic consistency and harmony underlying Asmat religion and magic. Write an essay suggesting how the aspects of

264

Asmat culture presented in this lesson reinforce and support each other. Also explain how these aspects may have contributed to the survival of this society.

2. The television program briefly describes the modern changes and cross-cultural contact now taking place in the forests of New Guinea. Summarize the changes which are taking place, and speculate about how they will affect the religious traditions of the Asmat which are described in this lesson.

3. The Asmat perception of the world is one of hostile forces, whether from physical enemies, ancestral spirits, or nature spirits. Their religious customs seem designed to protect the people from the omnipresent hostility and danger they perceive. Yet, the Asmat religion fulfills larger functions. Review the functions of religion as presented in Lesson Nineteen and text Chapter 12, and describe briefly how the Asmat religion performs each of these functions for the society.

Answer Key

Vocabulary Check

1. e   6. g
2. i   7. d
3. k   8. f
4. h   9. a
5. c

Completion

1. spirits, plants, sing (or chant), spears

2. killed, Bis, headhunting, avenged

3. severed head, trees, creation

4. ancestor poles, honor

Short-Answer Questions

1. Why do certain practices of the Asmat fall into the category of magic rather than religion? Your answer should include:

   Magic (as defined in the text) is an attempt to manipulate supposed "natural laws" by using certain formulas to compel supernatural powers to behave in certain ways.

All attempts to frighten ancestral or nature spirits, such as dancing or attacking them, are examples of magic.

Beheading an enemy is, in part, a kind of magic, since it is supposed to free an earthbound spirit.

The Bis ceremony is a ritual designed to force the ancestral spirits to leave.

2. In what ways are trees an important environmental resource to the Asmat? How is this related to the role that trees play in religion? Your answer should include:

Most of the resources the Asmat take from their environment come from trees: fuel, building materials, weapons, and food.

The sago palm provides about 90 percent of the Asmat diet.

Because trees and wood are central to their survival, so are they central to Asmat religious beliefs.

Trees are believed to have spirits just as humans do. The sago palm is believed to have the same spirit as a headhunter.

When a mangrove tree is taken for an ancestor pole, or a sago palm for feasting, it is "attacked" and overcome, not just cut down. Offerings are left for tree spirits.

3. Explain the religious significance of dancing, the ancestor pole, the mantis, and the coconut. Your answer should include:

Dancing is a magic ritual designed to frighten spirits. The costumes worn during the Bis preparation are designed to reflect the characteristics of plants which the Asmat admire.

The ancestor pole is a symbol of those killed in headhunting raids, and it is believed that, after appropriate ritual, the pole holds the spirits of those killed.

Due to its resemblance to plants, the mantis symbolizes a living plant. Due to the actions of the female mantis toward the male during mating (she bites off her mate's head), the mantis also symbolizes the headhunting act.

The coconut is a symbol of rituals connected with headhunting and is identified with eating the brains of an enemy.

Self-Test

1. d		8. c	
2. a		9. c	
3. c		10. c	
4. a		11. b	
5. b		12. c	
6. d		13. b	
7. c			

The Arts 21

Overview

Suppose you were asked to solve this puzzle: What do Leonardo da Vinci's *Last Supper,* Handel's *Messiah,* and Michelangelo's *David* share in common with the riddles we were fond of telling as children and the graphic designs we create on our home computers and television sets today? It is unlikely that you would say these are all forms of art; yet that is how anthropologists would answer the riddle.

Art, like language, is a uniquely human phenomenon and is present in some forms in all human societies. But what is art? There are as many definitions of art as there are forms of human expression or dictionaries to define them. William A. Haviland, the author of your text, defines art as "the creative use of the human imagination to interpret, understand, and enjoy life." It is in that context that you will be considering the arts in this lesson.

How do *you* define art? If you can at least tentatively agree with Haviland's definition, you can probably begin to think of riddles and designs as forms of art. But would you be ready to agree that an old urinal mounted on a pedestal and hung in a museum is art, simply because its creator says it is art? Just such a "work of art" was created by Marcel Duchamp, a leader of a 1920s school of art known as "dadaist" whose members delighted in mocking traditional ideas of beauty in painting and sculpture. When you have completed this lesson, it might interest you to compare both your conclusions about the definition of art and Duchamp's creation with what you think now.

Whatever the form of the art, the "raw materials" are symbols, and symbols make it possible for humans to communicate. In this lesson, you will—as anthropologists do—study riddles, myths, legends, folklore, poetry, tales, song, and even incantations as "verbal arts" which human societies use to communicate standards, preserve customs and values, and promote group solidarity. You will also learn something about the significance of body painting, music, and sculpture as forms of artistic expression which serve the same social ends. These art forms can tell us much about the world view and history of any society. Art, then, is an important and successful form of communication, and this vital function was probably the basic reason for the appearance of art early in human history and its prevalence throughout human societies.

But art must be considered from more than merely its functional perspective. The ability of the "artist" to give symbols different shapes (and meanings) provides the artist with the satisfaction of self-expression and gives the gift of enjoyment and a sense of something shared to those who comprehend. As you watch the television program, you may experience the creativity and dynamism of people and their culture. You will realize that art often expresses joy and happiness; other times it is a part of rituals and has more somber motifs. As you experience the mood and feelings revealed by each piece of art, you may come to feel that art truly does reach across boundaries and cultures. Indeed, art may be the closest humans can come to a universal form of communication.

Before leaving this lesson, look back at the question about Duchamp's "work of art." In view of what you've learned, what can you say about the function and value of this creation? Is it truly art?

Learning Objectives

When you have completed all assignments in this lesson, you should be able to:

1. Identify the definition of art presented in the text. (Text pages 379-380.)

2. Recognize that those involved in art make use of "symbols" in order to interpret, understand, or enjoy life. In other words, art is a form of communication. (Text pages 380-382; television program.)

3. Recognize that some form of artistic expression is found in all human societies and give examples which illustrate the diversity of forms and modes of artistic expression. (Text page 380; television program.)

4. Describe social cohesiveness and expression of creativity as functions of art. (Text pages 379-381, 385-386, 391-393; television program.)

5. List the forms of artistic expression included in the verbal arts. (Text page 384.)

6. Define and distinguish between folklore, myth, legend, epic, and tale. (Text pages 384, 386-388.)

7. Discuss some of the social functions of the verbal arts. (Text pages 384-390; television program.)

8. Define ethnomusicology. (Text page 390.)

9. Identify the social functions of music. (Text pages 391-393; television program.)

10. Describe the sculpture of West Africa as an example of a non-Western artistic tradition. (Text pages 395-397.)

Assignments For This Lesson

Before Viewing the Program

Read the overview and the learning objectives for this lesson. Use the learning objectives to guide your reading, viewing, and thinking.

Read the preview to Chapter 13 in the text, and look over the topic headings in the chapter.

Read Chapter 13, "The Arts."

View Program 21, "The Arts."

As you view the program, look for:

the variety of art styles found in societies around the world.

the close link between artistic expression and religious beliefs demonstrated by the monuments of the Egyptian Empire, the arts of Buddhist Tibet, and the dance in Bali.

the celebration of Vesak in Sri Lanka, a special Buddhist holiday, by the creation of paper lanterns.

the creation of art as an expression of ethnic identity in the barrio of Los Angeles and the music of Mexican-Americans.

After Viewing the Program

Review the terms used in this lesson.

Review the reading assignments for this lesson. A thorough second reading is suggested. Include the chapter summary in your study.

Complete each of the study activities and the self-test in this study guide; then check your answers with the answer key at the end of this lesson.

According to your instructor's assignment or your own interests, complete one or more of the suggested activities. You may also be interested in some of the readings suggested at the end of Chapter 13 in your text.

Study Activities

Vocabulary Check

Check on your understanding of terms by matching those on the left with the definitions on the right. Check your choices with the answer key at the end of the lesson.

1. _C_ functions of art
2. _H_ sea chanty
3. _J_ symbol
4. _A_ proverbs, riddles, and insults
5. _K_ legend
6. _I_ tale
7. _E_ motif
8. _L_ ethnomusicology
9. _F_ a social function of music
10. _D_ ritual mask

a. forms of verbal arts
b. a traditional narrative providing explanation of ultimate questions about human existence
c. interpretation, understanding, and enjoyment of life
d. an important form of sculpture found in many African cultures
e. a story situation in a folktale
f. a form of social behavior in which feelings and life experiences are shared
g. long oral narrative recounting glorious events in the life of a person
h. art form that originally had a practical purpose
i. a creative, fictional narrative
j. form that has a shared meaning among a group of people
k. a traditional narrative related in some way to history
l. the study of a society's music in relation to its culture

Completion

Choose the best word or phrase from the lists provided to fill the blanks in the paragraphs below.

1. Despite the fact that the Eskimo sculptor feels he is "revealing," rather than creating, a form in his piece of ivory, his activity illustrates one possible function of artistic expression: the expression of _creativity_. A group of Eskimos see one carver's work and share a feeling such as "that is an Eskimo seal portrayed there." This represents a group function of artistic expression: the promotion of _social cohesiveness_. This latter function is also illustrated by the original practical function of sea chanties, which set the _pace_ for cooperative work aboard ship.

   pace
   creativity
   social cohesiveness

2. Instead of the term "folklore," anthropologists prefer to use _verbal arts_ and _oral traditions_ when referring to unwritten stories, jokes, word games, and other creative expressions in this area. The "folk arts" are no less sophisticated than those found in highly literate or industrialized societies. Most of the examples of these arts are meant to bring enjoyment. In addition, myths function to answer _ultimate_ questions about human existence. Tales may illustrate a bit of practical _advice_. Legends and epics may rekindle _pride_ in one's ancestors. Music, as well, performs important social functions. Songs, for example, allow a group to share both experiences and _feeling_.

   verbal arts
   advice
   feelings
   oral traditions
   ultimate
   pride

Short-Answer Questions

1. From each of the three art forms (verbal arts, music, and sculpture) discussed in the reading for this lesson, or from the television program, give examples which show that art is a form of symbolic communication.

2. Briefly describe examples of West African realistic and abstract sculptures.

Self-Test

(Select the one best answer.)

Objectives 1 and 2
1. Art always includes an aspect of
   a. practical use.
   b. symbolic communication.
   c. religious belief.
   d. humor.

Objective 1
2. Art is defined in the text as contributing to
   a. interpretation, understanding, or enjoyment of life.
   b. preservation of historical information.
   c. illustrations of moral principles or practical advice.
   d. an explanation of a society's world view.

Objective 3
3. Artistic expression has been found by anthropologists
   a. chiefly in literate and semiliterate societies.
   b. primarily in hunting-gathering and complex industrial societies.
   c. in some form in all human societies.
   d. primarily in the Western nations.

Objective 4
4. Which of these is tentatively suggested by Haviland as a reason for the universality of art?
   a. Art is derived from religion.
   b. Art began as an attempt to communicate with spirits.
   c. Art began as an attempt to organize people's activities.
   d. Art is an expression of people's need for creativity.

5. Strictly speaking, which of the following is (are) *not* included in the verbal arts?
   a. word games
   b. written fiction
   c. carefully designed insults
   d. jokes

6. Which of the following distinctly relates to myth?
   a. It defines or illuminates the world view of the culture within which it is told.
   b. It is generally accepted as a fiction.
   c. It relates a lengthy story about the glorious deeds of an actual person.
   d. It is considered religion, rather than art, by anthropologists.

7. The epic is best described as
   a. a semihistorical narrative.
   b. a story generally accepted as fiction.
   c. defining or illuminating the world view of the society in which it is told.
   d. centering on the life of a real or legendary person.

8. Which of these is generally accepted as fiction, yet may carry moral or practical advice?
   a. myth
   b. tale
   c. legend
   d. epic

9. Ethnomusicology is defined as the study of
   a. music in relation to the culture in which it was developed.
   b. the forms and rhythms of music.
   c. the various tone scales developed for music by different cultures.
   d. the sharing of musical forms between different societies.

10. Which of the following is primarily an example of a social function of music in the television program?
   a. Tutankhamen's tomb
   b. Tibetan creation of a Buddhist mandala
   c. Christo's running fence
   d. Tex-Mex music

Objective 10

11. Ritual masks made in West Africa are
    a. of poor quality compared to those made in other areas of Africa.
    b. most often abstract or expressionistic.
    c. formed of clay.
    d. described by all of the above.

Suggested Activities

1. Read a myth from the Greek, Nordic, American Indian, or another culture that gives an account of the creation of the world. Attempt to answer these questions: How did humans come into being? What beings were instrumental in the creation of that culture? How do the creator's powers compare with those of later members of the culture? What features of the actual culture does the myth attempt to explain? Does the myth seem to have influence on the life of the culture at the time it was told?

2. Select four or five country-western songs and analyze their content. What do they reveal about current attitudes and values toward sex, individualism, loyalty, patriotism, love, authority, God, and self-reliance?

Answer Key

Vocabulary Check

1. c	5. k	8. l
2. h	6. i	9. f
3. j	7. e	10. d
4. a		

Completion

1. creativity, social cohesiveness, pace

2. oral traditions, verbal arts, ultimate, advice, pride, feelings

Short-Answer Questions

1. From each of the three art forms (verbal arts, music, and sculpture) discussed in this lesson's reading, or from the television program, give examples which show that art is a form of symbolic communication. Your answer should include:

   In verbal art, the subject of the myth and the story of the myth may symbolize the world view of the people. The hero of an epic or tale may provide a symbol of heroism or other quality which members of that society are expected to emulate.

Music, both in song and other forms, may serve as a symbol for feelings shared by the group.

Some ritual masks of West Africa symbolize dwellers in the afterlife, giving, as the text suggests, "shape and meaning to that which is unknown."

2. Briefly describe examples of West African realistic and abstract sculptures. Your answer should include:

The Benin bronzes are one example of realistic sculpture; each is a sort of portrait of a deceased ruler of Benin. Realistic art is also illustrated by many other examples, such as the royal statues of the Bakuba kings in the Congo River region.

Abstract art predominates in West Africa. Examples could include the *katanda* figure, a wooden figure of a person with changes in relative size of most body parts which are deliberately pierced with many holes. The figure symbolizes the effects of disunity. Ritual masks also may be abstract, and in some cases seem to emphasize that the spirit world is somehow opposite the earthly world.

Self-Test

1. b	5. b	9. a
2. a	6. a	10. d
3. c	7. d	11. b
4. d	8. b	

New Orleans Black Indians:

A Case Study in the Arts

22

Overview

You may have the impression that the arts of non-Western cultures, particularly those that are isolated, come from the ordinary people, while the industrial societies of the Western world acquire their art from professionals, who compose music or create another particular kind of art and make this art the major occupation of their lives. Many people share this impression.

Would you be surprised to learn that only a *fraction* of the art produced in Western societies is the creation of professional artists? Even today, "ordinary people" express themselves through the arts, and they account for by far the larger volume of artistic expression. Art so produced is usually created for pleasure, but often has aesthetic or artistic merit and qualifies as "folk art."

But folk art often serves broader purposes than mere pleasure. In a multicultural society like our own, for example, an ethnic group can employ its folk art to express its ethnicity and enhance group cohesiveness and solidarity. Such art can also chronicle notable events in the life of the group, serving as a kind of living history to be passed on from one generation to the next. The Black Indian Tribes of New Orleans have developed just such a folk art, one that not only affords them the pleasure of artistic expression, but also pays homage to their heritage and revitalizes group feelings of pride and solidarity.

Black Indians are a blend of American Indians and blacks, some of whom were West Africans brought to New Orleans as slaves in the service of wealthy white families. In this lesson, you will meet these unusual Americans and take an absorbing look at their art and the forms in which they express it during the famous and colorful Mardi Gras celebrations held in New Orleans every spring. You will learn about the historical roots of the black Mardi Gras and the importance of its traditions to the people themselves. And you will understand that the Black Indian Tribes, through their unique art, are doing more than merely entertaining themselves and others. They are making an intense and deeply personal ethnic statement.

Learning Objectives

When you have completed all assignments in this lesson, you should be able to:

1. Describe the social and artistic activities of the Black Indian Tribes of New Orleans. (Television program, Background Notes.)

2. Briefly describe the origins of art forms created by the Black Indian Tribes, noting the influence of American Indian, African, and Haitian cultures. (Television program, Background Notes.)

3. Identify the significance of the costumes and music of the Black Indians' Mardi Gras celebrations. (Television program, Background Notes.)

4. Describe in what ways the Black Indian Tribes and their ceremonies reflect the status of blacks in the United States. (Television program, Background Notes.)

Assignments For This Lesson

Before Viewing the Program

Read the overview and the learning objectives for this lesson. Use the learning objectives to guide your reading, viewing, and thinking.

Review Chapter 13, "The Arts," particularly taking note of the sections which describe folklore, legends, and music.

Read the background notes for this lesson in preparation for viewing the television program.

View Program 22, "New Orleans Black Indians: A Case Study in the Arts."

Documentary material in this program includes conversations by participants in Black Indian activities. Several of these comments help to illuminate the importance of these folk art forms to the community, and parts of the comments are reproduced here as an aid to your study. As you view the program, look and listen for:

the contrast between the "white" and "black" celebrations of the Mardi Gras.

the woman explaining as she watches a Mardi Gras parade in a black neighborhood, "If you want to be white today, you can be white today. . . Superman, Batman, Robin Hood. You can be anything you want to be today, but NOT tomorrow. You got to be a nigger tomorrow, 'cause that's what you is!"

a costume maker explaining something of the Indian tradition and describing the feelings he associates with Mardi Gras, "Mardi Gras is just something you got to be a part of. . .feeling what it's all about. It's just part of our heritage. You sittin' down, and the tambourines start ringin' up. Some people call it funk. It's strictly us, second-line us. Everything that's got that kind of beat is something to get your blood warmed up, and your feet begin to move, and you start being part of yourself, the *real you* . . . And the beautiful part of it is that no two people can express themselves the same way. Everyone is feelin' what *they* feel. And it's all basically a proud thing, and a happy thing. It's a sad thing. It's a joyous thing. It's all these things combined."

the historical roots of the Black Indians, illustrated through photographs and drawings.

costume makers describing how costumes are designed. One concludes that "no one goes to school to learn this. . . this is something you just have to automatically pick up."

the appearance of "Spyboy," brief glimpses of the many other participants in Black Indian parades, and two Black Indians describing how the tribes meet and confront each other in modern parades.

a father expressing the importance of the tradition, "This Indian thing is something I feel every black man should be into. And I have kids right now, and my kids is coming up, and I want to get all my kids into it. When I get to the point that I have to drop out, I want my kids to take over for me."

names of some of the Black Indian Tribes (Yellow Pocahontas, Wild Tchapatoulas, Black Eagles, Seventh Ward Hunters).

After Viewing the Program

Review the meanings of these terms:

folk art   mutual-aid societies
folklore   Spyboy
legend   second line
Mardi Gras   Big Chief
krewe

Review the background notes for this lesson.

Complete each of the study activities and the self-test, then check your answers with the answer key at the end of this lesson.

According to your instructor's assignment or your own interests, complete one or more of the suggested activities.

Background Notes

The Role and Meaning of Art in a Society

When we talk about art, we often visualize museums, like the Smithsonian in Washington or the Louvre in Paris, or wealthy collectors, like Norton Simon. But locking away art objects in museums is a comparatively recent development in human history.

All societies have aesthetic traditions. Men and women decorate their bodies, the tools they use, and their surroundings. Dancing and music are universal, or nearly so. In small-scale societies, everyone participates in creating art forms. Even in complex, stratified societies, art often begins in the streets, among the poor, and only gradually becomes accepted at all levels of society. Shakespeare aimed his plays at the masses of his day. Classical composers incorporated peasant melodies and themes into their music.

Art and aesthetic forms, like dance and music, are a vitalizing force in a society. They allow people to act out, invent, and reinvent cultural forms. Art can be a medium for telling stories about people or significant events. Or it can simply be decorative. Drama and dance can be ways of reflecting upon, rehearsing, and transcending real-life roles. Or they can simply be entertaining. But even entertainment tells something about the culture which produces it and the people who find it entertaining. All societies have decorative forms, but what is considered to be decorative may differ from culture to culture.

The Mardi Gras celebrations of New Orleans combine several decorative forms, among them music, dancing, and the making of costumes, as you will see and hear during this lesson. Mardi Gras began with the first French settlers in New Orleans in the early 1700s and is tied to the Roman Catholic calendar as a festival which precedes the season of Lent. Lent is, for Christians, a time of atonement and fasting in preparation for Easter. Mardi Gras is French for "fat Tuesday," the last day for feasting before Lenten fasting begins.

The Mardi Gras celebration began to develop its modern form in 1857 with the formation of the Mistik Krewe of Comus, a prestigious secret society. The Mistik Krewe's parade and ball are still a highlight of Mardi Gras, but now a number of other krewes have been formed, representing many segments of New Orleans society.

The krewes spend $10,000 or more on floats and sponsor elaborate balls. To be named king or queen of a krewe and preside over its ball is considered a great honor. Families of socially prominent debutantes pull strings to have their daughters named queens of the more prestigious balls. Thus, Mardi Gras reflects the New Orleans class structure and is a way of asserting status. The secrecy of the major krewes excludes all but the chosen from their membership, and, in this way, Mardi Gras emphasizes and reinforces class differences.

The Black Indian Mardi Gras

A Black Indian of New Orleans could never hope to become king or queen of one of the major balls. As descendants of slaves and perhaps also of Indians who were driven from their lands, they are doubly disenfranchised. Black Indians are poor and they are excluded from the society of those who control most Mardi Gras festivities. But the Black Indians hold their own Mardi Gras celebration, one which affirms their cultural heritage and asserts their claim on the artistic expression of the city. Under the guise of Mardi Gras, the Black Indians can openly pay homage to their cultural heritage.

Black Indians represent a unique cultural blend. In the nineteenth century black slaves met and mingled with Indians of various tribes (primarily Choctaw) when they went to the French Market to buy goods for white households. Indians also hid runaway slaves. Thus, the Indians became associated with freedom for the slaves. There was also intermarriage between blacks and Indians.

In the 1870s, after the Civil War, "free persons of color" began to form mutual-aid societies to support members at times of life crises, such as birth, death, and marriage. Blacks weren't accepted by white-owned insurance agencies, so they provided their own kind of insurance. Writing in the New Orleans newspaper, *The Courier*, Don Lee Keith asserts that these organizations provided "in reality what Lincoln's emancipation provided in theory."

These organizations may have grown out of earlier African tribal associations, which held dancing and drumming competitions in New Orleans's Congo Square on Sunday afternoons, the slaves' day off. These competitions were banned before the Civil War because of rebellions by slaves, but they went underground and thereafter were permitted only on Mardi Gras. After the Civil War, when these associations resurfaced, they quickly became oriented toward Mardi Gras. In the 1880s, Chief Becate presented the first Black Indian Tribe for Mardi Gras. Early tribes paraded through the black sections of New Orleans in American Indian costumes decorated with eggshells, turkey feathers, and broken glass.

In 1894, a dance teacher founded the "Illinois Club," modeled after white social clubs. Now divided into two clubs, the members of this group hold Mardi Gras balls which are similar to those held by whites, even to the presentation of debutantes in expensive gowns.

The most famous black Mardi Gras organization is the Zulu Social Aid and Pleasure Club, which was founded in 1909 by a group of laborers who had seen a vaudeville skit about Zulus. The club holds a ball and stages a parade through the black community. A main feature of early Zulu parades was a drunken king. Today the society is upwardly mobile and has taken on many characteristics of white clubs, but during its early existence the Zulu Club made fun of white Americans who tried to behave like aristocrats.

But the most colorful and authentically black Mardi Gras celebrations are the Black Indian parades, featuring elaborate Indian costumes and music. These processions are put on by a number of "tribes," having names like Wild Magnolias, Seventh Ward Hunters, Black Eagles, Golden Sioux, and Yellow Pocahontas. Each tribe has its own parade route, songs, and costume traditions. Beginning several months before Mardi Gras, practice singing sessions are held in bars every Sunday evening after church. These practices have become part of the Mardi Gras tradition, and each tribe practices in a particular bar. The chief of the tribe opens practice sessions by saying "Ma-Day, Cootie Fiyo." All present answer: "Tee-Nah Aeeey." Then tribe members practice the songs they will sing on Mardi Gras. The music is primarily West African, with some elements from Haiti and Trinidad. The songs often tell stories about previous Mardi Gras celebrations or about life in prison or the ghetto.

Each member of the tribe has a title and a specific role to play on Mardi Gras. Spyboy (the scout) starts the march. Next comes Flagboy, carrying the tribal banner. He may be accompanied by Gang Flag, who carries a flag or emblem on a "spear," or stick. Next comes Wildman, who may also be called "Witch Doctor" or "Medicine Man" and is supposed to keep the crowds back. Wildman may be followed by the second and third chiefs. A woman "queen" or perhaps several "princesses" may accompany these chiefs. Big Chief, the tribal leader, follows this group and, sometimes, a Trail Chief completes the procession. This central group may be followed by the "second line," hundreds of noncostumed adherents who sing and dance with the parade.

Until about twenty years ago, Spyboy's role in the parade was more than ceremonial. He was supposed to keep watch for rival tribes, because the parades were occasions for fights fought with knives and guns to resolve disputes and prove one gang to be the most powerful in the city. When rival tribes met, one chief would order the other to "humba," or bow down in deference. If the second chief refused the order, the tribes would fight. The Mardi Gras parade route thus came to be called the "battlefield." Two traditional Black Indian songs, "Meet Me Boys on De Battlefield" and "Corinne Died on the Battlefield," describe those early battles.

Early hostilities are still observed ritually. When two tribes meet on their parade routes, the chiefs begin a complex encounter ritual, dancing around each other and shouting threats. However, this hostility is purely for display, and the tribes try to outdo each other in the art of costume design, not with knives and guns. The style of sewing and materials used in costume construction vary from tribe to tribe, but all costumes are elaborate and display fine workmanship. Writing in *Black New Orleans*, Maurice M. Martinez notes, "The biggest disgrace to self and others is a 'raggedy' Indian whose costume displays 'short cuttin' '—something slapped together in a hurry with glue and paste."

Making a costume requires skill and years of practice in sewing. Costume makers use velvet, ostrich feathers, rhinestones and sequins. The "crown" is the most prized part of the costume. It is worn over a black wig with braids. It is made of feathers or ostrich-plumed marabou formed like a chieftain's headdress. Several fine examples are shown in the television program. The "apron" covers the body from the waist to below the knees. Usually the design is sketched on canvas and then "drawn out" by stitching on beads and stones. "Wings" are arm coverings that spread out like plumage when the wearer's arms are raised.

Hostility and Rebellion Stated in Art

As with folk art in other parts of the world, the various forms represented among the Black Indians in Mardi Gras—music, costuming, and dancing—are more than decorative. They are a social statement and a revitalizing force for the participants. In the case of the Black Indians, the social statement is about (1) class and racial consciousness, (2) feelings of powerlessness, and (3) the importance of maintaining social identity.

For example, even among the Black Indian Tribes, there are distinctions made between "uptown" and "downtown." Groups which perform "uptown" are considered by downtowners to be more "commercial" and less true to the racial and class origins of the art form. The downtown neighborhood groups are more concerned that the costumes and music remain within their neighborhood boundaries, be performed by group members, and be performed for their own pleasure and enjoyment.

All black Mardi Gras celebrations reflect a form of rebellion. The Zulu Social Aid and Pleasure Club began as a parody of white pretensions and gradually began to conform to the white institutions it had previously mocked. The Illinois Clubs were always modeled after white institutions.

Black Indian traditions also began as defiance, growing out of underground black societies and reflecting the social realities of their times. As social reality changed, so did the Black Indian celebrations. Real-life hostilities among tribes became ritualized and transformed into aesthetic competition. Some tribes have now released albums of their Mardi Gras songs, and most participate in the annual Jazz and Heritage Festival, which is a newly developed showcase for Black Indian music.

In early parades, men carried flaming torches to light night parades, but black high school marching bands have recently replaced traditional flambeaux carriers in the parades. These are now ceremonial flambeaux carriers that serve no functional purpose.

In stratified societies, folk art often begins as an act of rebellion or alternative form of expression among the disenfranchised, but it revitalizes the society as a whole. Expressive forms developed in the bars and ghettos of black New Orleans have found their way into the mainstream cultural patterns. But, because it is a living art form, folk art is continually being reinvented and transformed by the lives and experiences of those who produce it.

Like conventional art, however, folk art has rules and cultural traditions. A spyboy cannot dress or behave like a chief, for example. As in conventional art, folk art requires a body of knowledge and skills that must be transmitted to each successive generation. But, unlike conventional art, it is not produced by a class of artists for collectors and museums. It is art by and for the people.

Study Activities

Vocabulary Check

Check on your understanding of terms by matching those on the left with the definitions on the right. Check your choices with the answer key at the end of the lesson.

1. __G__ folklore
2. __J__ legends
3. __H__ Lent
4. __D__ krewe
5. __B__ tribes
6. __K__ mutual-aid societies
7. __C__ battlefield
8. __A__ second line
9. __F__ Spyboy

a. large groups, often without costumes, which follow behind tribal leaders in a parade

b. organizations of members of the black community for traditional celebrations of Mardi Gras

c. a name for Mardi Gras parade routes

d. organizations of members of the

white community for traditional celebrations of Mardi Gras

e. ritual encounter in which loud threats are exchanged

f. starts the march and heads the procession

g. the traditions that are preserved orally in all societies

h. in the Christian religion, the period of fasting and penance that precedes Easter

i. French for "fat Tuesday"

j. semihistorical narratives that tell the stories of past heroes and the establishment of local customs

k. organized as a form of insurance protection

Completion

Choose the best word or phrase from the lists provided to fill the blanks in the paragraphs below.

1. New Orleans Black Indian Tribes meet regularly in neighborhood ___bars___ to practice traditional ___songs___ throughout much of the year. The leader, known as the ___Big Chief___, conducts the practice sessions and occupies a place of honor in the parade. One of his functions is to ___challenge___ leaders of other tribes in the Mardi Gras parades.

   songs
   Big Chief
   bars
   challenge

2. The interest of the black community in Indians began in the years before the ___Civil___ War. There was intermarriage among the peoples, and the Indians aided the blacks by hiding ___runaway slaves___. The Indian influence on Mardi Gras festival art is seen chiefly in ___costumes___ and in the roles of tribe members.

   Civil
   costumes
   runaway
   slaves

Short-Answer Questions

1. Describe the origins and typical subjects of the music forms used by the Black Indian Tribes today.

2. In what way could the formation of the Zulu and Illinois Clubs be termed a form of rebellion against the dominant culture of New Orleans of that day?

3. In what ways can the costumes and music of the Black Indian Tribes be seen as an example of folk art?

4. According to the background notes for this lesson, what kind of social statement is made by the Black Indian Tribes through their folk art?

Self-Test

(Select the one best answer.)

Objective 1
1. Black Indian Tribe activities reach their high point each year in the celebration of which festival?
   a. Lent
   b. Mardi Gras
   c. New Orleans day
   d. Indian Summer

Objective 1
2. Today members of each tribe learn their songs while participating in
   a. high school band classes.
   b. practice sessions of social clubs.
   c. meetings held in members' homes.
   d. sessions held in a particular bar.

Objective 2
3. Why do the Black Tribes of New Orleans identify with the American Indian?
   a. Indian dances were seen by a group at a vaudeville show in the 1880s.
   b. Blacks associated with Indians freely in the early twentieth century.
   c. Blacks and Indians both were the victims of oppression and both had been moved from their homelands.
   d. The Black Tribes admired Indian costumes seen in early western movies.

4. The music of the Black Indians is *not* traced to
   a. music from gatherings held during the slavery years.
   b. Indian ceremonial music.
   c. West African music.
   d. the music of Haiti.

5. Selection of Mardi Gras costumes by the Black Indians relates most strongly to
   a. natural desire for a colorful and striking costume.
   b. desire to copy the white community traditions.
   c. memory of struggle against oppression.
   d. competition among the gangs in the city.

6. How are individual Black Indian costumes designed?
   a. The costumes have remained the same, being passed down to participants from one year to the next.
   b. Modern costumes are usually purchased from professional designers each year.
   c. All Black Indian costumes are identical except for color.
   d. Costumes are individually designed and prepared by costume makers in the community.

7. Words to Black Indian songs usually tell stories of all of the following except
   a. parade activities of earlier days.
   b. the forced migrations of the Indians.
   c. prison life.
   d. life in the black community.

8. When used in Black Indian songs, the term "battlefield" refers to
   a. the parade route.
   b. the Civil War.
   c. battles between American Indians and soldiers.
   d. the First World War.

9. Which of the following is the Spyboy's traditional role?
   a. to discover a rival tribe approaching
   b. to demand that a rival tribe bow to his tribe
   c. to discover the meanings of other tribal symbols
   d. to hold back the crowds during the parade

Objective 4

10. Where do the Black Indian Tribes stage their parades today?
    a. in the social center of New Orleans
    b. in the black community area of New Orleans
    c. in both the black neighborhoods and the white community centers
    d. in festivals held throughout the United States

Objective 4

11. At the time of their first meetings, blacks in Louisiana probably felt a strong similarity between themselves and the American Indian. What was the similarity?
    a. Both blacks and Indians felt powerless and under oppressive control of the dominant society.
    b. Both looked back on a long and war-like heritage.
    c. Each society had a culture and folklore similar to the other.
    d. Each society desired to return to its former lands.

Objective 4

12. The "Illinois Club" of New Orleans patterned itself after
    a. northern social clubs.
    b. mutual-aid societies.
    c. white society social clubs.
    d. the Zulu club.

Objective 4

13. Which of the following is most nearly the counterpart of the Black Indian Tribes in white society?
    a. insurance companies
    b. Mardi Gras
    c. social clubs
    d. krewes

Suggested Activities

1. In the television program, one brief section shows the "use" of art on American Indian shields and dwellings. The animal or god-animal pictured, for example, shared its "medicine" with the bearer. From suggestions given in the program and the background notes, try to identify some of the possible cultural values of the Indian symbols worn by the New Orleans Black Indians. Write a brief paper on this topic.

2. If a local pageant or festival is held in your area, gather information concerning the event, particularly information distributed by those responsible for staging the event. If possible, talk with someone associated with the festival to learn how it originated and what purpose it serves in the community. Write a report describing what you think is the cultural importance of this event. If you find evidence that the festival has changed over a period of time, suggest reasons for such change.

3. Compare the Black Indian costume maker of this lesson with the Eskimo artist described in the "original study" for text Chapter 13, "The Arts." How do both exemplify folk art?

Answer Key

Vocabulary Check

1. g	4. d	7. c
2. j	5. b	8. a
3. h	6. k	9. f

Completion

1. bars, songs, Big Chief, challenge

2. Civil, runaway, slaves, costumes

Short-Answer Questions

1. Describe the origins and typical subjects of the music forms used by the Black Indian Tribes today. Your answer should include:

   Music is based on West African rhythms brought to America by black slaves and on the rhythms of Haiti and Trinidad. Blacks and Indians fleeing oppression in those areas in the late 1800s brought their music with them.

   The songs relate to earlier Mardi Gras festivals, especially those that recount the "battlefield" days when competing tribes fought when they met each other during parades. Other songs relate to life conditions today, such as time in prison or life in the ghetto.

2. In what way could the formation of the Zulu and Illinois Clubs be termed a form of rebellion against the dominant culture of New Orleans of that day? Your answer should include:

   The Zulu Club was a kind of black answer to the white society's "krewes," and, at first, mocked white pretensions to nobility and courtly manners.

   The Illinois Club patterned itself after the white social clubs, giving dances and providing a "showcase" for debutantes.

   Both groups have provided a means of expression and self-identity for black society, since the organizations of the white society were closed to them.

3. In what ways can the costumes and music of the Black Indian Tribes be seen as an example of folk art? Your answer should include:

Black Indian Tribe art is handed down to succeeding generations by learning "in the street," rather than through formal teaching in schools or academies.

The arts and traditional ceremonies of these people have changed and adapted to the needs of the society.

The Black Indian traditions are a vitalizing force in the community.

4. According to the background notes for this lesson, what kind of social statement is made by the Black Indian Tribes through their folk art? Your answer should include:

Class consciousness, feelings of powerlessness, and maintaining social and ethnic identity.

Self-Test

1. b	6. d	10. b
2. d	7. b	11. a
3. c	8. a	12. c
4. b	9. a	13. d
5. c		

Culture Change **23**

Overview

Early in this course (Lesson Two) you learned a good deal about the various characteristics of culture. Two of these characteristics are especially important to remember as you study this lesson: cultures are integrated, and they are always changing. Change in one area of the culture will cause change in other areas because beliefs, activities, and traditions *are* integrated into a system. And, even though many topics presented in this course may seem to suggest that culture is static, cultures are, in fact, dynamic; change, not sameness, should be expected.

Nonetheless, for most of us, change does not come easily. But, perhaps you feel that *your* culture is more flexible than others you've learned about in this course. If you do, think for a moment about an example of "cultural stubbornness" that has made itself apparent in the last decade. Despite social, legal, and scientific incentives, the population of the United States has shown strong resistance to a simple change that offers many advantages—the adoption of the metric system of measurement. Moreover, other Western societies have long since adopted this change without adverse results.

Why are some changes adopted quickly and easily, yet others take a long time, cause turmoil, and are met with a great deal of resistance? Anthropologists have discovered that change is sometimes influenced by forces within the culture, sometimes by forces outside the culture, and sometimes by changes in the environment. William Haviland devotes much of text Chapter 14, the reading assignment for this lesson, to the influences of other cultures on change within one society. Cross-cultural contact is not the only cause of culture change, and does not necessarily cause harm to cultures involved. But you will probably agree that many of the severe culture crises in today's world result from the contact of Western industrial culture with less industrialized societies.

Pay particular attention to the concept of modernization as presented in this lesson, because there is danger of falling into a kind of ethnocentric view of change, even while appreciating the basic worth of all cultures. Haviland, in fact, ends his presentation on culture change on a rather gloomy note. "Modern" technological society may not really hold a positive promise for the future, either for its own people or for those others who, for whatever reasons, seek to imitate it.

Learning Objectives

When you have completed all assignments in this lesson, you should be able to:

1. Recognize that culture change may be stimulated by change in the environment; change introduced within the culture; and change introduced by contact with other cultures. (Text pages 405,432; television program.)

2. Define "invention" and explain the difference between "primary" and "secondary" inventions. (Text pages 407-408.)

3. Explain why "the firing of clay" may be considered a "primary invention." (Text pages 407-408.)

4. Define "diffusion" and recognize examples of this concept. (Text pages 409-414; television program.)

5. Recognize that diffusion is normally a selective process and that borrowed traits usually undergo some modification. (Text pages 409-412.)

6. Describe "cultural loss" as an aspect of culture change. (Text page 414.)

7. Define "acculturation" and explain how the Indians of Northern New England are an example of this concept. (Text pages 414-416; television program.)

8. Recognize that changes, such as colonialism and military conquest, are often forced upon a people from outside the culture. (Text pages 416-418; television program.)

9. Describe two examples of culture change resulting from rebellion and revolution. (Text pages 418-420; television program.)

10. Explain Haviland's definition of modernization. (Text pages 422-423.)

11. Discuss how the Pueblo Indians of the American Southwest have managed to retain important aspects of their traditional society while participating in modern American economic practices. (Text pages 424-425, 428-429.)

12. Describe the Skolt Lapps as an example of a traditional culture which has not been able to resist many aspects of modernization. (Text pages 429-430.)

Assignments For This Lesson

Before Viewing the Program

Read the overview and the learning objectives for this lesson. Use the learning objectives to guide your reading, viewing, and thinking.

Read the preview to Chapter 14 in the text and look over the topic headings for the chapter.

Read Chapter 14, "Culture Change," in the text.

Review pages 373-375 in Chapter 12 on revitalization movements.

View Program 23, "Culture Change."

As you view the program, look for:

culture changes that occurred on the island of Manus, now a part of Papua New Guinea during the twentieth century.

examples of culture change resulting, in part, from colonialism, in India.

the rapid and violent forms of culture change which occurred during the Islamic revolution in Iran in 1980.

technological and economic development occurring among the Indians of the Xingu River region of Brazil and the impact on the lives and cultures of the indigenous people.

After Viewing the Program

Review the terms used in this lesson. In addition to the terms found in the learning objectives, you should be familiar with these, which are associated with acculturation:

substitution   origination
syncretism   rejection
addition   revitalization movements
deculturation   "culture of discontent"

Review the reading assignment for this lesson. A thorough second reading is suggested.

Complete each of the study activities and the self-test in this study guide; then check your answers with the answer key at the end of this lesson.

According to your instructor's assignment or your own interests, complete one or more of the suggested activities. You may also be interested in the readings suggested at the end of Chapter 14 in your text.

Study Activities

Vocabulary Check

Check on your understanding of terms by matching those on the left with the definitions on the right. Check your choices with the answer key at the end of the lesson.

1. _G_ diffusion
2. _A_ invention
3. _C_ revitalization movement
4. _F_ acculturation
5. _D_ nativistic movement
6. _I_ rejection
7. _H_ syncretism
8. _B_ modernization
9. _E_ snowmobile

a. creation of a new practice, tool, or principle that becomes socially shared
b. the process by which developing societies acquire characteristics of industrialized societies
c. a deliberate attempt by a group in a society to bring about culture changes
d. revitalization that tries to reconstitute a destroyed way of life
e. example of a cultural borrowing that has increased, rather than resolved, a society's problems
f. major changes resulting from prolonged contact between societies
g. a selective process involving the spread of cultural practices from one society to another

h. a type of acculturation in which new traits are blended with old traits
i. loss by a culture of its individual members, so that the society can no longer function
j. a reaction to acculturation in which many persons cannot accept new traits

Completion

Choose the best word or phrase from the lists provided to fill the blanks in the paragraphs below.

1. Changes can be introduced into a culture from forces outside the culture, such as contact with other _cultures_ or changes in the _environment_ Changes can also come from _within_ the culture; an example is inventions. Primary inventions are those which result from the creation of _new_ principles, while secondary inventions are those which come from the application of _known_ principles.

   environment
   known
   cultures
   within
   new

2. Cultural borrowing is called _diffusion_ In this process, some cultural traits may be adopted rather readily by a society, although they are usually modified. There may be great resistance to borrowing some practices, no matter how much these might appear as "improvements" to the outsider. There are probably more obstacles to accepting innovations that come from outside a society than there are to those introduced from within the society. Examples of such resistance might be the _potter's wheel_ to the Chinautla Maya or the _metric system_ to the people of the United States.

   potter's wheel
   metric system
   diffusion

3. Culture change is often the result of various kinds of forcible change. Often _colonization_ has allowed foreign governments to impose changes with little or no appreciation of the traditional culture. A struggle against externally imposed authority may be a _rebellion_ in which the aim is simply to oust the incumbents in office, or it may be a _revolution_, in which case a change in the whole system of government is sought.

rebellion
revolution
colonization

4. The Pueblo Indians of Santa Clara have accepted many of the tools and conveniences of the United States industrial society that surrounds them. For example, most clothing is purchased, _trucks_ are used for transportation, and television provides entertainment. At the same time, the Pueblos have retained much of their traditional social organization. The community applies strong social pressure toward _conformity_ to traditional norms, the various groups of which each person is a member serve to _integrate_ the society, and the traditional Pueblo _religion_ is maintained.

religion
integrate
conformity
trucks

5. In contrast to the Pueblo, the Skolt Lapps, who adopted the snowmobile, have not been able to resist many of the _negative_ aspects of modernization. Mechanized herding has increased the costs of maintaining reindeer herds, and adversely affected the _behavior_ of the herds. Many men have ceased being herders, creating further economic and _cultural_ difficulties, because herding has traditionally been an essential aspect of male identity.

behavior
cultural
negative

Short-Answer Questions

1. Define and distinguish between diffusion and acculturation.

2. Define modernization, and list the four subprocesses which take place in this kind of culture change. Briefly note Haviland's "problems" with the assumption that modernization is desirable.

Self-Test

(Select the one best answer.)

Objective 1
1. Significant changes in culture can be stimulated by
   a. change in the environment.
   b. new inventions.
   c. forced or selective contact with other cultures.
   d. all of the above.

Objectives 2 and 3
2. Pottery manufacturing with fired clay is considered a primary invention because it
   a. involved the creation of new principles.
   b. caused formation of a substantially new culture.
   c. involved application of known techniques to new uses.
   d. was discovered by more than one culture.

Objective 4
3. Linton has suggested that cultural borrowing may account for _____ of a society's content.
   a. 30 percent
   b. 50 percent
   c. 70 percent
   d. 90 percent

Objectives 4 and 5
4. Which of the following is the best example of diffusion?
   a. boat making by the Canary Islanders
   b. public transportation by the Guatemalan Maya
   c. British colonization of many societies in the nineteenth century
   d. changes in the culture of slaves brought to North and South America

Objectives 4 and 5
5. The adoption of tobacco use by European settlers in North America is an example of
   a. acculturation.
   b. rejection.
   c. diffusion.
   d. origination.

297

6. Adoption of a new practice or new technology may lead to a culture loss
   because
   a. the older practice may be forgotten through disuse.
   b. any innovation usually leads to new innovations.
   c. Western technology and innovation may upset major segments of the
      society.
   d. the society may reject the new ways selectively.

7. An example of culture loss without replacement is
   a. Skolt Laplanders and snowmobiles.
   b. Canary Islanders and boat making.
   c. Northeastern American Indians and pottery making.
   d. Guatemalan Maya and pottery making.

8. Acculturation normally involves which type of culture contact?
   a. selective
   b. occasional
   c. intensive
   d. forced adoption

9. Following colonization by the British, the Indians of Northern New
   England
   a. rejected all the new ways brought by the Europeans.
   b. lost identity as a separate society and consequently lost all aspects of
      their culture.
   c. gave up Indian subsistence activities.
   d. acquired many practices from the new culture.

10. Instances of imposed change or forced change on a culture have
    occurred most frequently through
    a. acculturation.
    b. modernization.
    c. colonialism and conquest.
    d. economic exploitation.

11. Which of the following has been suggested as a situation which may
    lead to rebellion and revolution?
    a. the practice of shamanism in the society
    b. increased expectations of material wealth
    c. a change in environmental conditions
    d. loss of prestige by an established authority

Objective 9

12. Which of the following groups is *not* an example of a revitalization movement?
    a. Skolt Lapps
    b. Mormons
    c. Black Muslims
    d. Moral Majority

Objective 10

13. The concept of modernization does *not* include
    a. technological development.
    b. population growth.
    c. agricultural development.
    d. urbanization.

Objective 11

14. The Pueblo Indians of the American Southwest have retained all of the following aspects of their culture *except*
    a. religious traditions.
    b. an integrated society.
    c. a subsistence farming economy.
    d. traditional clothing designs.

Objective 12

15. What has happened to the culture of the Skolt Lapps as a result of the introduction of motorized equipment?
    a. The average reindeer herd size has increased.
    b. New economic opportunities have developed.
    c. The cost of maintaining herds has decreased.
    d. Fewer Lapp men can be herdsmen.

Suggested Activities

1. As you learned by reading the text, "modernization" is a term used to describe a particular type of acculturation that carries with it a suggestion of ethnocentrism. In your opinion, does this implied ethnocentric approach to culture change interfere with your understanding of what may actually be happening with formerly nonindustrial peoples, such as Lapps and newly emerging African nations? Can you suggest a different term to use for this present-day phenomenon that would be descriptive without implying ethnocentric attitudes?

2. As a library reference project, choose an area which is undergoing current strife or experiencing the aftermath of rebellion or revolution (for example, Northern Ireland, the Palestinian peoples, Iran), and locate several articles or books that deal with your topic. After your research, identify which of the conditions listed on text page 419 seem to have

operated in this particular situation. Can you identify from your reading other factors precipitating revolt?

3. Colonialism usually presents a picture of "one-way" acculturation, in which the subordinate peoples adopt cultural attributes from the dominant society; yet colonialism has been shown to be a "two-way" process. Do research on instances of colonialism (such as the Spanish in the Americas, the British in India, and the French in Africa), and indicate the cultural traits which have been adopted by the colonial powers from conquered or subordinate cultures.

Answer Key

Vocabulary Check

1. g	4. f	7. h
2. a	5. d	8. b
3. c	6. j	9. e

Completion

1. cultures, environment, within, new, known

2. diffusion, potter's wheel, metric system

3. colonization, rebellion, revolution

4. trucks, conformity, integrate, religion

5. negative, behavior, cultural

Short-Answer Questions

1. Define and distinguish between diffusion and acculturation. Your answer should include:

   Diffusion is the spread of customs or practices from one culture to another.

   Acculturation is a more comprehensive phenomenon referring to major culture changes that occur as a result of prolonged contact between societies. There are several types of acculturation, including substitution, syncretism, addition, deculturation, origination, and rejection.

While both terms describe a kind of culture change, they are not the same. As Haviland notes, one culture can borrow from another without being in the least acculturated.

2. Define modernization, and list the four subprocesses which take place in this kind of culture change. Briefly note Haviland's "problems" with the assumption that modernization is desirable. Your answer should include:

Haviland defines modernization as the acquisition of characteristics of Western industrialized societies by developing (or nonindustrialized) societies.

There are four subprocesses in modernization: (1) application of Western scientific knowledge and techniques; (2) commercial farming replacing subsistence farming; (3) industrialization, with "modern" or inanimate forms of energy replacing human and animal power; and (4) urbanization or movement of populations from rural areas to cities.

To Haviland, the term modernization is ethnocentric, fostering the idea that other societies must become more like Western industrialized societies.

The Western world's standard of living is based on a high rate of consumption of nonrenewable resources. It is probably unrealistic to expect that most peoples of the world will ever be able to achieve a comparable standard of living.

Self-Test

1. d	6. a	11. d
2. a	7. b	12. a
3. d	8. c	13. b
4. b	9. d	14. c
5. c	10. c	15. d

Cricket The Trobriand Way: 24
A Case Study in Culture Change

Overview

This lesson really isn't so much about *cricket* as it is about culture change and the important aspects of their *culture* which the people of the Trobriand Islands have creatively and vigorously retained despite the pressure of contact with other societies. Even so, you will see some exciting moments in a very real cricket match.

The Trobriand Islanders live in a part of Papua New Guinea and are horticulturalists. Historically, in the Trobriand culture, a man's power and prestige was based on several kinds of competition: success in growing yams, skill in the exchange of valuables, and prowess on the battlefield. However, when foreign missionaries and colonists from Britain and Australia arrived, the Islanders were forced to eliminate traditional warfare and make many other changes in their culture. For example, they were pressured to adopt cricket as a substitute for warfare and as "lessons" in British values regarding dress, religion, and sportsmanship. Cricket is a very old game which is similar to baseball and is played with bats, balls, and wickets.

Later, during World War II, Allied soldiers and airmen exposed the Trobrianders to still other cultural differences. In the intensive case study of the dynamics of culture change afforded you in this lesson, you will see how the culture of the Trobriand Islanders changed in response to strong external pressures such as these. The Trobrianders, as you will understand, were able to "borrow" selectively from foreign cultures with which they had contact, yet still keep faith with their own cultural traditions. This lesson does not, and cannot, provide any final answers for problems caused by acculturation, but it does give a view of what appears to be a "success story" in culture change.

Learning Objectives

When you have completed all assignments in this lesson, you should be able to:

1. Describe the circumstances of the introduction of cricket to the Trobrianders. (Television program, Background Notes.)

2. Define syncretism and explain how the Trobriand adaptation of cricket represents an example of syncretism. (Text page 415; television program; Background Notes.)

3. Identify three examples of how the Trobrianders transformed the game of cricket. (Text page 418, television program, Background Notes.)

4. Explain the significance of the following in terms of Trobriand culture:

   a. The games take place during the harvest period.
   b. The players wear "war dress."
   c. The use of war magic.
   d. The use of dances and chants.
   e. The host team is always the winner.
   (Television program, Background Notes.)

5. Explain how the game of cricket reveals political and economic aspects of Trobriand culture. (Television program, Background Notes.)

Assignments For This Lesson

Before Viewing the Program

Read the overview and the learning objectives for this lesson carefully. Use the learning objectives to guide your reading, viewing, and thinking.

Review Chapter 14, "Culture Change," in the text, particularly the information on Trobriand culture, acculturation, and syncretism (text pages 414-415, 418). You may also wish to acquaint yourself further with the Trobriander culture through other references in the textbook, especially the description of Kula trading on page 213.

View Program 24, "Cricket the Trobriand Way: A Case Study in Culture Change."

As you view the program, look for:

the description of the game of cricket as played by the British.

the motivations of colonial officers and missionaries as they introduced competitive games and attempted to change traditional Trobriand practices.

changes which Trobriand Islanders made in team organization and equipment for their version of cricket.

integration of traditional elements such as magic, dancing, and dress into the game of cricket.

the traditional *kayasa* competition, how it has blended with cricket matches, and the influence it has in determining the winner.

After Viewing the Program

Read the background notes for this lesson.

Review the meaning of these terms:

acculturation	patrilocal
syncretism	Kula ring
diffusion	kayasa
tradition	exogamous
matrilineal	

Review the reading assignments for this lesson. A thorough second reading is suggested.

Complete each of the study activities and the self-test, then check your answers with the answer key at the end of this lesson.

According to your instructor's assignment or your own interests, complete one or more of the suggested activities. You may also be interested in the readings suggested at the end of Chapter 14 in your text.

Background Notes

The Trobriand Islanders of the South Pacific

The history of cricket in the Trobriand Islands reflects the history and aftermath of colonialism. It illustrates attempts to eliminate local customs of compromise between traditional practices and modern developments.

The Trobriands, located off the northeast coast of Papua New Guinea, are a group of coral islands that circle a shallow lagoon. There are no fresh water rivers on the islands, but there is heavy rainfall throughout the year. Rain water soaks through the coral and collects in underground caves, providing fresh drinking water. There is no hard stone, clay, or metal on the islands, so the natives have to buy or trade for them.

The Trobriand Islanders are horticulturalists, planting their crops where soil has collected in cracks and hollows in the coral. On Kiriwina, the main island, crops are grown on a ridge along the east coast. Their primary subsistence crop is yams and yams play a key role in the exchange and prestige system. Breadfruit, taro, sweet potatoes, beans, bananas, and corn are also important food sources. The people also raise pigs, and they fish for mullet in the lagoon and for sharks in the deep sea waters. The Trobrianders are skilled navigators. They build outrigger canoes and can sail a hundred miles or more across the open sea to exchange goods with people on other islands in the area. Bronislaw Malinowski, the anthropologist who studied them extensively early in this century, called the Trobrianders the "argonauts of the Western Pacific" (*Argonauts of the Western Pacific*. London: Routledge and Kegan Paul, 1922).

Most of the Islanders live in raised wooden houses clustered in small villages. Parents, young children, and adolescent females occupy one house. Young males live in bachelor houses near their families. Every household has a yam house for storing yams for family use. The households are arranged around a central clearing, where ceremonies, dancing, and cricket games are held. Yam houses for displaying yams occupy a central place in the clearing.

The Trobrianders are matrilineal, but residence is patrilocal. Young people must marry outside their own lineage. Upon marriage, the bride's family must give yams to her and her new husband. This sets up an elaborate system of exchange obligations between the two lineages.

Most households garden for themselves, but several households sometimes pool their labor. An individual can also summon people to work for him, after which he distributes food to them. Leaders of high rank use this method to mobilize followers to build yam houses or canoes or other large-scale projects. Such leaders accumulate food surpluses for this purpose through gifts from their kin.

Each household grows a surplus of yams and the best yams are given away. Some of them are set aside as tribute to the village leader. Each man must also give yams to his sister, whose husband responds by giving a stone axe or clay pot to his brother-in-law. Since the Trobriand lineages are exogamous, this means that yams move along paths of alliance among several lineages.

Only chiefs are entitled to marry more than one wife, and they can claim tribute from the kin group of each wife. Therefore, they are able to accumulate a surplus of yams, which adds to their prestige and influence.

When a man dies, the women of his lineage (that is, his sister, mother, sister's daughter, etc.) give woven bundles and skirts made of banana leaves to his wife's lineage. Note that during his lifetime, a Trobriand man is continually paying out yams to his sister and receiving ceremonial objects in return. The stone axe blades or clay pots a man receives from his brother-in-law and the bundles and skirts given to his wife's lineage on his death are not put to practical use. However, the axe blades can be exchanged for pigs, magic spells, and yams.

A leader gains prestige and, therefore, influence by being able to give away large quantities of food at a mortuary feast or other ceremonial occasion. Traditionally, a chieftain would sponsor a feast, a war, or a work project as an occasion to add to his renown by distributing food and other valuables.

The Importance of the Exchange System

Inland villages exchange yams with villages along the coast that specialize in fishing. The exchanges take place as part of traditional alliances between villages.

Men may also belong to the *Kula* ring, an exchange network that links the Trobriands with other islands in the Western Pacific. The Kula involves specific non-utilitarian trade goods, decorated necklaces, and armbands that are too elaborate for everyday use. Their worth is entirely symbolic. Some of the more prized necklaces and armbands have names and histories. In the Kula, a man publicly and ceremonially presents his partner on another island with a necklace. Some time later, the partner is obliged to give his benefactor an equally valuable arm shell. In this way, the necklaces, or *soulava*, travel in a clockwise direction around the islands, while the armbands, or *Mwali*, travel in a counter-clockwise direction. A map on page 213 of the Haviland text shows trade routes in the Kula ring.

Figure 24.1 The game of cricket played by Trobriand Islanders demonstrated ways they have retained traditional practices while accepting new practices from foreign cultures.

A man may have a number of Kula partners, but each partnership lasts for a lifetime and a man may not exchange Kula valuables with anyone but his Kula partners. The Kula establishes alliances throughout the area and provides a setting for trading other kinds of goods, since other kinds of exchanges take place on Kula expeditions. But acquiring a particularly valuable Kula article is also a way of gaining prestige. A man may use magic and sometimes subterfuge to help him in his bargaining.

Exchange, both as a means of cementing social obligations and of acquiring prestige, is a central part of Trobriand life. The exchange system promotes distribution of goods in an area where no single group has access to all the material goods its people need. Thus, people in inland villages send yams to coastal villages and receive fish in return. The Trobrianders acquire stone and clay items through partnerships set up in Kula expeditions. Some anthropologists have also suggested that the exchange system encourages the Trobrianders to produce a surplus and establish alliances which could prove useful in a fragile environment subject to natural climatic hazards.

Cricket as "Warfare"

Some of the traditions underlying the exchange system were challenged around the turn of the century when missionaries and colonial government officials traveled to the Trobriand Islands from Port Moresby on mainland Papua New Guinea. The missionaries hoped to eliminate what they considered to be pagan customs. In particular, they tried to stamp out warfare, the use of magic, and erotic native dances. Warfare was stopped by force and mission games were introduced as a substitute. As noted in the television program, cricket was introduced by a missionary, the Reverend M. K. Gilmour, in 1903.

The aim of the missionaries in introducing cricket to the Trobrianders was to encourage them to conform to correct British comportment in dress, religion, and "sportsmanship." But the Islanders weren't used to the British style of "bowling" (pitching) or friendly competition. They preferred a bowling style closer to their traditional way of throwing a spear, and their version of competition, more aggressive than that of the British, sometimes ended in war.

Early games pitted the Islanders against mission teams comprised of men from Fiji. But the Trobrianders gradually changed the game to conform to their earlier warfare system, as a means of settling disputes and adding to the prestige of powerful leaders. To the Australian and British game of cricket, the Trobrianders added battle dress and battle magic, and they reincorporated erotic dancing. Just as chieftains once called for warfare, they now scheduled cricket games. Following the game, they hold massive feasts, where their wealth is displayed to enhance their prestige. Cricket, in its altered form, fits in with traditional systems of prestige and exchange.

In the television program, the Trobriand elders say that cricket is now "our kind of competition—*kayasa*." Traditionally, a kayasa helped settle quarrels through competitive food display and distribution. When a dispute arose, the matter was solved by holding a kayasa to see which of the disputants could supply the most food. The ability to produce a great deal of food indicated that a man was powerful or had strong magic.

One of the people questioned by Malinowski during his fieldwork in the Trobriand Islands told him, "The reason for the custom of kayasa is that we should see that one man is the more powerful, his magic sharp"

(*Coral Gardens and Their Magic.* Vol. 1. London: George Allen and Unwin Ltd., 1935, p. 212). Thus, a man could win a dispute by demonstrating his ability to produce food.

Cricket has now taken the place of warfare in settling disputes. It is a new type of kayasa, combining the British game of cricket with traditional battle customs and Trobriand practices of prestige and exchange.

Cricket played the Trobriand way is an example of syncretism. Syncretism is the fusion of two or more cultural elements. In groups which have been dominated by foreign cultures, it can be a way of preserving traditional practices and social relationships. Traditional ways of life are usually destroyed or severely disrupted when one culture is overpowered politically, socially, or militarily by another. People who were formerly autonomous generally become powerless, because they cannot be absorbed abruptly into the new system. Syncretism allows such people to integrate new beliefs and practices selectively with ones to which they are accustomed, giving them a new identity and way of coping with change they have no other power to control. Trobriand spears may have been no match for British guns, but traditional competition as a way of establishing power and prestige survives in Trobriand cricket.

Study Activities

Vocabulary Check

Check on your understanding of terms by matching those on the left with the definitions on the right. Check your choices with the answer key at the end of the lesson.

1. _E_ Methodist missionaries
2. _I_ sportsmanship and decorum
3. _B_ exchange obligations
4. _D_ acculturation
5. _G_ syncretism
6. _A_ erotic and boastful dancing
7. _J_ village chiefs
8. _C_ kayasa
9. _F_ Papua New Guinea
10. _K_ matrilineal
11. _H_ Kula ring

a. element of Trobriand culture missionaries sought to eliminate; a way of demonstrating "importance" in Trobriand culture

b. a form of distribution of food and goods resulting from kinship and local village politics in Trobriand culture

c. a display and gifts of food to demonstrate power and importance

d. major changes that occur as a result of prolonged contact between societies

e. introduced cricket to Trobriand Islands

f. South Pacific country of which the Trobriand Islands are a part

g. blending old cultural elements with new "outside" practices to form a new system

h. a trading system between islanders of the South Pacific which involves goods of symbolic value

i. an aspect of British culture that colonial powers wished to teach the Trobrianders

j. formerly demonstrated their status through warfare, now do so with cricket matches and kayasa

k. lines of descent traced through women

l. the spread of customs and practices from one culture to another

Completion

Choose the best word or phrase from the lists provided to fill the blanks in the paragraphs below.

1. Warfare among Trobriand villages had been a series of highly _ritualized_ engagements, motivated chiefly by the desire for prestige and status. Missionaries and colonial officials, however, sought to end village _wars_, stamp out the "immoral" _chants_ and dances, and introduce British standards of religion, _dress_, and _sportsman._ The Trobrianders enthusiastically adopted cricket as a sport, but they incorporated it into their own values and traditions, preserving significant

dress
chants
wars
ritualized
sportsmanship

areas of their own culture in what was, in effect, a new system for intervillage competition.

2. Cricket, as it has been developed by the Trobrianders, is a confrontation of communities. The number of players may be as many as _desired_ . The games are held in the harvest season, because the contests are a part of the food display and giving called _kayasa_ . The Trobrianders adopted a different style of "bowling," more like _spear_ throwing. The winner is always the _host_ team, because the _visiting_ team shows respect for the sponsoring chief by losing.

kayasa
spear
desired
host
visiting

3. As adapted and refined by the Trobrianders, cricket matches proved a means of achieving two important social needs. _Village Cheifs_ and team members are able to demonstrate their own power and status, and all members of the community share in this. The contests also make it possible to continue the tradition of distributing _food_ and items of symbolic value, a pattern or style important to Trobriand culture long before cricket appeared. The system of exchange has probably developed over the centuries to meet the need of _distributing_ resources and to establish _alliances_.

alliances
village chiefs
distributing
food

Short-Answer Questions

1. In the television program it is stated that syncretism involves "keeping important traditions alive by integrating them with elements borrowed from another culture," while the Haviland text and the background

notes for this lesson define it somewhat differently. Taking all three definitions into account, discuss briefly how Trobriand cricket illustrates the concept of syncretism.

2. List several ways that cricket has been changed into a different game by Trobriand society.

3. Explain how the use of war dress, magic, dance, and song in their cricket matches helped the Trobrianders to maintain cultural integrity.

Self-Test

(Select the one best answer.)

Objective 1
1. Cricket was introduced to Trobriand Islanders by _____ around the year _____.
   a. missionaries, 1903
   b. servicemen, 1942
   c. government officers, 1903
   d. missionaries, 1942

Objective 1
2. Colonial government and missionary activities were able to stop which of the following practices?
   a. erotic dances and chants
   b. widespread exchange of food and symoblic goods
   c. warfare between villages
   d. use of magic spells and rituals

Objective 1
3. The motive which lead the Europeans to introduce cricket to the Trobriand Islanders was to
   a. provide the Trobrianders with a social means for acquainting themselves with other villagers.
   b. provide opponents for Europeans who enjoyed playing the games.
   c. encourage British standards of dress and behavior.
   d. allow the Trobrianders to retain most of the aspects of their culture.

Objective 2
4. Which of the following statements about syncretism is the most accurate? Syncretism is a form of
   a. acculturation in which a substantial portion of former cultural traditions is lost.
   b. acculturation in which old patterns are meaningfully blended with new ones.

c. diffusion in which a society borrows only the behaviors or technology it desires.

d. diffusion in which a society adopts many of the practices and customs of an entirely different culture.

Objective 2

5. Which one of the following is a fundamental aspect of Trobriand culture which was threatened by the outside culture, but retained in part through the new cricket matches?
   a. marriage practices and taboos
   b. horticultural practices
   c. Kula ring trade
   d. prestige and status determination

Objective 2

6. Many of the activities and practices which Trobrianders have incorporated into cricket were formerly associated with
   a. marriage and mating festivals.
   b. intervillage warfare.
   c. selection of village chietains.
   d. trade between islands.

Objective 3

7. How did the Trobrianders change the rules governing team size as they turned cricket into their own unique game?
   a. Trobriand teams became smaller than British teams.
   b. Trobriand teams could have twice the number of players allowed British teams.
   c. The exact size of Trobriand teams became unimportant.
   d. Opposing teams were not required to have the same number of players.

Objective 3

8. The primary purpose of the Trobriand cultural custom called kayasa is to
   a. provide the islanders with an alternative to warfare.
   b. furnish a means of demonstrating who has the greater prestige and magical power.
   c. determine the exchange obligations between families.
   d. represent the obligations of home team members to the visiting players.

Objective 4

9. Cricket matches are set up during the harvest period because
   a. the weather is more favorable during this time.
   b. harvest time is the traditional mating season.
   c. harvest time coincides with the Kula trading.
   d. yams for display and gifts are available at this time.

Objective 4

10. The fact that they were associated with _____ was the missionaries' major objection to traditional Trobriand dances and chants.
    a. ritual warfare
    b. pagan religion
    c. explicit sexuality
    d. anticolonial feelings

Objective 4

11. How is the winner determined in Trobriand cricket?
    a. The winner is selected on the basis of audience approval of both dancing and playing skill.
    b. Scoring, which is recorded on a palm frond, determines the winner.
    c. The visiting players are traditionally winners because they will distribute gifts.
    d. The host team is traditionally winner because the chieftain will distribute gifts.

Objective 5

12. Which of the following applies to both kayasa and Kula?
    a. Exchange is a central part of Trobriand life.
    b. Warfare between villages had both ritualistic and violent aspects.
    c. Open sexuality is a vital part of Trobriand culture.
    d. Yams have both practical and symbolic value.

Objective 5

13. Village chiefs acquire what advantage from hosting cricket matches?
    a. approval from the present colonial government
    b. increased prestige in the view of a chief's village and others as well
    c. an invitation to be the umpire for the next game
    d. open display of the battle potential of the chief's male villagers

Suggested Activities

1. The anthropologist who studied the Trobrianders and their cricket matches, Gerry W. Leach, has observed that Trobriand cricket can be seen as a "creative adaptation of tradition to contemporary circumstances." In what way is their adaptation of the game "creative"? What were some aspects of their culture which they were in danger of losing? Discuss these questions in a brief paper. Check the Haviland text for references to the Trobriand Islanders other than those in the reading assignment for this lesson.

2. For additional information, read about the Trobriand Islanders in Bronislaw Malinowski's *Argonauts of the Western Pacific* (London: Routledge and Kegan Paul, 1922) and *Coral Gardens and their Magic* (London: George Allen and Unwin Ltd., 1935).

3. Suppose that the government of Venezuela had tried to force the Yanomamo to give up their fierce, warlike behavior, stop using the hallucinogenic drug ebene, and take up the game of cricket in order to learn different values governing religion and behavior. Do you think the Yanomamo would accept or reject the changes? In *either case*, what do you think might happen? Create a scenario and describe in as much detail as you wish what you believe might happen if the Yanomamos' drugs and weapons were confiscated and they were presented with players' uniforms, balls, cricket bats, and wickets instead. Review Lessons Two and Three—especially the latter—to refresh your memory about the Yanomamo. For greater depth, you might read selections from Chagnon's writings or consult other references of your own choosing. If you wish, use a culture group other than the Yanomamo (or an imaginary one) and any object, event, or force which might stimulate culture change.

Answer Key

Vocabulary Check

1. e	5. g	9. f
2. i	6. a	10. k
3. b	7. j	11. h
4. d	8. c	

Completion

1. ritualized, wars, chants, dress, sportsmanship

2. desired, kayasa, spear, host, visiting

3. Village chiefs, food, distributing, alliances

Short-Answer Questions

1. In the television program it is stated that syncretism involves "keeping important traditions alive by integrating them with elements borrowed from another culture," while the Haviland text and the background notes for this lesson define it somewhat differently. Taking all three definitions into account, discuss briefly how Trobriand cricket illustrates

the concept of syncretism. Your answer should include:

Text definition of syncretism as a blending of old with new and Background Notes description as a "fusion" of two cultures.

Trobriand cricket as an example of syncretism because cricket: was accepted enthusiastically; has been revised to accommodate traditions and customs which are vitally important to the society; enabled Trobriand Islanders to retain an identity and a style or pattern that was familiar despite the introduction of much that was new and the loss of old customs, such as warfare; can be viewed as providing continuity, rather than resulting in disruption of the society.

2. List several ways that cricket has been changed into a different game by Trobriand society. Your answer should include at least a minimum of three of the following:

The Trobriand Islanders adopted their battle dress and face paint for the cricket matches.

Their version of the game incorporated traditional styles of dance and chants.

Magic rituals formerly associated with warfare are employed before and during the game.

The contests are associated with kayasa feasts.

Instead of twelve players, the number of players is unlimited and more members of the community may participate.

The stumps and bats were modified, partly because of certain traditional cultural skills of the Trobriand Islanders.

Bowling style was changed, so that it now resembles the Trobriand spearthrowing technique.

Out of respect for the host chieftain, the host team is always allowed to win.

3. Explain how the use of war dress, magic, dance, and song in their cricket matches helped the Trobrianders to maintain cultural integrity. Your answer should include:

Trobriand Islanders transformed cricket into a competition that replaces the earlier function of warfare between villages.

The costumes and facial paint used in the games are associated with magic, which frees the players from inhibitions and bolsters courage—traits sought both in the former wars and in modern cricket.

Magic rituals formerly associated with weapons are now employed for the playing equipment; thus, the rituals themselves are retained, even in the face of loss of the traditional context for the rituals.

Trobriand dancing was opposed by the missionaries, but the Trobriand Islanders preserved their dances by incorporating them into the cricket matches introduced by the missionaries.

Self-Test

1. a	8. b
2. c	9. d
3. c	10. c
4. b	11. d
5. d	12. a
6. b	13. b
7. c	

The Future
Of **25**
Humanity

Overview

What will the world be like fifty years from now? Not even anthropologists have "crystal balls" for predicting the future, of course. However, specialists in anthropology do lay claim to skills in synthesizing relevant information from a variety of sources with which they can compare similarities and differences among cultures and identify important factors. Armed with these skills, anthropologists can identify some problems which threaten to become critical, such as conflicts between cultures, inadequate food production, and population expansion. Anthropologists do not offer solutions, only possibilities. It would be well to remember that what the world is like fifty years from now depends largely on the decisions that our generation is making and will make during those years.

The information presented in this lesson and the preceding one strongly supports a hypothesis that modernization and its accompanying developments have created problems that may be difficult to solve. In fact, there appear to be many traits in present-day Western cultures that make self-evident solutions seemingly impossible.

However, in the text chapter for this lesson, author Haviland offers evidence that indigenous, previously isolated peoples *can* adapt to the modernized world if they are allowed time and space to do so. As you study this lesson, perhaps you will find grounds for believing that Western cultures, if they are allowed time and space, can find new solutions to some current, unsolved problems which could become critical to future generations if not solved by our own generation.

Learning Objectives

When you have completed all assignments in this lesson, you should be able to:

1. Explain the difference between "one-world culture" and "cultural pluralism" as predictions for the future. Describe possible problems and advantages associated with each of these predictions. (Text pages 439-447.)

2. Describe the following as reasons why there is a continuing worldwide food shortage: a limited amount of land suitable for agriculture; and the large amounts of fossil energy required by modern agricultural methods. (Text pages 450-455; television program.)

3. Explain how the problem of limited food production is compounded by various cultural practices and give at least one example. (Text pages 453-455; television program.)

4. Compare the general world views of Western and non-Western people toward the earth and its resources. Explain why it has been said that the Western world view makes it difficult to control pollution. (Text pages 455-458; television program.)

5. Explain how the beliefs in various cultures make adoption of birth control practices difficult. (Text pages 458-459.)

6. Describe the situation which has created a "culture of discontent." (Text pages 432, 459-460; television program.)

Assignments For This Lesson

Before Viewing the Program

Read the overview and the learning objectives for this lesson. Use the learning objectives to guide your reading, viewing, and thinking.

Read the preview to Chapter 15 in the text, and look over the topic headings in the chapter.

Read text Chapter 15, "The Future of Humanity."

View Program 25, "The Future of Humanity."

As you view the program, look for:

a summary of the overlapping problems of hunger, poverty, urbanization, and population throughout the world.

interviews with gerontologist Roy Wolford about extending the human life span and with space engineer Peter Vajk about "mining" resources from outer space, and the effects of both these developments on human cultures.

comments by cultural anthropologist Joan Halifax regarding the need for a change in the world view of people in Western developed nations.

After Viewing the Program

Review the terms used in this lesson.

Review the reading assignments for this lesson. A thorough second reading of the text chapter is suggested. Include the chapter summary in your study.

Complete each of the study activities and the self-test in this study guide, then check your answers with the answer key at the end of this lesson.

According to your instructor's assignment or your own interests, complete one or more of the suggested activities. You may also be interested in some of the readings suggested at the end of Chapter 15 in your text.

Study Activities

Vocabulary Check

Check on your understanding of terms by matching those on the left with the definitions on the right. Check your choices with the answer key at the end of the lesson.

1. _I_ one-world culture
2. _J_ cultural pluralism
3. _E_ marginal lands
4. _H_ fossil fuels
5. _C_ global apartheid
6. _D_ hunting and gathering societies
7. _K_ starvation
8. _G_ green revolution
9. _F_ culture of discontent

a. a belief or attitude that nature exists to be exploited
b. valuable farmland appropriated for other uses, such as construction
c. condition in which a small percentage of the world's wealth goes to almost half the population
d. tend to view themselves as integral parts of nature
e. virtually the only places available today for enlarging farmland
f. a result of aspirations exceeding available opportunities
g. produced new high-yield strains of wheat, rice, and corn
h. required in large amounts for intensive agricultural techniques

i. has been predicted to occur in as little as 300 years
j. more than one culture exists in a given society
k. a form of structural violence in the present-day world

Completion

Choose the best word or phrase from the lists provided to fill the blanks in the paragraphs below.

1. Cultural pluralism seems to be one present pattern of world cultures which may continue into the future. The efforts of such groups as the American Indian to assert and retain their _cultural iden_ is one evidence of this. In order for multiple cultures to exist side by side, however, a deep _respect_ for the cultural traditions of others is required. This seems difficult to achieve in practice, as is illustrated by the revolt of the _Ibo_ in Nigeria.

   Ibo
   respect
   cultural identity

2. At the same time, the hopes for a single, world-wide culture seem to be diminished by such recent events as the Islamic revolution in _Iran_, which sought to break the influence of _Western_ culture. The "original study" on the _Kwaio_ in the Solomon Islands is further evidence that there can be determined resistance to modernization.

   Kwaio
   Western
   Iran

3. "Global apartheid" is a term coined by anthropologists to describe a structure they perceive in the world's economy and power systems. The affluent of the world, some _20_

   power
   white
   nonwhite
   20

percent of the global population, take about 70 percent of the world's income. The majority of those living in poverty are from _nonwhite_ groups. The affluent _white_ minority possesses by far the larger share of _power_.

Short-Answer Questions

1. Define and give an example of "structural violence."

2. Give two reasons for the apparent failure of the "green revolution."

3. Explain why the potential for enlarging lands available for food production is limited, and list two practices in the United States which decrease the amount of land available for food production.

4. Describe the Western world view that has been accused of making pollution an almost insolvable problem.

Self-Test

(Select the one best answer.)

Objective 1
1. Which one of the following statements is *not* correct?
   a. Over the past 5,000 years, there has been a trend toward fewer separate political units in the world.
   b. Some anthropologists have predicted total political integration of the world by 4,850 at the latest.
   c. Separatist movements resisting acculturation are becoming stronger and more frequent.
   d. Overall, there is little resistance to Westernization or acculturation through contact with neighboring societies.

Objective 1
2. The Kwaio of the Solomon Islands provide an example of
   a. cultural loss through contact with Western society.
   b. cultural resistance to birth control.
   c. resistance to modernization.
   d. modernization of agricultural methods.

Objective 1
3. "Cultural pluralism," seen in a constructive, peaceful manner, requires

a. rapid intermingling of cultural traits in neighboring or integrated societies.
b. total separation of each group, in effect segregating them from one another.
c. rejection of ethnocentrism.
d. both a and c.

Objective 1
4. Until recently, the United States would best be described as a(n)
   a. "melting pot" society.
   b. pluralistic society.
   c. agricultural society.
   d. unchanging society.

Objective 2
5. Which of these statements is true about the world's land that is best suited for farming?
   a. Virtually all land still available is now used for food production.
   b. Virtually all land still available is used for farming, but not all for food production.
   c. About half the potential land available is now used for farming.
   d. Intensive agricultural techniques could increase crop yields indefinitely.

Objective 2
6. Fossil fuel energy is required for all these aspects of intensive agriculture except
   a. nitrogen fertilizers.
   b. pesticides.
   c. light radiation.
   d. machinery.

Objective 3
7. A cultural practice that is removing land from food production is
   a. growing corn in North America.
   b. slash-and-burn agriculture in Guatemala.
   c. the green revolution.
   d. production of tobacco.

Objective 4
8. Reduced to its simplest terms, the attitude of many hunting and gathering peoples toward nature is _____, while the attitude of industrialized societies toward nature is _____.
   a. fearful, hostile
   b. respectful, exploitive
   c. religious, indifferent
   d. exploitive, utilitarian

Objective 4

9. What has occurred following the ban on fluorocarbon aerosol sprays?
   a. Ozone layer destruction has increased.
   b. Ozone layer destruction has decreased.
   c. Scientists have learned that the sprays were not the problem.
   d. Americans have demonstrated willingness to give up comforts to prevent pollution.

Objective 5

10. In developing countries in recent years, as the death rate
    a. declines, birth rate declines.
    b. increases, birth rate declines.
    c. declines, birth rate remains unchanged.
    d. increases, birth rate increases.

Objective 5

11. Two cultural situations that make acceptance of birth control difficult in many societies are
    a. government policy and desire for status.
    b. rejection of Western ways and fear of starvation.
    c. religious principles and love of family.
    d. desire for status and need for manual labor.

Objective 6

12. According to the Haviland text, what is a solution to the problem of the "culture of discontent"?
    a. no ready solution, because the resources to improve standards of living are being depleted
    b. improved methods of birth control
    c. rapid urbanization of populations, so that most will be available for industrial work
    d. intensifying agricultural production to increase food supplies

Suggested Activities

1. Use your library resources to make two maps or graphs, one to show relative food production on each continent, and one to show relative food consumption per capita on each continent. How do your findings compare with your impressions about the distribution of poverty and affluence in the world?

2. Consult the *Reader's Guide to Periodical Literature* in your library to find articles appearing during the last two years which describe the economic development, demographic changes, and problems resulting from modernization affecting the Ibo of Nigeria, the Kwaio of the Solomon Islands, or the agriculture of Guatemala. Pick one of these societies and summarize your readings on the topic.

Answer Key

Vocabulary Check

1. i
2. j
3. e
4. h
5. c

6. d
7. k
8. g
9. f

Completion

1. cultural identity, respect, Ibo

2. Iran, Western, Kwaio

3. 20, nonwhite, white, power

Short-Answer Questions

1. Define and give an example of "structural violence." Your answer should include:

   Structural violence is that human suffering which is perpetuated by a variety of institutions and structures, rather than by individuals.

   The example emphasized in the Haviland text is that of death by starvation, because blame is directed at the structures and systems which produce and distribute food.

   Another example cited in the Haviland text in another context is those for whom no work exists when they come to cities in search of a better life. There are institutions encouraging these persons to seek the benefits of industrialization, but the structures are not creating opportunities for them.

2. Give two reasons for the apparent failure of the "green revolution." Your answer may include two or more of these:

   Increased food production did not continue to match population growth.

   Fishing regions have been over harvested, making lower catches in the future probable.

   Further intensification of agriculture using modern machinery and fertilizers costs more than many poorer countries could afford.

Intensification of agriculture would conflict with the cultural values of some societies.

Reliance on single crops, necessary in intensive agriculture, increases crop vulnerability to insects and disease, and use of pesticides leads to more resistant insects.

3. Explain why the potential for enlarging lands available for food production is limited, and list two practices in the United States which decrease the amount of land available for food production. Your answer should include:

Most of the available land now not farmed is marginal land. Such land is more costly to farm, and more easily eroded or depleted.

In the United States, some land previously used for farming is converted to urban use, reducing the amount available for food production.

Some lands in the United States are used to grow nonfood crops such as tobacco. These crops may bring the farmer a better and more consistent profit.

4. Describe the Western world view which has been accused of making pollution an almost insolvable problem. Your answer should include:

The view of Western industrialized societies is that nature exists to be exploited. It is possible that the philosophical roots for this concept are based in the religious heritage which says man is to have dominion over everything that grows and lives on the earth. The practice also arises from an intensive agriculture subsistence pattern.

Combined with this world view is the additional problem that people are reluctant to end practices that previously have seemed to work well. Such an attitude persists even if conditions change, or if the practice is changed so that its effects are more adverse.

Self-Test

1. d	7. d
2. c	8. b
3. c	9. a
4. a	10. c
5. b	11. d
6. c	12. a

Anthropology And The Future **26**

Overview

One principle you are most certain to have learned throughout your study of "Faces of Culture" is that change is inevitable in the lives of all human individuals and in the societies we organize. This universal principle underlies not only your own studies, but the entire discipline of anthropology as well. It is inevitable, then, that the roles of anthropology and the professional anthropologist are changing, just as societies change. But anthropologists would not want their discipline to remain static, since the need for studying and understanding human behavior is never satisfied and does, in fact, become even greater as the world becomes "smaller" and the population greater.

In this final lesson for the course, anthropologists look at some problems and potentials for their own field and share with you their thinking on important kinds of contributions they can make to human societies in the future. It shouldn't be surprising that anthropologists are concerned for the survival of those remaining societies that are in danger of being overwhelmed by modernization and for the protection of threatened archaeological sites which contain the priceless last vestiges of our earliest human heritage.

Most especially, anthropologists fear for the human rights of individuals in so-called third world countries where industrialization and exploitation by outside interests all too often force some social groups into a deprived underclass. Carried to its extreme, this kind of exploitation has at times lead to genocide, or the extinction of an entire social or ethnic group. You would probably agree with anthropologists that people so endangered should be allowed the freedom to work out their own destinies. If this is to happen, anthropology as a discipline needs to focus on the process of modernization as it affects not only small ethnic and social groups, but whole nations. Anthropologists must also continue to collect data on societies threatened with extinction and help to make sure that these data are preserved.

Greater attention is being given to social and cultural developments in America, especially the industrialized and urban areas of the nation. And justifiably so, for we need to know far more about matters such as the effects of urbanization on our cities and their inhabitants, slums, poverty, the formation of class structures and ethnic enclaves in large cities, and the adaptation of migrants to urban areas as well as the effect of the migrants themselves on these areas. Armed with data from studies such as these, anthropologists could take an effective role in social planning.

As you complete this introduction to cultural anthropology, you should experience a feeling of enjoyment as well as enlightenment. It is hoped that you have also gained new and worthwhile perspectives for scrutinizing, evaluating, and understanding your own culture, as well as all others that you may encounter in the future.

Learning Objectives

When you have completed all assignments in this lesson, you should be able to:

1. Explain why anthropologists are concerned about the human rights of the world's remaining tribal peoples in an era of rapid social changes and development. (Text pages 466-467; television program.)

2. Describe the efforts and goals of Cultural Survival, Inc. and the Anthropology Resource Center, Inc., on behalf of native peoples. (Text pages 467-468.)

3. Explain why anthropologists are concerned by the disappearance of traditional cultures and anthropological sites. (Text pages 468-470; television program.)

4. Identify some of the nonacademic career opportunities available for persons with training in anthropology. (Text pages 474-476, 479-484.)

5. Recognize some of the ethical implications of anthropologists' research and findings. (Text pages 476-479; television program.)

Assignments For This Lesson

Before Viewing the Program

Read the overview and the learning objectives for this lesson. Use the learning objectives to guide your reading, viewing, and thinking.

Read the preview to Chapter 16 in the text, and look over the topic headings in the chapter.

Read Chapter 16, "The Future of Anthropology," in the text.

View Program 26, "Anthropology and the Future."

As you view the program, note the following points made by panel participants Napoleon A. Chagnon, professor of anthropology at Northwestern University; Laura Nader, professor of anthropology at the University of California, Berkeley; and Ira Abrams, anthropologist and producer of the "Faces of Culture" series:

topics for future study by anthropologists: changes in gender roles and relationships, mass migration, warfare, sources and distribution of power, and technology.

the issue of "westernization" and homogeneity of the world's cultures versus recognition and support of ethnic and cultural diversity.

the ethical complexities of anthropologists supporting or threatening the status quo and existing power structure in a community or a society.

After Viewing the Program

Review the terms used in this lesson.

Review the reading assignments for this lesson. A thorough second reading is suggested. Include the chapter summary in your study.

Complete each of the study activities and the self-test in this study guide; then check your answers with the answer key at the end of this lesson.

According to your instructor's assignment or your own interests, complete one or more of the suggested activities. You may also be interested in the readings suggested at the end of Chapter 16 in your text.

Study Activities

Vocabulary Check

Check on your understanding of terms by matching those on the left with the definitions on the right. Check your choices with the answer key at the end of the lesson.

1. _D_ Cultural Survival, Inc.
2. _C_ genocide
3. _G_ applied anthropology
4. _H_ Weston La Barre
5. _F_ urban anthropology
6. _E_ Project Camelot

a. has done significant research on the Native American Church
b. studies of entire city complexes
c. deliberate extermination of ethnic groups
d. concerned about the survival of indigenous cultures around the world
e. a study on armed rebellions
f. concerned primarily with the adaptations of subcultures
g. work done in anthropology for a specific client
h. research on wood sculpture of North American Indian groups

Completion

Choose the best word or phrase from the lists provided to fill the blanks in the paragraphs below.

1. _Anthropologists_ are showing increasing concern for the well-being of peoples who are adversely affected by industrialized societies. Territories formerly the home of traditional societies have become sites of development and exploitation; some examples are the Amazon Basin of South America and parts of Alaska and Canada. Frequently, there is little provision made for helping such people to _adapt_ to new social and environmental conditions. They seemed condemned not only to remain on the _lowest_ step of the

lowest
adapt
anthropologists

socio-economic ladder, but to lose their cultural practices, values, and identity.

2. Anthropologists perceive traditional societies and archaeological sites as an important part of the human _heritage_. If they disappear or are destroyed, potentially valuable information is forever lost unless an adequate _record_ is developed. Preservation of some records has been valuable to ethnic groups that wish to recapture part of their cultural heritage. One example of this is the value of traditional _wood_, which has been placed in museums, to the Northwest Coast Indians of the United States.

wood sculpture
heritage
record

Short-Answer Questions

1. Briefly summarize the attitude of Cultural Survival, Inc., and the Anthropology Resource Center, Inc., toward preservation of individual cultures.

2. List at least five kinds of nonacademic job opportunities available to professional anthropologists.

Self-Test

(Select the one best answer.)

Objective 1
1. According to Haviland, which of the following is true about the incidence of genocide in conflict between dominant and minority societies? Genocide is
   a. increasingly common.
   b. far less common than other abuses of human rights.
   c. the most frequent solution to such conflicts.
   d. common among traditional societies.

2. Which of these experiences is typical in major land or resource developments that involve territories of indigenous cultures?
    a. Governments move swiftly to fully integrate the smaller societies into the larger society.
    b. Members of the smaller societies generally experience a loss of status, traditional ways of living, and sense of identity.
    c. Governments try to relocate such groups into new areas where they can continue traditional ways.
    d. Government policies usually involve deliberate extermination of the peoples.

Objective 2

3. Cultural Survival, Inc., and the Anthropology Resource Center, Inc., provide which of the following for indigenous peoples?
    a. projects designed and established in indigenous societies with the approval of the national government involved
    b. financial aid for development
    c. advice and assistance upon request
    d. preservation of records of disappearing cultures

Objective 2

4. An organization that is active in public information and education activities designed to help traditional societies facing destruction is
    a. Cultural Survival, Inc.
    b. Anthropology Resource Center, Inc.
    c. described in both a and b.
    d. neither a nor b.

Objective 3

5. Identify the statement that does *not* explain why anthropologists wish to record and, if possible, preserve archaeological remains and living societies.
    a. Archaeological remains and living societies have great potential economic value.
    b. Archaeological remains and living societies are viewed as components of the human heritage.
    c. All possible data is needed to make eventual generalizations about "human nature."
    d. Information preserved can be important to descendants of that society.

Objective 4

6. As practiced by anthropologists today, urban anthropology primarily deals with
    a. ethnography of the city.
    b. archaeological studies.
    c. cultural subgroups and neighborhoods.
    d. preindustrial cities.

Objective 4

7. Anthropologists are finding new opportunities to use their skills in
    a. government studies and projects.
    b. business and industrial projects.
    c. media and entertainment industries.
    d. all of the above areas.

Objective 4

8. Generally speaking, from an ethical standpoint, the predominant concern for anthropologists is the
    a. welfare of the people under study.
    b. dissemination of knowledge to the profession.
    c. personal academic freedom.
    d. responsibility to the client or funding agency.

Objective 5

9. Project Camelot was criticized by anthropologists because
    a. data was drawn from inaccurate secondary sources.
    b. it dealt with suppressing groups that would be studied.
    c. large-scale destruction of archaeological remains was possible.
    d. it involved moving large groups to allow for development of hydroelectric power.

Suggested Activities

1. Periodically, incidences involving anthropological ethics make the news. Read "Battle in the Scholarly World" in *Time*, 14 March 1983 (Volume 121, page 72), which reports dismissal of a doctoral candidate in anthropology by Stanford University. After reading the article, identify the several ethical questions involved. The issue concerned is a complex one, because the reactions of the Chinese government and the question of academic freedom are mixed with questions of anthropological ethics.

2. Write for information from the Anthropology Resource Center, Inc., 59 Temple Place, Suite 444, Boston, Massachusetts 02111, or Cultural Survival, Inc., 11 Divinity Avenue, Cambridge, Massachusetts 02138, about their current projects. Identify ways that you or others could participate in the effort to protect impacted indigenous peoples around the world.

Answer Key

Vocabulary Check

1. d
2. c
3. g

4. a
5. f
6. e

Completion

1. anthropologists, adapt, lowest

2. heritage, record, wood sculpture

Short-Answer Questions

1. Briefly summarize the attitude of Cultural Survival, Inc., and the Anthropology Resource Center, Inc., toward preservation of individual cultures. Your answer should include:

   Both organizations seek to help individual societies preserve and strengthen their own identities and work out solutions to their own problems.

   They are not seeking to preserve such groups as "living museums" that are unable to change or adapt. Nor do they favor integrating these groups into the mainstream of the dominant culture.

   Their efforts are through suggestion and assistance, rather than by imposing projects on a society.

2. List at least five kinds of nonacademic job opportunities available to professional anthropologists. Your answer might include these or others:

   Working on behalf of specific societies or subcultures.

   Government studies and programs dealing with different cultures and subcultures.

   Businesses with extensive international projects.

   Businesses that plan extensive communication with ethnic groups.

   Government or private projects involving preservation of archaeological sites.

   International agencies such as the World Bank.

Self-Test

1. b
2. b
3. c

4. c
5. a
6. c

7. d
8. a
9. b